What a Tale My Thoughts Will Tell: Words Not to Be Forgotten

A Memoir of Happiness, Sorrow, Pain, and Regret

John Edwards

Copyright © 2023 John Edwards
All rights reserved
First Edition

Author Photo by:

Luminis
PHOTOGRAPHY • STUDIO

Folsom, California

PAGE PUBLISHING
Conneaut Lake, PA

First originally published by Page Publishing 2023

ISBN 979-8-88960-000-8 (pbk)
ISBN 979-8-88960-057-2 (hc)
ISBN 979-8-88960-003-9 (digital)

Printed in the United States of America

To my ex-wife, Robbin, the love of my life, and to my beautiful children, Johnny and Jessica. I hope you will hold onto this tale as I long to be a part of your life, praying that we will find a way.

As far as we can discern, the sole purpose of human existence is to kindle a light of meaning in the darkness of mere being.

—Carl Jung

Acknowledgments

This book evolved through the help of many of my longtime friends and acquaintances that diligently offered insightful, intelligent, and valuable feedback. I am enormously grateful to Andrea Fike, Mike Grover, Bob Grover, Donna Boots, Randy Barker, Bill Sherwood, Dean Souza, Jim Stuart, and Nancy Ojeda.

Special thanks to Angela Brace.

Additionally, I owe a special debt of gratitude to Courtney Winder, Page Publishing Publication Coordinator, and her production management staff and departments. They applied exceptional guidance, editorial insights, and meticulous standards that guided me through the specific steps required while publishing my book. In addition, their work ethic and commitment to excellent customer service through exceptional follow-up attentiveness and dedication to producing a customized effort to achieve optimal product quality from beginning to end were outstanding. I am so thankful.

John Edwards, Author
What a Tale My Thoughts Will Tell—Words Not to Be Forgotten
First Edition, 2023

Prologue

I began writing this memoir shortly after the unforeseen end of my second management career with Enterprise Holdings Inc., in Roseville, California. At sixty-eight years of age, having completed thirteen years of service with this exceptional organization, I planned to devote another seven years to achieve a twenty-year career and retire at age seventy-five to match my father's work-life commitment. However, the ending of my career at Enterprise was bittersweet as the World Health Organization announced the spread of a mysterious coronavirus-related pneumonia in Wuhan, China, in January 2020. By March, President Trump had declared COVID-19 a national emergency, and the NBA had indefinitely suspended their season.

In April, I accepted a voluntary buyout as Enterprise battled the financial turbulence caused by the virus. In May, the CDC announced the sobering development that over one hundred thousand COVID-19 deaths had occurred in the United States, reminding people over sixty-five were particularly susceptible and at a higher risk for a severe life-threatening illness if they had an underlying health condition. As pandemic lockdowns began and virtual medical appointments became standard, transitioning into an isolated lifestyle with PPE (personal protective equipment) was recommended until pharmaceutical organizations could develop an agent-based vaccine.

During this time, the virus was unprecedented, causing fear and anxiety. However, I found this time to be a welcoming break from my hyperconnected life, feeling comfortable with the prospect of isolating for an extended period. Seclusion became an interval of restoration, reflection, and self-evaluation. I reflected on my life which deepened my appreciation of my life successes and failures. For example, when reviewing my first thirty-four-year business management career with United Parcel Service, I felt blessed to have worked for such an iconic organization that championed a well-defined career pathway and promotion from within policy. Having secured a lucrative pension plan after retiring at the age of fifty-five allowed me the option to start a second management career with Enterprise. Additionally, self-reflecting on the lessons learned from failed marriages and family estrangement helped me realize my role in the cause and effect of dissolution. Being socially isolated started my journey into renewal and the search for meaning through personal contemplation.

Having plenty of time on my hands and after finishing several genres of unread titles collecting dust on my bookshelves, I decided to purchase Jessica Simpson's memoir, *Open Book*. I was inspired as she wrote a compelling, honest, uniquely candid, vulnerable reflection of her life disruptions. Influenced by Ms. Simpson's book, I decided to throw "machismo masculinity" characteristics out the window to write a personal storytelling rendering of my life experiences that turned my joys and heartaches into wisdom gained. First and foremost, I wanted to give a vulnerable, honest, and personal story describing the emotional roller coaster of my life experience. Then, where possible, I wanted to take readers on a compelling storytelling journey of how life's transitions can shape and disrupt the decisions, choices, and path of our lives. Finally, and most importantly, I wanted my ex-wife, Robbin, and my children, Johnny and Jessica, to know how much I love them.

Being graced with seventy years of human existence so far, taking inventory of all the encounters and exploits accumulated throughout the years, I realized that life's meaning is the story you tell yourself. That story includes multiple possible interpretations of feelings, emotions, and actions that eventually lead to an awareness and comprehension of that meaning. Reflection left me more open and compassionate toward life's high and low points and also gave attention to how I adapted to personal, socioeconomic, and cultural changes. My inspiration for writing a book began.

It is a story of where I came from, what hopes and dreams I fought for, and what single dynamic is most important regarding the true meaning of life. It's the story of my life.

WHAT A TALE MY THOUGHTS WILL TELL: WORDS NOT TO BE FORGOTTEN

A story of happiness, sorrow, pain, and regret follows. Over the last two years, while grappling to find the right words to put on the pages, what I didn't anticipate through creating and completing the task of writing a book was how it led me to discover the true meaning of life.

Jessica Simpson commented on why she devoted her time to writing a memoir, saying, "I did it for my family. I did it for myself."

I wrote a personal narrative for the same reasons. Additionally, reexamining the past helped my heart remember and relive the human spirit of happiness, hardship, and sorrow. Repeatedly, my memories would guide me to a deeper understanding of what transpired and how I contributed to the joys and disappointments of my earliest beginnings and family life. Finally, I also wrote for the reader, hopeful that my story might guide you to navigating through the painful experiences of life's disruptions and discover the true meaning of your life.

I mentioned in my prologue that my goal was to match my father's achievement of retiring at the age of seventy-five. That goal is still alive. After being vaccinated multiple times, updated Pfizer bivalent boosters became available in 2022, helping me feel more comfortable reentering the workforce and readjusting to in-person interaction post-pandemic.

Wanting to connect with my local community, I thought it might be helpful to apply my extensive management and customer-service skills to an organization that could provide a clean, welcoming environment and an occupation that required some form of physical activity for beneficial health outcomes. The perfect choice became my local grocery store chain, Safeway.

Safeway operates under the banner of Albertsons Companies, one of the largest food-and-drug retailers in the United States, which hired me as a part-time courtesy clerk.

My new workplace is where I met Angela Brace. After sharing positive and negative lifetime experiences, I was impressed with her open-minded, imaginative, creative, and insightful personality traits. Angela's warm and caring nature made me feel comfortable sharing some of my book's most intimate written passages to gain her input and feedback. Her energetic enthusiasm, humor, and unswerving ability to impart constructive feedback to my writings were encouraging and motivating factors to complete my book.

Angela would enthusiastically ask, "John, send me the next passage. I can't wait to find out what happens next!"

Thank you, Angela. I am eternally grateful and forever indebted to your positive input, advice, and friendship.

Lightness into darkness. I remember when the most traumatic consequence of my life took place in 1996.

After a hard day's work, I eased into my soft leather reclining chair. It was a warm spring night in March, a few days before my forty-third birthday. I reached over and placed my glass of merlot wine on our 1960s antique-style wooden end table while a *Seinfeld* episode was playing on the television. Your mother wordlessly entered the room with a worried expression, displaying a drained sadness. We made eye contact. Robbin rubbed her forehead with both hands, pausing as if she was disturbed. As she lowered her hands, she calmly declared without any emotion, "I want a divorce." Robbin's voice dropped to a whisper as she continued, "I know this is difficult, but I don't want to be married to you anymore."

Robbin quickly exited the family room and headed down the hallway toward the master bedroom. I reacted clumsily, stumbling forward as if I had detached my body entirely from my mind. My eyes started to well up. Her words not only stunned me but took my breath away. Suddenly, I felt frozen in dismay and trapped in an out-of-body experience. I asked myself, *Did I hear that correctly?* I felt my knees buckle, feeling dizzy and shocked. I had to sit back down with my hands covering my face. I leaned forward and closed my eyes, thinking, *This is the most dreadful day of my life.* I was suddenly drowning in the darkness of despair, looking for any glimmer of lightness.

During this distress, I attempted to collect my thoughts as consternation and nausea became unrelenting. Then deep in contemplation, a familiar voice in my head says, *After almost eighteen years of marriage, she wants a divorce?* I had always believed that marriage was forever. Marriage was the beginning of a family and a long-life commitment. You don't uproot and toss away a long-term marriage. In my mind, marriage was more than a physical union; it was also a spiritual and emotional union. Therefore, my adherence, acceptance, and faith in the sacrament of marriage and its vows were of great significance.

"I, John, take thee, Robbin, to be my wedded wife to have and to hold from this day forward, for better, for worse, for richer, for poorer, in sickness and in health, to love and to cherish, till death do us part, according to God's holy ordinance, and thereto I pledge thee my faith."

For several weeks after your mother's divorce request, everything would become dark, bewildering, painful, and so unfocused that I wasn't sure I would ever find my way out of the utter confusion. Even though there were early warning signs, unsupportive behavior, and infidelity during our fifth year of marriage, it was challenging dealing with the contradiction that a love I had worked on and sacrificed for unexpectedly felt like all hope had vanished. Your mother's emotions toward me became lifeless and indicated her love for me was dying. The next thought that filled my anxiety was how this would affect my children's well-being. Suddenly, I realized that your mother's plea would drastically alter our lives. It would become a life I would have to fight for or come to terms with the harsh reality that our relationship and family bond would end as Robbin refused any willingness to work on our marriage. My search for meaning began.

Since our divorce, our disconnection and abandonment from each other as a family unit have been heartbreaking and unsettling. I have never been the same. Losing her love has been the most painful experience of my life. Deliberately, I will reenact some joyful and agonizing life experiences from a fair-minded and soul-searching point of view. I became a victim of betrayal. However, I never became a sufferer of victimhood. I chose to stay. I never sought self-pity or to use your mother's infidelity as an excuse for anything. Through forgiveness and compassion, I wanted to save our family. Regrettably, our family unit was broken, our family environment where our needs are satisfied was broken, and your needs for family access to immediate emotional and communicative support were broken. These are just some of the ramifications of a marital breakdown. All I ever wanted was unwavering support and unconditional love from your mother. I wanted to grow old with her and fulfill our marriage vows. In retrospect, there was always an underlying premise that your mother wasn't there for me, often letting me down and never becoming my best friend. After surviving infidelity and just before you entered high school, our marriage relationship became one-dimensional.

Your mother became emotionally unavailable, and loving support sometimes seemed beyond reach. I became a ghost; I felt trapped, unloved, and insignificant to my wife. I did my best, considering I had to overcome your mother's affair with a college student and her affirmation a few years later that she was sexually abused by her father. I chose to forgive and work through these dark chapters of our marriage. I made this personal sacrifice for your well-being and will never regret this decision. However, many questions have remained unanswered through all these years. Why did your mother decide to endure thirteen more years of marriage considering her earlier infidelity? Why was your mother so aggressive during our divorce settlement, not willing to compromise? Where did her love go? Robbin never explained why she fell out of love. If I could only read her mind, what story would her thoughts tell?

Consequently, I felt compelled not to leave any words behind to tell my story. It is sad for me to ponder that you don't know that much about me or even bother to care about our estrangement. I have attempted to reach out to you several times by different means, with no success. I want you to understand how life transitions and disruptors influence our choices and decision-making process. I want you to hold me accountable for my actions and mistakes of judgment. Therefore, I hope my memoir will help you understand my genuine motives and feelings regarding what led to our alienation from a non-critical and objective viewpoint. With that fact in mind, how does one become the person one will be? What causes us to make individual decisions and choices that can change the path of our lives? These questions and subject matter involve very complex and varied interpersonal life experiences that sociologically and psychologically provide the framework for how, why, and what we will become later in life. Therefore, another Carl Jung quote seems appropriate here,

Who looks outside, dreams; who looks inside, awakes. There is no coming to consciousness without

pain. The privilege of a lifetime is to become who you truly are.

Since nobody experiences or sees the world precisely the same way, our behavior and human nature are effectuated by the interaction between our fundamental biological heritage and life transitions. The struggle of human nature has always been a push-and-pull proposition. We make choices, we make decisions, and we make mistakes. It's hard to be human. But more importantly, understanding how the family unit provides the warmth, shelter, care, love, and long-lasting bonds that shape our evolution.

Divorce shatters the family unit, and everything changes. Divorce is incredibly problematic, especially when children are involved. Therefore, let me give my best shot at explaining who your father is and how life's transitions influenced my decision-making. This written work will be a memoir of my life story and an interpretation of my developed humanity. My hope and desire are that my written portrayal will help you understand not only who I am as your father but how malignant family estrangement emerges and why open-minded love, forgiveness, and support are so important. Where possible, I want to offer you a sense of what it was like to be in my shoes and how I have lived through the happiness, sorrow, pain, and regret of not only my divorce from your mother but your disaffection concerning me. This testimony is nothing more than a personal rendering of my story. To tell the truth with no hidden agendas and to explain things from my point of view and a place of personal integrity. I never wanted to be perceived as an emotional obstacle to your growth. All I ask is that you have an open mind. Therefore, we are empowered to interpret our past and create a story that maximizes the meaning and purpose we get out of life. So here it is, the story of my life.

WHAT A TALE MY THOUGHTS WILL TELL: WORDS NOT TO BE FORGOTTEN

I always loved checking out my baby pictures during my childhood because the human mind generally can only recall limited events in one's earliest beginnings. Newborn photographs connected me to my earliest past and put into perspective all the shared stories about my evolving existence.

I was a chubby baby with a round face and big hazel-colored eyes. My parents often told me I looked like Telly Savalas from the *Kojak* 1970s TV series. My all-time favorite infant snapshot of myself was taken when I was two years old. The portrait shows me and my brother, Frank, in a short suit. The short suit consisted of a formal jacket (with large round white buttons), and short trousers were known back then as britches. That picture would inspire relatives and family members to coin the phrase at get-togethers, *Frankie and Johnny were lovers*, an old traditional folk song made famous in 1912, but several remakes would follow. My parents liked the 1946 version by Lena Horne. To this day, I can remember my parents singing their song lyric variations when we were old enough to understand, "Frankie and Johnny were lovers. Oh Lord, how they loved each other. Swore to be true to the other and the stars above. They were boys who could do no wrong."

Interestingly, my first memories were recalled from either an emotionally charged situation or a pleasurable occurrence I experienced at the age of three. My parents, attempting to provide a positive, supporting, loving environment, moved next door to your great-grandparents, Howard and Betty Barter. Thus, my older sister, Judy, younger sister, Mary, twin brother, Frank, and I started our lives being squeezed into a small bedroom in a modest two-bedroom apartment on School Street in Oakland, California. The year was 1956.

One of my most traumatic memories included the limited space, darkness, and emotional turmoil triggered by four small children living and sleeping together in close quarters within a ten-foot by ten-foot bedroom. The room was unusually dark even during daylight hours because it had an undersized window with light-concealing blinds that were closed most of the time.

One afternoon, while Dad was at work, Mom was vacuuming our bedroom rug when suddenly she turned the vacuum off to say that she had forgotten something and needed to take a quick jaunt to see Grandma next door. Before leaving, Mom instructed Judy, "Stay with the children and keep the front door locked. I will be back within five minutes." Like typical kids, we immediately started playing together in our bedroom, with the only illumination provided by a ceiling light fixture as the window blinds were closed. Mom had left the vacuum cleaner in our bedroom with the long extension cord stretching to a hallway's plug outlet. Playing peekaboo and red light/green light simultaneously, we somehow triggered the wall light switch to the off position and slammed the bedroom door shut over the vacuum cord. Suddenly, total darkness.

Frantic and panic-stricken, Judy reached out blindly with her arms, trying her best to find the doorknob and light switch. Once she felt the doorknob, she tried to open the door, which proved futile. Immediately, uncontrollable hysteria. I vividly remember the sounds of fraught emotions, impressions scrambling in the darkness, and screams for help. That was the longest five minutes of my life as Mom finally came back home to rescue us from the darkness into the light. Even at that young age, the feeling of claustrophobia and fear of darkness was natural and initiated an underlying fear of confined spaces for the rest of my life. The emotional turmoil from my siblings bursting into distressing tears while cohabitating within that compact living space would shape my psychological yearning for peace of mind and serenity. The short-term absence of my mother not being available evoked a childhood fear of abandonment and internalization of stressful events. The craziness of having such a large family would prove to have its benefits and disadvantages.

As our primary caregiver, Mom wanted to nurture the relationship between family bonds and lineage by having the wisdom, unconditional love, and support that grandparents provide. I clearly remember the joy and excitement of sprinting over to Grandpa and Grandma Barter's apartment every Sunday morning for breakfast. As I approached their front door, I could smell the wonderful scent of Aunt Jemima's pancake batter and maple syrup cooking. The best part was getting a big bear hug from Grandpa Howard while sitting in his lap as he read me the funny papers. Grandpa would tell me later that I seemed to respond and enjoy the newspaper comic strip featuring *Animal Crackers* the best. The *Animal Crackers* funnies featured animated various animal life coping with different half-baked situations of human nature. Whenever we had to leave Grandpa and Grandma to go home, I remember Grandpa always saying, "Be a good boy, and I will see you in the funny papers." Being a good boy would become an inspiring goal of mine.

My father was an adopted child. His adoptive parents named him Garth Delmane Edwards. Being raised in the small California farm town of Morgan Hill, my father attended Live Oak High School where he played the drums in the school band and was a star one-hundred-yard dash track athlete. He eventually graduated from San Jose State University before serving his country and entering the Korean War. After the war, Dad started his career at the Naval Air Station in Alameda, California. His workmates nicknamed him "Steady Eddie" for his unyielding work ethic.

My mother grew up in the Bay Area and met my father about four years after graduating high school. Dad was thirteen years older. In 1950, he married your grandmother at the age of thirty-three. Mom quit her job at the Montgomery Wards Department Store in Oakland to devote her time to raising her children as a stay-at-home mom. My father preferred it that way.

Dad's favorite pet name refrain for Mother was *Dee Dee Baby Boo Boo's* as her first name was Delores. Late in 1957, a few years after the Korean War had ended, my father served as a Military Police Army Officer. He started his career as a metal-casting patternmaker at the Alameda Naval Air Station. Dad was an excellent handyman because of his natural mechanical skills, including competent carpentry and automotive aptitudes. At that time, my parents also decided to move away from our grandparents and purchase their first and only home in San Lorenzo, California. A three-bedroom, two full bath, single story, 1,350-square-foot corner-lot home on Via Catherine. The GI Bill helped my father by subsidizing low-cost mortgages for returning soldiers, which meant that it was often cheaper to buy a suburban house than rent an apartment.

The neighborhood homes were all built on small lots with similar construction attributes among large sycamore shade trees lining the streets. San Lorenzo was known for its ideal mild climate. Homes in San Lorenzo did not need air conditioning. September is typically the hottest month of the year averaging only seventy-five degrees, with cool breezes in the late afternoon from nearby San Francisco Bay. In later years, I found out that the small town of San Lorenzo was one of our nation's first planned communities, with land parcels designated for schools, churches, parks, police/fire stations, a theater, a library, a small industrial area, and several retail centers. I still remember the day we pulled up to the curb in front of our new home in my parent's light blue 1955 Chevy Station Wagon. Trying to get out of the car's back seat, the song "A White Sport Coat (and a Pink Carnation)" was still blaring on the car radio. My brother, Frank, could not contain his excitement as he bolted out of the vehicle before my father could turn off the engine so he could be the first to observe and run full speed through our new residence.

As the rest of the family trailed behind and entered the house a few moments later, we could not find Frank anywhere. It was as if Frank had vanished into thin air. Suddenly, mother heard a faint and weak cry for help from the hallway bathroom. Mom thought Frank might be severely injured, screaming, "My little baby! My little baby!" Frank survived with just a few abrasions and bruises. Running around in the dark, Frank had fallen into the basement/cellar space opening (about a four-foot drop) uncovered in the bathroom floorboard. My brother's overzealous behavior seemed familiar enough to any visual understanding. However, as Frank grew older with each passing year, his evolution of symptoms, such as inattention and impulsivity, would progress and extend through middle school, providing many remembrances and cherished stories. Yet falling through the floorboard would not slow Frank down.

Growing up in San Lorenzo was an ideal and safe middle-class community for growing families and workers hired into cold-war-related Bay Area industries in the mid to late 1950s through the 1960s.

WHAT A TALE MY THOUGHTS WILL TELL: WORDS NOT TO BE FORGOTTEN

In those days, you could walk the streets at night and leave your front doors unlocked and windows left wide open. San Lorenzo, located between San Leandro to the north and Hayward to the south, is classified as a small unincorporated town. Its land area is only three-square miles, limiting its new housing growth and population. Typically, San Lorenzo's community population stays around twenty-four thousand, demographically housing primarily White, Asian, and Hispanic ethnicities. You knew your neighbors by name, contributing to the supportive, friendly, family-valued community environment. Most people felt comfortable with the comings and goings in the neighborhood. It was common practice to have your milk delivered fresh once weekly in the early morning hours throughout the early sixties.

Often you would hear the noise from clinking milk bottles placed into metal milk crates on your front porch. The milkman, postman, and garbage personnel were known by their first names and became family friends. Interstate Highway 880 is the main freeway extending from Oakland to San Jose. During my childhood, three other exciting features and memorable landmarks of San Lorenzo were a large park named *Tot Town*, which eventually would become known as San Lorenzo Park Community Center. The Lorenzo Theater was a popular cinema landmark with its art deco fluorescent murals and stadium seating arrangement. And the South Pacific Coast Railroad tracks were just a few blocks west of our home. These three landmarks would spark an inquisitive mind that would energize our social development. I would stay put in my hometown until 1979.

Before the end of the 1950s decade, we had replaced our red tricycles with Schwinn Sting Ray bicycles as my parents would enroll Frank and I into the local Bay School Kindergarten class at five years old. Frank and I were separated as we had different teachers. My teacher, Miss Carpadakis, provided a teaching environment that furnished age-appropriate activities to nourish and encourage my eagerness to learn. Dr. Seuss's *The Cat in the Hat* was my favorite book, a story that heightened my imagination and interest, enhancing my enjoyment of school. As I lost my chubby-cheeked face, I could proudly recite my ABCs and count up to one hundred at five years old. In addition, I noticed how my developing motor skills allowed me to skip, hop, run, and jump. Understanding our developing physical power and movement, Dad purchased our first thirty-two-inch plastic baseball bat and wiffle ball to keep us occupied. Having a bat and ball set complemented the other classic toys we possessed in 1958 (e.g., GI Joe plastic toy soldiers, Matchbox Hot Wheels, and Wham-O super balls).

Getting ready for school, I had the freedom to get dressed after Mom insisted on picking my clothes for the school day. Mom always combed my hair to make me look like one of her favorite actors, Clark Gable, from *Gone with the Wind* movie fame. First, Mom ensured my hair was combed perfectly to one side with a part on the other. Next, she used a small amount of water with Brylcreem hair cream to hold my hair in place. Then, with loving self-satisfaction, Mom would look at me with admiration and declare, "Johnny, you are so adorable!" This hairstyle would serve me well through eighth grade. My mother's affectionate bond would give me a head start in establishing the character traits of self-confidence, affection, and empathy. Mom would become our protector, our defender, and our disciplinarian.

Before entering first grade, my older sister, Judy, had completed second grade. St. Joachim's was about two miles from our home, located in the neighboring city of Hayward. Entering the same school, Judy became a support system for knowing what to expect. Catholic school enrollment was very expensive at the time. My father, the only breadwinner earning money to help support our large family, was provided financial help from my grandparents so all the siblings could attend private schooling together. Our mother, being of an active Roman Catholicism faith background, greatly influenced the importance of participating in the guidance of faith and spirituality the church provided. As infants, we all received our first Holy Sacrament of Baptism in the Catholic Church. Mom ensured we knew the sign of the cross, Our Father, the Hail Mary, the Creed, and Glory Be prayers. Mom enriched us with the gift of a rosary, saying, "Praying the rosary every night will purify your souls from sin."

WHAT A TALE MY THOUGHTS WILL TELL: WORDS NOT TO BE FORGOTTEN

As a family, we attended the 8:30-a.m. worship ceremony on Sundays. Our mother's main objective was for all of us to lead a virtuous life through prayer and adhering to the Ten Commandments. Mom demanded that our preparation before attending mass be timely and disciplined. Her instructions were similar to that of a Marine drill sergeant and as effective as a reveille trumpet call to wake up military personnel at sunrise. Mom would decisively yell "Get your butts in gear," waking us up in the early Sunday morning hours, still exhausted while trying to roll out of bed. Making the rules of engagement clear and sticking to them was a critical tactic for my mother. Attempting to discipline four young children was nothing short of an arduous task. We quickly realized that our mom was the controlling figurehead of the family and would manage our autonomy with ridged but loving authority. Even though the act of worship started at 8:30 a.m., we would arrive at 7:30 a.m. to ensure our family always obtained the front-row pew closest to the altar. It would become known as *the Edwards Family Pew* for several years.

Dad was of Protestant faith, adherent to Christian beliefs and rarely attended service with us. Dad's main focus was providing for his family and being a masculine role model and teacher. Steady Eddie was a man of routines and sacrificed all his opportunistic choices and autonomy for us. Dad would allow us to make mistakes and learn from them. He was always supportive and protective in an understated, calm manner. Dad demonstrated his unconditional love for his family through his hard-work ethic and doing whatever he could to provide his family with the security and necessities we required. Dad represented the perfect example of what personal sacrifice for his family means. For me, this type of role modeling was reflective of Dad's depth of love for his family. His main concern was that we all did well in life. He was always there when we needed his support or help. He was selfless, staying married to my mother for over sixty years. Regrettably, I could not follow my father's example of marital commitment to one woman for his entire life.

Early childhood of first-grade through fourth-grade schooling was relatively uneventful. During elementary school, regular contact with other students daily would influence the importance of reinforcing friendships and wanting to be liked and accepted. Having my twin brother, Frank, in the same class and grade levels helped with this transition, and my sister, Mary, followed one grade level behind. Even though my mother was a strict disciplinarian, she encouraged us to participate in school activities and team sports as she recognized early on that we all had above-average athletic abilities. Furthermore, Mom wanted to ensure we had a balanced and nutritious diet. She emphasized the importance of ensuring we ate various vegetables, fruits, and whole grains. For eight consecutive elementary school years, we could count on having an apple, orange, and banana included in our brown-bag lunches.

Mom and Dad were exceptional athletes in their time. Mom was an outstanding baseball player, and Dad was an impressive high school track-sprint star running one-hundred-yard dashes in a ten-second flat measured time by a handheld stopwatch during his senior year. My parents' athletic abilities would be a passed-along trait that enhanced our ability to maintain friendships and understand the importance of teamwork. Our primary source of fun early on was playing hide-and-seek outside in the streets or neighbors' yards. I can still hear my mom saying, "Go outside and play, and don't talk to strangers." Ultimately, the streets would become a secondary priority, eventually replaced by the available baseball/football fields and basketball courts.

Family life before the end of the 1950s decade was changing rapidly. Home sizes were growing. Frank and I shared one bedroom as Judy and Mary would share the other. That did not last long as Mom and Dad had a fifth child. Susan, out of necessity, would occupy the same bedroom with Judy and Mary. In some respects, an esprit de corps or tribalism evolved as we shared a sense of family unity and fair values.

Mom and Dad were satisfied furnishing their home with modest amenities using a mismatch of hand-me-down furniture pieces or decorating with tasteless framed art and wall ornaments purchased through the saving of Green or Blue Chip stamps. The home improvement fad or interior design help for homeowners did not arrive until the 1970s. We had a cozy fireplace that we enjoyed snuggling up to as a family during the cold winter. Pets were continually being introduced into our family as well.

Our first pet was a seed-eating parakeet, constantly chirping all the time. Soon, a couple of goldfish made a home entrance in a large glass bowl my mom placed on top of the TV console. Some of the pets were short-term visitors. I remember when Mary brought home a chicken and a hamster. Dogs and cats were long-term family members. During this time, my parents started to take more significant roles in valuing conformity by teaching appropriate boundaries and to obeying the rules to stay out of trouble. As a result, some household rules became nonnegotiable.

Mom was the principal administrator of punishment for misbehavior. She was very good at temporarily withdrawing privileges or affection as a means of discipline: the paddle or the strap treatment became predictable. The consequences would be equal. For example, while playing "hide-and-seek" outside with Mary and Frank, we accidentally ran through my mom's flower garden, flattening down and breaking several of her tulips and rose plants. Later in the afternoon, Mom went to tend to her flower bed and became aware of the damage. "Frankie, Johnny, Mary!" she shouted at the top of her lungs while scanning and stalking the front-yard landscape like a trained investigator. She found our hiding place behind a large rhododendron plant. She yelled, "Get in the house. Now!"

Mom lined us up near her kitchen stove and asked us to "Turn around" with a stern voice. Mom then used her disciplinary instrument of the strap on our behinds. Later in life, to our detriment, I would realize that this type of physical discipline directly resulted from her upbringing and cultural norms that stayed in effect for a long time before being banned. It was called *corporal punishment*. After the spanking, I went to my bedroom sobbing. I wanted to believe that my mom, who loved us, taught us the difference between right from wrong, respecting others, and possessing a conscience when you do something wrong. So I never got spanked by that strap again and became that "good boy" my grandpa Barter asked me to be.

After getting a ride home from school in the early fall season of 1960, I handed Mom a signup sheet from my teacher for Frank and I to enter second-grade CYO Basketball. CYO stands for Catholic Youth Organization. Even today, CYO Basketball remains the most extensive youth program in the United States. Mom laid her hand on my shoulder, "Dad and I already signed you and Frankie up to play. Daddy and our neighbor, Mr. Daly, will be your coaches. So finish your homework before Dad gets home from work. He is going to take you shopping for some new tennis shoes." Even today, I remember the excitement and joy of getting new tennis shoes. They seemed to help me run faster and leap higher. I was so happy I ran and jumped up and down all over our front yard in those new sneakers until exhaustion set in.

When we got our red basketball jerseys with white numerals, my brother and I couldn't wait to start playing. Dad worked with us endlessly on proper dribbling and shooting skills with an adult-size basketball. Our first sports team adventure would lead us toward the love of competition and team sports. Mom and Dad realized that sports activities would help build self-confidence and self-esteem. That meant that basketball, baseball, and track would become our primary participative sports. Mom objected to us playing football because she viewed it as aggressive and violent, risking severe injury.

If it wasn't sports occupying our time, it was the radio or record player. However, with the upcoming television improvements, transitioning from black-and-white screen to color would significantly impact our lives revolving around the TV set. My maternal uncle Eddie was a TV service repairman and owned his business shop in San Leandro. In 1960, most American households had black-and-white TV sets or wood cabinet radio consoles with a record changer and inside-mounted speakers. Listening to the radio was very popular throughout the 1960s. Our family had both. My parents had a large Philco Radio Wood Cabinet/record-changer brand and a Westinghouse wood console television with a ten-inch screen. My father would continuously be on the roof, adjusting the TV antenna. He frequently mumbled swear words under his breath, trying to improve TV reception. Ultimately, he would call my uncle Eddie to stop by to replace the glass vacuum tubes.

During that year, my parent's favorite boob-tube programs were *Rawhide*, *Wagon Train*, *I Love Lucy*, *American Bandstand*, and *The Ed Sullivan Show*. My first visual exposure to politics happened during the presidential campaign of Richard Nixon and John Kennedy in 1960. Devoted Democrats, Mom and Dad were engrossed in watching the debate between them on their small black-and-white TV screen. After the contest, my father would exclaim, "Jack just kicked Nixon's ass in that debate!" I wanted Kennedy to win because my parents supported his campaign.

Shortly after Kennedy's inaugural speech, my uncle Eddie stopped by, pulling into our driveway in his blue-and-yellow-colored business stenciled *Eddie's TV Repair* Dodge cargo van. He gave my parents a great deal on a used large-screen RCA Victor Color TV he had repaired at his shop. Uncle Eddie would say, "Television will overtake radio as the most popular form of home entertainment." We were in complete happiness and wonderment as we watched television programs, movies, and our favorite cartoon TV show, *The Flintstones*, in color.

Before completing third and fourth grade, I became more aware of how the outside world would shape my social and emotional development. I read and wrote at nine years of age but still worked on correct spelling and grammar. I was a good student. My understanding of how to relate to peers and adjust to social rules became more advanced. My parents did an excellent job of balancing sibling rivalry and equal treatment. The household rules were set uniformly identical for all and put in place not to be broken; stepping beyond these rules brought consequences. However, arguing my point of view and negotiating with my parents for something became more commonplace. Being a part of a group and being popular was critical to avoid bullying and intentional meanness from other kids. My more-advanced athletic skill and size at a young age would protect me from such emotional stress as name-calling and exclusion in my childhood years. My mother and father's natural loving bond and physical affection would create and reinforce my confidence and awareness of the differences between boys and girls. The scent of my mom's feminine perfume, called Yardley Flair, compared to my father's masculine aftershave lotion, Old Spice, for example, would become a chemical signal that would trigger my emotions and recollections. The power of human touch and smell would raise my interest and curiosity about gender perception.

Dad and Mom loved music. My mother particularly loved to sing and dance to music. My parents were excellent swing, twist, and jitterbug dancers. Music was often played throughout our home, stimulating our family's joy, emotions, and imagination. Music would always arouse my most profound memories and sentiment. In 1962, the song "The Twist" by Chubby Checker became a number-one Billboard hit and a famous dance routine worldwide as demonstrated on Dick Clark's *American Bandstand*.

Grandma and Grandpa Barter would visit every Sunday afternoon, greeting each grandchild with a silver-dollar handout. The love and emotional closeness they provided could not be understated. Their qualities of empathy, self-understanding, kindness, and acceptance were the building blocks of our loving and empathetic character traits.

While Uncle Eddie was always concerned about our TV set's working condition or lending a helping hand to my parents, our uncle Gil and Jordan were born entertainers. Uncle Jordan would always make us laugh by contorting his face like the famous 1960s comedian/actor Jerry Lewis by making funny facial expressions. He was a natural mimic. Uncle Gil would pull out his bag of magic tricks and corny one-line jokes. One of Uncle Gil's jokes went like this: "Why did the student eat his homework? Because the teacher told him it was a piece of cake." My uncle Jordan would say: "Why use jokes and magic tricks, Gil, to make the kids laugh? All you got to do is make a funny face." They provided precious childhood remembrances that reinforced the importance of family and sharing love.

Throughout the early 1960s, my parents played the traditional Western-pop music favorites that predated rock and roll, such as Andy Williams, Bing Crosby, Steve Lawrence, Frank Sinatra, Nat King Cole, Doris Day, and Dean Martin. Mom and Dad had an extensive record collection. They introduced me to the beautiful melodies and romantic lyrics of the songs "Moon River" by Andy Williams and "Pretty Blue Eyes" by Steve Lawrence. Listening to musical melodies and lyrics would provide the framework and evolution of emotional tenderness. These two songs were immediately unique to me as my mom sang the vocals and seemed to repeat playing these two songs more often on the record player. Listening to the lyrics and watching my mother's pleasure singing with the musical refrain would constantly stimulate heartfelt sentiment and happiness. My music appreciation would become a powerful instrument for experiencing and relating to human emotions. The beautiful harmonies influenced my social interactions during my childhood and later years by merely listening and using my imagination.

Music would become my escape from the stressors of everyday life. After attentively listening to the lyrics of Steve Lawrence's "Pretty Blue Eyes" song, I wondered, *What's the big deal about a girl having pretty blue eyes?* questioning the rationale as I began asserting my gender identity.

My father was devoted to his full-time job. He would come home from work at 4:30 p.m. every late afternoon like clockwork. Dad often dozed off, taking a quick nap on the living room couch before eating dinner or playing with us kids. He was a fitness fanatic during his younger years, mostly weight lifting and learning some boxing skills at his local hometown gym. He passed on his fitness ethic to my brother and I at a young age. We could easily do twenty push-ups and understand some rudimentary boxing offensive and defensive maneuvers. Dad never pressured us to play sports as Mom did, but he did a lot to encourage us by being an early role model/coach and teacher. He always made himself available to play catch and be our underhand toss pitcher for our wiffle-ball game at-bats in the front yard. At the same time, Mom was busy playing hopscotch or teaching my sisters how to use the hula hoop. The round plastic hoop was the craze in the 1960s.

In March of 1962, my parents gave me a nine-volt Sony AM/FM transistor radio for my ninth birthday after receiving the sacraments of Confirmation and Holy Communion. It was one of the most popular communication devices of that time. I enjoyed listening to music on Bay Area radio station KFRC AM channel 610 and my favorite professional baseball team broadcasts on radio station KSFO AM channel 560 on the dial. Additionally, our family would enjoy Giant baseball game TV broadcasts on independent KTVU channel 2, just one of four available stations. My brother, Frank, and I grew up becoming instant fans of professional baseball, basketball, and football stars. Willie Mays, Wilt Chamberlain, John Brodie, Reggie Jackson, Daryle Lamonica, and Kenny Stabler would become essential role models for kids growing up in the Bay Area.

During baseball's "Golden Age," the Giants were in the World Series competing against the New York Yankee greats of Mickey Mantle, Roger Maris, Whitey Ford, and Yogi Berra in 1962. Professional sports were a microcosm of society that could unite a community, impart an inspirational passion for emulating, and bestow an example of accomplishing your dreams and goals. CYO youth baseball was definitely in our near future.

Before the year ended, the Cuban Missile Crisis would bring intense anxiety as Walter Cronkite on the CBS evening news seemed to be on our TV set 24-7. Angry images and disturbing news clips of raving oratory from Cuban revolutionary leader Fidel Castro and Soviet Union President Nikita Khrushchev caused fear. Classroom duck-and-cover training drills were practiced daily for safety, teaching us to dive under our desks and cover our heads. Civil defense air-raid sirens blaring in our neighborhood were unsettling. The event exploded worldwide, and reports of the tensions between the United States and the Soviet Union over Cuba would leave a lasting impression that atomic war and global destruction were possible. I remember going to bed at night, worrying about if I would live to see another day. My inner voice would say, *I am too young to die.*

Spirits replenished after President Kennedy's naval blockade worked and reduced tensions. My parents rallied behind Kennedy even more. "Kennedy just saved our lives and the world from obliteration," Dad said. I remember taking a deep breath of relief. However, the Cold War was at its peak during the aftermath of the Cuban Missile Crisis.

WHAT A TALE MY THOUGHTS WILL TELL: WORDS NOT TO BE FORGOTTEN

Uncle Gil would tell my father, "What do the kids want to be if they have a chance to grow up?"

I thought, *Lousy joke, Uncle Gil.*

In later years, understanding the extraordinary historical significance of that fateful event, I purchased the written work by Robert F. Kennedy called *Thirteen Days*, a memoir of the Cuban Missile Crisis. I grew up with the fear that nuclear war was a real possibility.

Later childhood encompassing fifth through eighth grade was extraordinarily eventful as my understanding of how world events can impact life's meaning combined with the onset of male puberty. School environments, friendships, sports participation, music, and TV news broadcasts became more influential. Being born after World War II, our baby boomer generation experienced a dramatic change that transformed the rules of everything that had gone before. Developing my values, cultural norms, boundaries, and ability to decide on conflict management became important. My capacity to give an outward appearance of poise and self-control was essential. I vividly remember having to deal with hormonal changes that caused my voice to deepen, accelerate the growth of my body and facial hair, and become taller with muscle and bone development. Personal achievement and academic records became permanent.

My parents emphasized the urgency of achieving good grades through unwavering study habits with the school curriculum. I remember the feeling that I was no longer anything special, now becoming one in a crowd. Spending more time with my peer group's influence became more important as my parent's guidance diminished. Punctuality and neatness, learning to be still, keeping quiet, and not being distracted were required while attending a Catholic school classroom. Catholic school uniform clothing requirement policies, classroom rules/discipline, and gathering at God's house for worship helped with these conduct standards. Even though I was not a big fan of wearing the same salt-and-pepper black pants, a green sweater, and a white shirt every day to school, I begrudgingly accepted it.

Playtime was always a high priority. I would keep myself occupied for hours by imitating my favorite baseball player, Willie Mays.

I used to stand outside on our front lawn facing our home's large front bay window. Mother typically had the drapes closed, leaving my reflection within the glass. After watching many Giants baseball games on television, I soon realized that my batting stance and swing looked like Willie's. So I practiced my batting stance and stroke repeatedly, watching myself through the front window glass.

My brother would often flash out of the house, breaking my concentration and asking me to play pitch and hit. We would throw the wiffle ball high and try to catch it or take turns as a hitter. I would usually be the first batter and Frank the pitcher as he would float in underhanded pitches while I tried to hit the ball with that thirty-two-inch plastic bat Dad had bought us.

One afternoon, I was in my batting stance, waiting for Frank to toss a pitch when I heard a faint feminine voice saying, "Can I play?"

As I turned, glancing over my left shoulder, I saw a pretty blond-haired girl with large blue eyes, dressed in a cute blue overall outfit with a pink-and-white small checked shirt and white sneakers. Pleasantly befuddled, I dropped the plastic baseball bat as my brother's underhand pitch hit me in the head. She appeared to be around the same age as me. I found out later; she was one year older—eleven years old.

I asked, "What is your name?"

She responded, "Nancy... Nancy Peterson."

Within a short time, we became inseparable friends. We would ride bikes together, play card games, or hang out. Nancy would laugh and smile at my innocent teasing and the corny one-line jokes I learned from my uncle Gil. I would look into Nancy's big blue eyes while having a conversation. Instead of listening, I would get distracted, noticing my emotional feelings changing as I focused on her blond hair and full lips—my first crush. From then on, I was anxious to get home from school to be with Nancy after finishing my homework.

On a beautiful and warm fall day in October, we slowly danced to the song "Our Day Will Come" by Ruby and the Romantics for the first time. We were awkwardly attempting a two-step dance movement, moving back and forth as we would clumsily step on each other's toes as our jitters would melt away. We would laugh with heartwarming delight and could see the happiness in each other's eyes. As the song lyrics captured our tender affection and innocent attachment to one another, "No one can tell me. That I'm too young to know, I love you so, and you love me," we sang the lyrics in unison.

After a couple of months had passed, my platonic affection for Nancy grew. One day, I nervously entered back into my mother's flower garden on a weekend afternoon. Carefully, I cut the bottom of six yellow tulip stems and six red roses (hopeful that Mom wouldn't notice) and prepared the floret by wrapping them in a green-colored sheet of craft paper. Then I thought, *What message should I write for her that I could attach to the flowers?* I thought about this for quite some time. And then suddenly, that inner voice of mine said, *The lyrics from the song by Steve Lawrence, "Pretty Blue Eyes." Perfect!*

So my note to Nancy contained this message,

> *Thought I was in love before*
> *And then you moved in next door*
> *Pretty blue eyes, pretty blue eyes*
> *All the guys from the neighborhood*
> *Keep sayin' you sure look good.*
> *With your blue eyes, pretty blue eyes*
> *Saw you from my window*
> *My heart skipped a beat.*
> *Going to sit by your doorstep*
> *So that I can meet*
> *Pretty blue eyes, please come out today*
> *So, I can tell you what I have to say*
> *That I love you, love you*
> *Pretty blue eyes*

After Nancy read my note, her innocent smile and gazing eye contact expressed a deep emotion that made my heart flutter. Then she reached out to me with her arms and hugged me. After that, Nancy and I became devoted to each other. I thought to myself, *This must be how love feels.*

Being the strict disciplinarian, my mom always demanded that playtime end no later than 5:00 p.m. Knowing I was at Nancy's house, my mom would whistle when I would be late, even a few minutes after the 5:00-p.m. hour. The whole neighborhood was familiar with my mom's whistle. I was not too fond of that whistle. I said to Nancy, "I don't want to go." Nancy responded, "I don't want you to go, but I don't want your mom getting mad at me either."

As the weeks passed, Nancy and I developed strong feelings of attachment and infatuation for one another. Looking back, I remember how we both enjoyed listening to the song "Puppy Love," released by Paul Anka, as it reminded us of how our first romantic love stage progressed.

A few weeks later, while Nancy and I were playing a card game on her front porch, she said, "John, I have something to tell you." Having difficulty, Nancy said, "I was afraid to tell you this, but we are moving out of the neighborhood next weekend. My father got a new job" It was 5:10 p.m.

I heard my mom's annoying whistle; I had to go. In the moonlight that night, I cried myself to sleep. Nancy's father had received a job promotion that would require him to move his family to the East Coast. When we met for the last time a few hours before her departure, sitting under the giant sycamore shade tree on my front lawn, Nancy reached over, touched my hand, and held it tightly for the first time. My young heart swelled with an emotion that I had not experienced before. As I looked into her eyes, I noticed a small tear from the corner of her right eye rolling slowly down her cheek. As I tried to hold back my tears, getting choked up, I couldn't talk, never uttering a word, motionless. I was transfixed on Nancy's pretty blue eyes, conveying her warmth and bond with me. Releasing her hand from mine, she looked down, placed a folded paper note in the underside/palm of my left hand, and closed my hand with her fingertips to secure the message. Before I realized it, Nancy was no longer next to me. Quickly, I looked up, only seeing her backside as she ran back toward her home. I reached out my arms in vain. Nancy was gone.

WHAT A TALE MY THOUGHTS WILL TELL: WORDS NOT TO BE FORGOTTEN

When I opened the note, it read, *You are here*. Nancy's words were handwritten inside the drawing of a heart. If I had the forethought about writing a message to her, my words would have come from the lyrics of our favorite song, "Puppy Love."

And they called it puppy love
Oh, I guess they'll never know
How a young heart how it really feels
And why I love her so
I hope, I hope, and I pray
That maybe someday
You'll be back (you'll be back) in my arms (in my arms)
Once again

My young heart experienced love for the first time. I learned about having an affectionate bond and how an interpersonal connection with the opposite sex can evolve into a shared attachment. Of course, my heartbreak and emotions were real. But in reality, Nancy was my first stepping stone to discovering what love is or isn't. Looking back on it now, I will never forget the beauty of our loving innocence, honesty, spontaneity, and purity of our companionship. Love would become the instrument of my self-growth and understanding. And I understood how a girl's pretty blue eyes could make love grow.

Kids living in our small town of San Lorenzo grew up with a wide range of recreational activities and sports programs in the 1960s to partake. San Lorenzo provided a boy's club, recreation facilities/parks, Little League baseball, swimming pool use at local high schools during the summer, Boy/Girl Scout programs, and bowling alleys. These programs furnished the ability for kids to create new friendships outside of a structured school schedule. Fortunately, we participated in most of these youth programs during our childhood. My parents wanted us to have the same opportunities they had experienced throughout their lifetime.

Most of the neighboring families were practicing Christians. We all shared many of the same values, and sports were very prominent, almost like a second religion. Walking the neighborhood streets during the baseball or football season, you could hear the radio play-by-play broadcast of Lon Simmons calling the Giants or 49ers game out of open garage doors. Listening to Lon Simmons would ignite my passion and interest in playing baseball and rooting for my favorite professional baseball and football teams. My mother wanted to register us to play baseball in the next upcoming CYO season. Mom preferred CYO baseball over the San Lorenzo Little League at the time. I didn't care at the time; I couldn't wait to play in the upcoming season in March.

During sixth grade, my physical growth was accelerating. I was considered well above the clinical-based CDC Growth Average Charts for a 10–11-year-old child moving into adolescence. Frank was smaller and a little under the average. I was the firstborn twin, and studies suggest that being the firstborn could slightly influence height. However, our intelligence difference was the opposite regarding the comparison of standardized Stanford Binet IQ Tests results. Frank scored the highest in our family at 131. I landed a little above average at 119.

Frank was hyperactive, having difficulty paying attention in class, and was easily distracted, interrupting the teacher, or causing problems with bursts of energy. Frank was basically "bouncing off the walls." During fifth-grade English class, our teacher, Sister Maria, would have a particular term each day from our homework assignments handwritten on the blackboard. The word of the day was "INQUIRE." Sister Maria called on my brother and asked him to give the definition. Frank knew the word's exact meaning but answered instead, "It's when you sing in church." Everyone started laughing as Frank completely disrupted the class intentionally. Mischievous and unruly misbehaviors resulted in Frank staying back and having to repeat fifth grade.

In contrast, I noticed myself becoming more independent with a quiet temperament and preferring to spend more time alone focusing on homework or listening to the top 20 Billboard hits on the radio in my bedroom. I was starting to understand what I am doing now could have long-term effects on my future. My interest would grow in reading fictional and nonfiction books. Studying American history became an obsession. During this time, I discovered that I could close my eyes and see objects and memories just as clearly as if I had taken a photograph. My parents often commented on my ability to retrieve memories in such vivid detail.

This aptitude served me well when studying for a test and comprehending reading material by easily memorizing information. However, the downside was that my brain occasionally became overloaded with unneeded thoughts when reflecting on past experiences.

One of the books that became assigned reading for sixth graders was *The Underground Railroad*. This novel depicted the struggles of the enslaved people in their efforts for freedom. It quickly became a favorite of mine, reading it three times. The book stirred my empathy and heartache for Black Americans' plight and the terrible human cost of slavery during the Civil War. Reading *The Underground Railroad* was enlightening and ignited my initial interest in American history. I was well on my way to becoming a person of acceptance and appreciation of all ethnic and cultural backgrounds. So when my turn came around to give my interpretation of the book, I said something along these lines, "I enjoyed reading this book. I became sad over the harm and pain enslaved people had to go through. I learned so many things that I did not know. Enslaved people helped build our country and the nation's capital. It was awful to learn that disagreements over slavery caused the war."

Then, on November 22, 1963, during an early morning recess break, playing in the jungle gym, I noticed a commotion near the flag pole by our school offices' front entrance. Father Hannigan was attempting to calm some sobbing nuns. Immediately over the PA system, students were instructed to return to their classrooms. It was a little before 11:00 a.m. Our teacher, Sister Maria, trembling and crying, spoke one sentence, "President Kennedy has been shot in Dallas, Texas."

Christine Shively, who sat next to me in class, started shedding tears and reached out for me to comfort her. I did my best to calm her. I was stunned and comforted others as many kids were scared and started weeping uncontrollably. I couldn't resist my natural desire to jump in and fix other people's problems. I took great pleasure in being coincidentally placed into the savior role.

All of it was hard to believe. It felt as if the world was ending. A few moments later, we all gathered as Sister Maria led us in prayer, reciting the Apostles' Creed and praying the rosary. About thirty minutes later, President Kennedy was pronounced dead. Father Hannigan dismissed all classes early that day. When Mom picked us up from school, we realized that she had been crying and was visibly upset. All of us kids remained silent during the ride home, with respect for our mother's grief and President Kennedy's family. My inner voice asked the question, *Why? How could this happen?* This event would continue to spur my interest in studying past-chronicled events to seek understanding.

*****

After finishing another successful CYO basketball season, coming in second place behind St. Bede's Catholic, baseball practice started in the early spring. I loved our baseball uniform colors of white and gold with black lettering/pinstripes. As uniforms were being handed out to the players, I asked my coach for the number 24 and wanted to play center field. My coach granted both requests as I was considered the best athlete in my class. During practice sessions, it was evident that I could hit the ball further, run faster, and overall have more advanced athletic ability than my counterparts. As my coach would say, "You sure can run fast, John."

I practiced and perfected the basket catch that Willie Mays made famous. When I would run the bases stretching a single into a double, I would intentionally hit the baseball cap bill with my right hand, knocking it off halfway between first and second base, just like Willie used to do. But I remember most about the season was how involved my mother was. She never missed a game. Her words of encouragement from the stands were more forceful and energetic than other parents attending our games, often screaming at the umpire or opposing players. Coaches and players from both sides would turn their heads, sometimes wondering, "Whose mother is that yelling in the stands?"

I loved my mom's support, but it was sometimes a bit embarrassing. One of her famous opposing heckles was "Come on, Johnny… I've seen better pitchers at my Tupperware party" or yelling to the umpire, "Hey, Blue, I've heard better calls at our Friday night Bingo game." It was an omen of things to come as my athletic progression continued.

My love of playing sports and being a good athlete started the internal self-conscious feeling that I was talented and unequaled. Being part of a peer group and team made life more reassuring. Mike, my best friend, was a baseball teammate among another group of guys who became friends. We all had nicknames: Mike "The Machine" Grover, Kenny "Slick" Meyers, Chris "Slim" Davis, Dave "Peanut" Ahern, and Dean "Sticks" Souza. They called me "Fast Eddie."

We hung out together and even created our neighborhood baseball field. We came up with the idea of going over to the open field grounds of Tot Town, just two blocks south of Mike's house from the Via Catherine entrance, to construct our ball field.

Tot Town consisted of hills, lumps, burrows, and five feet tall ragweed. The ragged footprints of jackrabbits were everywhere over a ten-acre lot. With my father's guidance, we got together a couple of hand-pushed lawn mowers and garden-tilling tools (shovels, wheelbarrows, pruning shears, pickax, hoes, and rakes) and put a plan together. We got to work, including the help of Mike's brother, Bob, brother, Frank, and my sisters, Judy and Mary, chipped in to help. It was so much fun as we toiled amid the vibration of the ground underneath our muddy shoes, recognizing the rumbling roar of an approaching Southern Pacific train from a distance away. It filled us all with anticipation and awe as its light grew brighter and clanging louder. The railroad tracks were about a hundred yards west of our construction site. An eight-foot cyclone fence protected the area with circular barbed wire and clusters of short, sharp spikes on top. As the train passed by, we watched the tracks light up with sparks underneath.

It took almost a month, but we cleared all the obstacles and carved out a sizable flat dirt surface. My father paced off the area and measured the space. "Nice job, guys! For your hard work, here are base bags and a bag of limestone chalk so you can line the baselines and home plate batter's box," Dad said. "Welcome to your field of dreams."

Besides having fun playing on our new baseball field, the pure joy about our accomplishments and the brotherhood established by working together taught me two precious lifelong lessons. First, accomplishing a goal through teamwork and putting in the hard work to achieve that objective was rewarding, and second, realizing that there is a lot of beauty in ordinary things.

After a few years had passed, our field of dreams ended up being bulldozed as construction crews began renovations. Ultimately, once redevelopment was completed, Tot Town would be renamed San Lorenzo Park Community Center. Improvements included a significant human-made lake/duck pond, community center, playground, baseball fields, and grounds to accommodate picnic tables and barbecue pits.

Better late than never, my parents started providing us with an allowance. All of us would alternate, taking turns doing everyday household tasks. Mowing the front or back lawns, raking leaves, folding clean clothes, or washing Mom and Dad's car provided a paid allowance. Mom and Dad took the time to instruct the proper methods to ensure we did a particular job the right way. If you did not keep up with your assigned nonpaying household duties, you automatically forfeited your option of getting an allowance-paying chore. If your allowance-paying job hadn't been completed to our parents' satisfaction or standard of excellence, you would have to either redo the task or not get paid.

Dad would say, "Save your money over time for things you want to buy. Your allowance will be $5 per week."

My nonpaying household responsibilities included helping wash the dishes after dinner and ensuring my bedroom stayed clean. I had my eye on a pair of Chicago Roller Skates and a blue-colored Schwinn Continental twenty-eight-inch wheel size 10-speed bicycle. However, I knew it would take a long time to save enough money for those desired items by doing some simple math. Our best friends, Mike and Bob, already had 10-speed bikes while Frank and I were still getting around on our small twenty-inch wheeled Schwinn Sting-Rays.

One Saturday afternoon, while trading baseball cards at Mike's house, Mike asked Frank and I if we could help him deliver his *San Francisco Chronicle* 120 households paper route on Sunday mornings.

We quickly found out why Mike needed help. The Sunday *San Francisco Chronicle* newspaper included several advertisements inserts and entertainment sections that made a single paper weigh over 4 pounds each. Mike guaranteed that he would pay us both $15 each week. The requirements involved being at Mike's house at the predawn hour of 5:00 a.m. sharp (papers and inserts were delivered to Mike's home at 4:00 a.m.). Responsibilities included helping with folding and rubber banding and, the number-one rule, newspapers had to be placed on the customer's front porch.

On rainy days, we had the extra step of having to wrap the papers in a clear plastic covering. Frank and I were all in as long as Mike could guarantee that we would be finished in time, not running us late for the 8:30 a.m. Sunday service at St. Joachim's Church. This new moneymaking adventure would drastically reduce the time needed to save enough funds to purchase the bike and roller skates we wanted. It was a godsend.

We had just completed our first month helping Mike with the paper route being reliable, on time, and providing good customer service by placing every paper on the front doormat. We had saved up about $80 each. However, we needed $125 each to purchase both items we wanted.

The following Sunday, arriving right on time, Mike showed us a written customer complaint from his station manager that described that a customer that lived on Via Harriet had complained about not getting his paper on the front porch. It was an address that was my brother's responsibility. Frank had the odd-numbered side of the street, and I had the even-numbered side. Unbeknownst to me, Frank had been throwing this particular customer's Sunday newspaper for the last couple of weeks onto the front driveway, attempting to save time. One of those weeks was a windy-misty morning when the customer's Sunday paper, rubber band snapping, came apart, with the wind blowing newspaper pages and advertisements all over the client's front yard.

Before Mike could finish asking Frank about the complaint, Frank said, "It won't happen again."

Knowing I was delivering on the opposite side of the same street, Mike asked me to watch Frank and make sure he placed the customer's paper on the porch! "No problem, Mike," I responded.

As we approached the customer's house, I hit the brakes, yelling at Frank, "Make sure to place it on his porch!"

Frank got off his bike, leaving it on the sidewalk, pushing down the kickstand; he grabbed that big heavy Sunday paper out of his trolley tote basket attached to the rear of his bike as he headed toward the complaining customer's front door porch. I lost sight of Frank temporarily as he disappeared behind a tall hedge-type plant.

Suddenly, I heard an ear-splitting clacking sound, like a screen door slamming against a door frame. I got off my bike to get a better view of what was happening. I saw Frank winding up to launch the customer's newspaper against his screen door for a second time. Then, *boom*, this second deafening sound was even louder than the first. Frank returned to retrieve the newspaper with a determined look on his face, preparing to throw it again. It's six in the morning. Standing in shock, I saw Frank bending down to pick up the newspaper; suddenly, a stocky bald man with the facial expression of an angry psychopath bolted out of the front door in a bathrobe.

Frank turned and ran for his life down the street, with the much older man bowlegged and barefooted, with arms pumping up and down, running at his top speed, trying his best to catch my brother. Then his bathrobe strap abruptly came undone, causing his bathrobe to swing wildly in the wind, exposing his bare butt. Frank expertly dodged the man with quick double moves and post maneuvers that any professional football wide receiver would be proud to accomplish. The image of that man chasing my little brother, I couldn't help but laugh as he was unsuccessful in his pursuit. When we got home and retold the events to my father, fearing the worst, Dad paused for several moments before responding, looking directly into our eyes with an imposing stare. Then he smirked with a pinched mouth, trying to hold back the big grin that gradually appeared on his face.

Finally, Dad broke out in a deep, loud belly laugh and said, "How much are you, boys, short of getting those 10-speed bikes you want?"

Frank and I said in unison, "About $25."

Dad responded, "Don't worry, I got you covered."

There was a lot of beauty in those brand-new roller skates and 10-speed bikes we bought. Cycling and roller skating would provide not only fun but also maturing self-confidence, fitness, and the responsibility of maintaining their proper operating condition daily. Valuable lessons learned. Frank grasped the consequences of his substandard customer-service episode, and a few weeks later, Frank was hired as a paperboy for a smaller news publication out of San Leandro called *The Morning News*.

My mom had hobbies that kept her busy as a stay-at-home mother. She was a great cook. New kitchen gadgets were becoming more commonplace, appliances like electric can openers, food mixers, electric toasters, coffee percolators, and electric carving knives. She prepared many traditional comfort food dishes like meat loaf, beef stews, steak dishes, soups, casseroles, and homemade chicken pot pies, always complemented with vegetables and rice or potatoes. Mom always said, "Make sure to eat everything on your plate, especially vegetables."

She was also quite skilled at sewing. She would sew several shirts and pairs of pajamas for Frank and I by following easy-to-use clothes-sewing pattern blueprints supplied by Simplicity or McCalls. She took joy in teaching my sisters how to sew and knit. Another hobby our mother enjoyed was putting together her White Mountain one-thousand-piece jigsaw puzzles while watching her beloved TV soap operas. Her favorite soap operas were *As the World Turns* and *General Hospital*. Mom was hooked, stimulating her imagination, as the frantic storylines would change daily, displaying various human emotions and interactions that made the themes intriguing and true to life. One of the fictional characters in *As the World Turns*, who played the role of a traditional housewife, was Nancy Hughes. Mom empathically said while watching an episode, "No, Nancy. He is a waste of time. You can't measure love. Don't be fooled, girl!" Watching periodically with her, I started getting addicted to the stories, often coming home from school anxiously asking, "What happened to Luke and Laura at *General Hospital* today?"

For exercise, Mom loved roller skating. She would skate around the block in our neighborhood. The path's starting point was Via Natal, making a left on Via Walter, another left on Via Amigos, and then completing the final left turn on Via Catherine for the homestretch run. That route was a little bit over one-half mile in length. Once we got our Chicago Roller Skates, which fit over your shoes with adjustments and straps to hold them in place, we could join our mother on that course. Mom beat us on our neighborhood roller-skating course for about one year before we could easily pass her as we noticed her breathing with more difficulty. Smoking and cigarette advertisements were prevalent in the 1960s. Being a chain smoker (she started smoking at fourteen), our mother would go through a two-pack-a-day habit of smoking her favorite Benson and Hedges cigarette brand.

Our required bedtime back then was 8:00 p.m. One of Mom's favorite pastimes was watching her Bay Bombers Roller Derby team on KTVU channel 2. The videotaped games were broadcast in the Bay Area at 8:30 p.m., just past our bedtime. Occasionally, I snuck out of my bedroom and asked her, "Can I watch the game with you?" Since I was always such a good boy, Mom would say, "Okay…just for a little while. You need to get your rest."

So I would quickly snuggle next to her in a comfortable position hugging her arm and placing my head on her shoulder while wearing my Simplicity Sewing Pattern *Super Man PJs* she handmade for me. I loved the rough-and-tumble action of the game. The Bay Bombers had two units, male and female. They alternated teams while skating for several periods on a circular banked track. The team would field five players at a time. Their colorful orange, white, and black uniforms with stripped helmets were fun to watch on our color TV. Like football, offensive linemen and individual players were called blockers. Jammers were potential scorers, and the pivot man was usually the team's captain and best player. Number 40 Charlie O'Connell and number 38 Joan "The Blonde Bomber" Weston were the star players for the Bay Bombers. She was mom's favorite player. The fun was the famous fights between them and their main rival, the Los Angeles T-Birds. The knockdowns, chair-throwing assaults, and entertaining personalities made it exciting to watch. Once I turned twelve, my bedtime was extended, allowing me to enjoy the games with her until completion.

In early 1964, my sister, Judy, was very involved in the fan frenzy over the Beatles called "Beatlemania." Watching *The Ed Sullivan Show*, Judy couldn't sit still as she was mesmerized watching the Beatles perform, "I Want to Hold Your Hand." Judy's favorite was Paul McCartney. Images of screaming young female fans seemed over the top as their intensity surpassed any previous fan adoration. The Beatles would be followed by other popular London groups that exploded on the scene, including The Rolling Stones and Dave Clark Five. I couldn't understand what the fuss was all about. I focused more on the upcoming Cassius Clay versus Sonny Liston Heavyweight Title Fight. My father did not like Cassius Clay because of his audacity and outspoken stance on the Vietnam War, saying, "That Clay is a loudmouth."

In contrast, I liked Cassius Clay's proclamation "Floats like a butterfly and stings like a bee," which was amusedly poetic. I remember Cassius being a huge underdog as Sonny Liston was feared as a devastating puncher. Some analysts said Cassius could be risking his life in the ring, increasing the hype before the match. Unfortunately, it would not be broadcasted on our local TV channels, so my dad and I listened to the blow-by-blow on the old Philco radio. Listening to the fight was magical. The radio broadcast was live, with Les Keiter calling the punch-by-punch action. Howard Cosell, Rocky Marciano, and pro football star Jim Brown contributed commentary between rounds. Clay won a seventh-round technical knockout. From then on, I followed the fantastic career of the greatest professional boxer of all time as he proclaimed his allegiance to the Nation of Islam by changing his name to Muhammad Ali.

My first professional venture was on the near horizon. One of the most solemn and highly regarded roles within the Catholic Church was becoming an altar boy. It was a serious responsibility as your role was to become part of the clergy by serving the priest at the altar during the Mass sacrifice. We were given a packet that included the required functions, responsibilities, dress codes, and Latin prayer replies. We studied for hours, learning proper pronunciation and memorizing adequate responses to the priest's Latin prayers. "*In Nomine Patris, et Filii, et Spiritus Sancti. Amen*" was the sign of the cross in Latin. You had to be proficient and accurate before being allowed to join.

One of my favorite roles and traditions being an altar boy, besides the prayerful participation and attentiveness, was when the priest would complete the Lord's Prayer and then say, "May the peace of Christ be with you. Let us exchange the sign of peace."

WHAT A TALE MY THOUGHTS WILL TELL: WORDS NOT TO BE FORGOTTEN

Most parishioners would say either "Peace be with you" or "May God bless you." After the sign of peace and greetings ended, this initiated the congregation's preparation to approach the altar and receive Holy Communion. Those individual's conscious of grave sin cannot accept the body and blood of the Lord without prior sacramental confession. When the priest or deacon moved from the sanctuary to distribute communion, all altar boys would rise and stand reverently at their seats unless the priest motioned for help. When this happens, one altar server would stand next to the priest and process or assist them in any way. I was often called upon to help by holding the large chalice of wine while the priest distributed the consecrated bread by saying, "The body of Christ." I would serve the consecrated wine by saying, "The blood of Christ." You had to have received the sacraments of Confession and Communion to be allowed an offering of wine.

While offering the sacred chalice of wine, one of my seventh-grade classmates, Eileen Eggers, came up to accept her sip of wine. Before receiving the wine, she looked into my eyes and gave me a sweet, approving smile. I recognized that familiar adoring smile and what her welcoming gaze implied. My heart fluttered as I was lovestruck. We quickly developed a devoted affectionate connection. Eileen was considered the prettiest girl in our seventh-grade class. She would become my second stepping stone in learning how to interact within a loving relationship. Our close connection was more mature as going steady was commonplace. Our bodies were simultaneously undergoing typical hormonal and secondary sex characteristics that produced more robust fascination, emotion, and libido. The independence and mobility to get around riding my 10-speed bike to school or Eileen's house without adult supervision advanced my ability to spend more time with her. We shared many special moments at school, church, and home, finding commonalities with sports and music, working on homework assignments, and watching television.

We enjoyed watching *Dr. Ben Casey* or *Dr. Kildare*'s TV episodes in Eileen's family room, enjoying homemade chocolate chip cookies and milk. We would pass each other folded handwritten love notes during class at school. As our bond evolved, one of Eileen's notes said, "Will you lend me a kiss? I promise to give it back." We would safeguard our love notes, binder paper, and homework assignments in our "Pee-Chee folders," which had two internal pockets and printed reference information inside. The outside of the Pee-Chee folder would have illustrations of engaging sports figures. Our written exchanges initiated conversations about more romantic behaviors, such as hand-holding or how to kiss, as our affection for each other grew. However, my love of playing sports was a priority before anything else.

As I was nearing my twelfth birthday, my best friend, Mike, told me that he had decided to switch from playing organized CYO baseball to the San Lorenzo National Little League.

Early registration and scheduling for the Majors division started in February, and tryouts began in March. Frank and I pleaded with Mom asking if we could make the same switch. After a week had passed, waiting for Mom to decide, Dad intervened and said to Mom, "Dee Dee, I think the shift from CYO baseball to the San Lorenzo Little League would be good for the boys. They have the talent and ability! A change would be a good challenge for them."

Mom finally gave in. Afterward, we followed Dad's statement by saying excitedly, "Mom, we want you to root for us during the tryouts!"

During my previous CYO baseball season, I led the team in batting with a .390 average with three home runs. I had great unwavering confidence in my abilities and was looking forward to the tryout challenge.

Major League baseball's player draft and tryout was a two-day weekend event of about 120 participants. The League's board of directors chose the Major division team managers to grade the player's tryout evaluations based on five competencies: hitting, throwing, fielding grounders/fly balls, and situational running. The San Lorenzo National Little League had four well-manicured fenced baseball fields. Fence dimensions were 175 feet to the left- and right-field corners and 203 feet to straightaway center field. Colorful advertising boards were on the outfield fences, and a large concession booth was selling beverages and food to increase revenue.

WHAT A TALE MY THOUGHTS WILL TELL: WORDS NOT TO BE FORGOTTEN

On tryout day, the smell of hot dogs cooking saturated the afternoon air. The Minor League and Major League flags and banners were blowing majestically in the breeze. Festive bunting decorations and reading the Little League pledge before the tryout added to the day's excitement and anticipation. Mom, Dad, Eileen, and Eileen's father were in the stands to watch Frank and I perform. Frank and I were good to go, practicing together for three weeks before the tryout date.

Evaluations on the skill of throwing, fielding, and situational running came first on Saturday. We performed well above average, not making errors, throwing accurately and making correct decisions in the situational base running drills. We couldn't wait for the final evaluation on Sunday, hitting.

One of the coaches would operate a Louisville Slugger mechanical pitching machine to accommodate the hitting segment of the tryout. As a result, you were allowed only fifteen pitches, mostly 45 to 60 mph fastballs.

While waiting in the on-deck circle, I imagined Willie Mays and how often I practiced his stance and home run swing. Next, I visualized myself hitting long moon-shot home-run balls over the fence. Then my name and jersey number were announced over the PA system, breaking my concentration. As I approached home plate, I looked up into the stands and saw Dad chewing on a hot dog, Eileen and her father clapping encouragement, and my mom vigorously bouncing up and down in the stands, emphatically yelling, "Show them what you got, Johnny!"

I started by hitting several stinging line drives in the gap, smacking the outfield fences after a couple of hops. Then I hit the next pitch on a line that pounded the center field wall on the fly. I momentarily stepped away from the plate, taking a deep breath, knowing I was getting down the pitching machine's timing. Then I hit three consecutive moon-shot home runs over the left-field fence. Again, I could hear my mom hollering emphatically, "That's my boy! That's my boy!"

Mom's face was proudly beaming with gratifying satisfaction during the drive home. Dad would say, "Nice job, boys!" Then Mom interrupted Dad with a raspy and hoarse voice strained from yelling encouragement, excitedly said, "Garth, did you hear the other parents in the stands? They were buzzing and asking 'Where did these Edwards boys come from? Did they play in the league last year?'"

Frank and I sat in the back seat, slapped, and exchanged high fives during the ride home. Finally, Mom said, "How does strawberry shortcake sound for dessert tonight, boys?"

It would be at least a week before determining if we made the cut and what team had selected us. Only Mom, Dad, or Judy, now a freshman in high school, were allowed to answer the pink-colored rotary telephone. Mom seemed more anxious than we were, waiting for the San Lorenzo Little League offices' phone call. The phone rang while watching *The Jetsons* Saturday morning cartoon show. When Mom answered, you could tell it was an official from the Little League. After Mom hung up the phone, she turned toward us and proudly announced, "Congratulations, boys. You both got drafted onto the same team, Mac's Produce, in the Majors division." She continued, "Your coach, Mr. Kruger, will call later in the week with your practice schedule."

We went on to have a great year, taking second place in Major League play, posting a 14–2 record one game behind league champion Bohannon Homes. I led the league in batting average and was selected to the All-Star team, designated to play center field like my idol, Willie Mays. The great thing about making the All-Star team was that my teammates and coaches got complimentary tickets to attend a San Francisco Giants game at Candlestick Park in South San Francisco. In 1965, the Giants had an outstanding team but fell two games short of winning the pennant over the hated Los Angeles Dodgers. We had upper-deck nosebleed seats, but I will never forget watching my hero, Willie Mays. The Giants won the game easily, beating the Pittsburgh Pirates as Mays, McCovey, and Jimmy Ray Hart hit home runs. Unfortunately, our All-Star team fell short by winning only a few games before being eliminated just before qualifying for the regional playoffs. We lost a one-run ball game to a team from Albany. After the loss, sullen and sad sitting in the dugout, I changed from my cleats into sneakers.

WHAT A TALE MY THOUGHTS WILL TELL: WORDS NOT TO BE FORGOTTEN

Leaving the dugout, I went through the right-field line gate opening; I noticed an older man standing just outside the gate with a red baseball cap with a large black letter "A" logo embroidered on the front crown of his hat. He approached me and said, "Hey kid… nice game!"

I responded, "We lost?"

He acknowledged me by nodding and said, "I have been watching you play for a while. You have some natural talent, kid. By the way, my name is Verl Thornock. I am the varsity baseball coach at Arroyo High School."

"Nice to meet you, Mr. Thornock, my name is John Edwards," I responded.

He chuckled as he walked toward the parking lot. Then he stopped, turned around, and said, "I know who you are. Keep learning and working on the fundamentals of the game. I'll be watching."

Later, I discovered that Coach Thornock was a typical visitor, often attending San Lorenzo Little League games. In addition, Coach Thornock would scout for talented players entering high school. There were two high schools in San Lorenzo, Arroyo and its main rival, San Lorenzo High School. Geographically, my home address on Via Catherine would require me to attend Arroyo.

After explaining my encounter to my father, he said, "Verl Thornock has been the varsity baseball coach at Arroyo since 1957 and has won several Hayward Area Athletic League championships. He is an excellent coach, well-known, and highly respected."

Mom, listening to our conversation as she was heading out the door to attend her favorite Friday night ritual, playing bingo at St. Joachim's Church hall, asked, "Wasn't it Coach Thornock that said 90 percent of the game is half mental?"

Dad, laughing, said, "No, Dee Dee, that was Yogi Berra."

The church's bingo hall held winner pay-out games every Friday and Saturday night and was a huge moneymaker. However, St. Joachim's most successful fundraiser was its annual Carnival Festival. The three-day event included an entertainment tent, game/food booths, a portable dance floor, a water dunking tank, carnival rides, and a large rotating Ferris wheel.

All church members were asked to volunteer and participate. I volunteered as a dunking subject for the water tank machine. It consisted of a large circular tank of water with a collapsible seat. Participants would throw softballs at a round metal target with a bull's-eye painted in the center. When the ball strikes the target, it collapses the chair, dunking you into the water.

Eileen was utterly delighted after dunking me several times. Our favorite carnival ride was called "The Scrambler." You could seat up to three people in a locking carriage. There were twelve cars distributed among three long arms that rotated the cars clockwise at high speeds so you could experience centrifugal force. It was fun because the ride-deviating pressure would slide you next to your partner, causing you to snuggle close to each other. Heading for the next ride with Eileen, I tried to avoid the Ferris wheel because I was afraid of heights. Trying to walk past the ride's entrance, Eileen stopped and said eagerly, "Let's go on the Ferris Wheel, John." Attempting to make weak excuses to go on a different ride, Eileen said, "You aren't afraid to go on the Ferris wheel, are you?"

I said, "I'll go on it with you."

Eileen could tell I was nervous reading my emotions, having an anxious expression on my face as we buckled into our seats. She leaned closer to me reassuringly, reaching out to hold my left hand. She placed her cheek on my left shoulder momentarily before pulling away to give me a kindhearted kiss on my left cheek. She said, "We will get through this ride together."

The sweetness of that moment, Eileen's concern expressed through reassuring words and gestures of tenderness, put me at ease, calming my fear. Sharing this loving moment strengthened our relationship and created a different version of myself. We both looked forward to summer vacation before entering our final year at St. Joachim's.

During summer vacation, Eileen and I spent as much time together as possible, knowing that a relationship separation was possible after completing eighth-grade graduation. Eileen's home address would require her to attend San Lorenzo High School or Monroe Catholic High School in Hayward. The thought of possibly being separated from Eileen once we moved on from St. Joachim's was a lingering apprehension.

Mom allowed me to use the telephone within limits to communicate with Eileen. During one of our phone conversations, we talked about going steady. Eileen asked me to speak to my parents to get their approval. I didn't think there was a chance that my parents would approve. Therefore, I decided to ask Eileen's parents first. In the 1960s, a "polite boy" would first seek permission from the girl's parents. To my surprise, Eileen's parents accepted my request, as did my parents, but it would be under parental supervision. Eileen and I were delighted. Entering eight-grade and going steady meant that we would become more popular among classmates and were committed to one another without thoughts of beginning an intimate relationship.

Eileen and I spent our first date together after my parents dropped us off for a Saturday afternoon matinee at the Lorenzo Theater. Our parents seemed a little more enthusiastic than usual for us to go to the movies that day. Once we approached the theater, we found out why and saw the large marquee signs above the box office that read, TODAY'S SHOWING: THE TEN COMMANDMENTS, STARRING CHARLTON HESTON, YUL BRYNNER, AND ANNE BAXTER. After the movie, we exchanged friendship rings and our seventh-grade class pictures.

Entering eighth grade, I was five foot eleven inches tall and 158 pounds. I was in the ninety-fifth percentile according to the pediatric growth and weight chart. I was as tall as my father and now towered over my mother. In March, I would be turning thirteen years old and was already having to shave as my peach fuzz was turning into more visible hairs on my face, chin, and above my upper lip. At this age, you discover that specific issues like whether I should begin shaving are as clear-cut as you might think and could be construed differently. For example, my father took pride in showing me how to shave, whereas my mother thought I should wait at least another year, concerned that shaving too early could lead to infections or facial skin disorders. I opted to shave, realizing that I was maturing toward more independence and building a solid sense of self.

In the 1960s, most kids learned about sex from their peers. My parents never talked to me about sexual intercourse. Often, friends replaced my parents for information and advice. I never felt comfortable talking to my parents about this topic even though my puberty hormones were going crazy. My parents knew that the Catholic diocese provided eighth-grade students with sex-education-based learning programs and films, including a wide range of topics on what type of physical changes to expect during puberty.

The documentary provided nuanced guidance about building healthy relationships with the opposite sex and messages containing proper spiritual and emotional attitudes toward the marriage act's reverence. I followed these guidelines as my catholic faith emphasized that boys must respect girls because they are God's chosen to create human life. Boys who learned to respect womanhood would respect women later in life. At times, I was caught off guard by some of my eighth-grade classmate's self-exploration and curiosity about sexual issues and body parts. My inner voice said, *Eighth grade is going to be interesting.*

My sister, Judy, was now attending her sophomore year in high school. At the same time, Mary and Frank started seventh grade and Susan entered second grade. During the eighth-grade school year, I would have the opportunity to attain more responsibility and social awareness. You learned how to manage leadership roles through a team effort concept by campaigning and running for individual elected positions within the Class Student Council. The student council included a president, vice president, and secretary nominated and elected by voting classmates. I was voted into the student council as the vice president. Being my first influencer role, I started building the human skills of time management, problem-solving, and leadership.

Regarding academics, I recognized my increasing command and understanding of the English language. I enjoyed reading and writing. Furthermore, in eighth grade, we learned how to compose an essay with proper sentence structure, grammar/punctuation, and subject, verb, and object usage. Our teacher, Sister Mark, gave us an essay assignment length of no more than five paragraphs, and your essay had to include an introduction, body, and conclusion. The topic was "How would you survive if left isolated on a deserted island."

Sister Mark said, "I will read the top five essays to the class on Friday. Essay composers will remain anonymous."

In our eighth-grade class, we had a total of forty-five students. I was a little disappointed that my essay was not chosen. However, I enjoyed listening to my classmates' creative written work. One paper, in particular, would be unforgettable and heartwarming. Based on the word selection and descriptive adjectives used, you could tell that the author was a female. Her opening introduction statement and thesis grabbed everybody's attention right away. It read something like this: "Feet firmly planted on the ground, I look up desperately into a cloudless blue sky to say a prayer as something catches my attention… Is it a bird? Is it a plane? No, it's my hero."

The first paragraph restated her introduction statement by telling us that it was only a mirage. Then, being discouraged, she described how she was determined to survive. Within the following three paragraphs, her essay's body included supporting evidence with smartly worded transition statements that seamlessly led to each of the other sections as she explained the survival strategies she would employ. Her concluding paragraph would re-empathize her thesis. Finally, she ended her essay with a thoughtful knight-in-shining-armor reflection.

As my memory serves, it read like this: "I continue to survive as my cries and prayers for help go unanswered, my sense of distress and anguish being unrelenting, one thought keeps me hopeful and optimistic. John Edwards will be my hero and come to my rescue."

My desk was positioned in the middle of the classroom. Suddenly, all approving eyes were upon me. It was such a remarkable feeling that someone would single me out that way.

I asked Eileen if she had written the essay, and she responded, "No, my essay wasn't selected." Being a curious adolescent kid, I did my best to find out which classmate wrote those words. I never found out. However, those words would carry an indelible signature within my heart.

St. Joachim's had a firm code of discipline, but each teacher had the authority to decide what punishment would be imposed on a child who broke any rules. Unfortunately, this led to a wide disparity in the decision-making process about the severity of the discipline being dished out. My brother was a victim of this disproportionate inconsistency by his seventh-grade teacher, Miss Anderson. In private Catholic schools, it was pretty standard practice to spank a child with a paddle or wooden ruler for disrupting the class or misbehaving. The punishment regimen seemed to happen to boys much more than to girls. Our classrooms had a designated "punishment corner." The teacher would instruct you to sit in a chair facing the corner of the wall with your backside view displayed to your classmates for thirty minutes for violating the rules.

One day in class, Frank disrupted the classroom rules by starting a conversation with a couple of his friends while Miss Anderson attempted to communicate homework assignments. In front of the whole class, Miss Anderson, visibly upset, walked over to Frank's desk and struck him with a wooden ruler on the back of his head. Being humiliated and angry, Frank immediately devised a retaliatory attack plan while Miss Anderson returned to writing assignments on the chalkboard. Frank immediately grabbed three-ring binder paper from his Pee-Chee folder, handing out sheets to other classmates. Suddenly, you have ten other classmates tearing off pieces of paper, putting them in their mouths, chewing and mustering as much saliva as they could while rolling spitballs into a small ball, making sure they were wet and gooey. The participating classmates had at least five to six spitballs to aim and fire each. Frank, taking his time, had to have the ultimate spitball by chewing on two whole paper sheets, creating a spitball of enormous magnitude. It was the atomic bomb of spitballs. They were armed and ready to fire with their mini weapons of mass destruction. Winding up, classmates started hurling in unison while Miss Anderson faced the chalkboard. Small spitballs started pelting and sticking to the blackboard.

Frank, who had not thrown his mega spitball yet, aimed with mathematical precision, quickly estimating velocity and distance to hit just above Miss Anderson's head. Miss Anderson, noticing the sound effects, realized what was happening. Turning around slowly, she sees Frank releasing his spitball. Unfortunately, it was too late to pull back as Frank missed his target. Instead, his spitball splattered all over Miss Anderson's left shoulder. The whole classroom erupted in laughter, everyone except for Miss Anderson.

One classmate yelled, "You cannot be serious!"

Frank's best friend, Bob Grover, said "Oh my god!" as Miss Anderson, a large, heavyset woman, made a beeline to Frank's desk within a few seconds. With a determined bulging eyeball expression on her ever-increasing red face, she grabbed Frank by his left earlobe and unceremoniously dragged him to the front of the class. Clutching Frank's ear, she started aggressively pounding his head against the blackboard, splitting open his left ear's outer external back side cartilage, causing it to bleed. The whole class was sitting motionless in stunned silence. Frank was bouncing off the chalkboard wall.

Whatever the punishment, an unwritten rule discouraged students from telling their parents what discipline was administered during class. Frank followed this rule, attempting to keep it quiet, not wanting to be the butt of humiliation or have his parents visit Father Hannigan's office. Regrettably, that effort failed as Frank came home from school and did not notice that he had bloodstains all over the back side of his white shirt.

Mom caught sight of the blood. Alarmed, she screamed, "What in God's name happened to you!"

Being our protector, Mom showed up at the school offices within twenty minutes, fighting mad and going into battlefield mode on Frank's behalf like "Old Blood and Guts" General George Patton. It was not a pleasant scene. Frank required six stitches to mend his injured ear. Consequentially, Miss Anderson got fired.

The only positive of this incident was that it seemed to help Frank outgrow his high-strung attention deficit disorder. As historical lore would document, Frank became a model student for the rest of his school years.

During emotional stress or anxiety, music would always comfort my mind. My appreciation and understanding of music were evolving. Awareness and interpretation of musical lyrics, melody, tones, and how they would provoke emotional memories and feelings were lasting. During the summer months of 1965, Mom brought home two new record albums performed by The Supremes. The titles were *Where Did Our Love Go* and *More Hits by the Supremes.* I fell in love with the Motown sound. Distinctive harmonies, lyrics, and the introduction of different musical instruments for background sound effects, such as the playing of tambourines, horns, and violin strings, created a beautiful, unique sound. One of my favorites from the album *More Hits from the Supremes* was a song called "Honey Boy."

The lyrics went like this:

> *He's my honey boy, my ever-loving pride and joy*
> *He's my honey boy, my ever-loving pride and joy*
> *Sweet kisses are his claim to fame*
> *In my heart, he'll always remain*
> *True fine loving is his game*
> *Honey boy is his name. He's sugar; he's spice*
> *He's everything that's nice*
> *He is my honey boy, my ever-loving pride and joy*

Even today, listening to this song brings me back to a time, a place, and a moment that stirred the emotions of my adolescent years.

Music was a powerful subconscious influence that illuminated my conception of romantic love. When Eileen and I began our relationship, we found each other personally and physically attractive. But it was a different kind of love. My relationship with Eileen involved physical signs, such as increased heart rate, an obsessive focus on one person, and romantic love thoughts being a soul-stirring emotion. Eileen was the first woman I got up with enough courage to kiss. Our early interpersonal affectionate experiences helped mold and unfasten family bonds. My total absorption with Eileen facilitated a commitment transfer from my existing family to a new family of emotional love and self-identity. With eighth-grade graduation only a few months away, Eileen and I contemplated transferring to Monroe Catholic High School together or deciding to attend our home-address-required public high schools of Arroyo and San Lorenzo.

My best friends, Mike Grover and Dean Souza, had already decided to attend Arroyo High School. My other friends, Ken Meyers, Chris Davis, and Dave Ahern, all chose to enter Monroe Catholic. My parents and grandparents would play a role in my final decision, which I was not looking forward to, knowing that Eileen and I would be separated in all probability. I couldn't help but think that our relationship would be short-lived and headed in different directions. Thank God I had sports that helped distract me from these emotional thoughts and worries.

I could play Babe Ruth baseball or enter the San Lorenzo National Senior Division. I chose the senior division league because it would reunite me playing baseball with my brother. We would be competing against sixteen-year-old boys and moving up to a ninety-foot diamond and a pitching distance of sixty feet. Our principal baseball diamonds would be at Arroyo High School Varsity and JV baseball fields. Frank and I got drafted to play on the same team, Turner's Sporting Goods. Frank would become the starting shortstop as I would play my expected position in center field.

Meanwhile, Mike and Dave Ahern got drafted onto a competitive team in the same division. We defeated them both times we played, one game being a blowout by a 12–2 score as we went on to win the league championship. But the thing I remember most about that championship season was one play set in motion by my mother. It was a game against Moeller Brothers Body Shop and the league's top pitcher, Mickey Lopez. Mickey was a left-handed flame thrower with a complimentary Sandy Koufax type curveball that kept you off balance. Mickey had already thrown two no-hitters during league play. Mickey was one year older and had already completed one senior division season. Even at the young age of fourteen, he could throw an 80-mph fastball.

Knowing that Mickey had control problems consistently getting his un-hittable curveball in the strike zone, I would sit on his fastball. I would let him throw four to five pitches, waiting until the pitch count would reach a favorable hitters' advantage of three balls and one strike. In the third inning, anticipating that fastball on a three-ball one-strike count, I hit a home run to the deep-left center field gap, giving us a 1–0 lead. Mickey was visibly pissed off. He took off his glove and slammed it to the ground in frustration. Our starting pitcher was Tom Renville, the second-best pitcher in the league who would duel with Mickey, keeping the game at a 1–0 score through the late innings. They tied the game on a throwing error with two outs in the top of the seventh inning.

Being the lead-off hitter in the bottom of the seventh, Mickey threw four straight balls out of the strike zone, giving me a free pass. My base coach gave me the steal sign. Trying to extend my lead from first base carefully, Mickey made a quick snap throw, picking me off and causing a rundown between the first and second base infield running path. Mickey tagged me out with force, knocking off my batting helmet and causing me to lose my balance and fall to the ground. Getting up to dust myself off, suddenly, I see someone charging out of the bleachers and heading toward the field in my direction. After recognizing who it was, I said, *Oh my god, Mom, what the hell are you doing?*

Running around our dugout and onto the field of play, I thought she must be coming out to ensure I wasn't hurt. She rushed past me and the infield umpire heading in a straight line toward Mickey, standing on the pitcher's mound, yelling, "That was a cheap shot!"

Mickey yelled back at my mom, saying, "Get the fuck off the field, Mrs. Edwards."

Coaches and players from both teams started laughing as the home-plate umpire calmed my mom down and escorted her off the field and back into the bleachers. Embarrassed, this delayed our game for fifteen minutes before play resumed. We went into extra innings. Leading off again in the bottom of the tenth inning. I had one thought: Hit Another Home Run.

WHAT A TALE MY THOUGHTS WILL TELL: WORDS NOT TO BE FORGOTTEN

Mickey threw three straight curveballs outside the strike zone. I step out of the batter's box to look at my third base coach, who gives me the take sign. Then I hear my mom in the stands screaming at Mickey, saying, "Hey, lunch meat, Mickey, keep serving up that baloney."

Mickey stepped off the pitching rubber and gave my mom the middle finger! Getting upset, I thought to myself, *Nobody flips my mother off.* Mickey's next pitch is way off the plate, bouncing past the catcher, hitting the backstop, and putting me on first base with a walk. Being mad at Mickey for disrespecting my mother, I didn't even look at my third base coach for the steal sign. I was going to steal bases with or without his approval.

I said, "We are going to win this game. It's mine to win."

So I take off, stealing second base first and sliding safely into third base. After standing up, my coach asked with aggravated sarcasm, "Did you see me give you the sign to steal?"

Mickey then struck out the next two batters. I noticed that when Mickey struck out a batter, his natural tendency to bend down and grab the rosin bag to improve his grip for the next pitch, taking his eye off the base runner momentarily.

I prepared for a running start as he returned to the pitching rubber with his back facing me. My timing was perfect, taking off as soon as Mickey started to bend toward the rosin bag, catching him off guard. I ran as fast as I could to score the winning run, beating his throw to home plate with a headfirst slide as the home plate umpire yelled, "Safe!"

After the game, Mom kept yelling at Mickey repeatedly, "How do you like that, Mickey? That's my boy!"

My inner voice said, *Don't ever mess with my mom, my protector.*

Before graduating from eighth grade, we were required to take a proficiency examination assessment test to determine grade-level reading, writing, and math skills before entering high school. I remember the sense of urgency suggested by Sister Mark to study hard to make sure you do well on the test. Her hint implied that not doing well could keep you from entering high school. So cramming for that exam became a priority. I devoted myself to my bedroom for one whole week without watching television or listening to my favorite music radio stations preparing for the test. The hard work paid off as I scored very high on all three tests, learning that good study habits and hard work can lead to self-confidence and the idea that the effort was worthwhile. It is incredible how much I learned in those first eight school years. Most of my teachers were excellent. More often than not, they were inspirational and made going to class exciting and engaging, which motivated my interest in learning and being successful.

Being part of the student council, we were responsible for planning our eighth-grade graduation party. First, we needed to develop a theme and an off-site location to accommodate enough room for serving food and dancing. After determining the composition and location, our next step would be coordinating decorations and awards. Since parents chaperoned the event, we found volunteers and donations within our church community, making this undertaking very easy. One of the parishioners let us use his swim club business for our graduation party location. Parents volunteered to bring a record-playing sound system with speakers and a black light. Finally, we organized a potluck spread along with decorations. Our graduation theme was "*Glow in the Dark: Headed to High School.*" I remember dancing to "Good Loving" by The Rascals and "You Can't Hurry Love" by The Supremes.

The graduation party was a bittersweet occasion because Eileen told me she had decided to go to San Lorenzo High School. However, she also took the opportunity to explain that since we would be attending different schools, it would be in our best interests to break up and go our separate ways. I was already mentally preparing myself for this potential outcome, but hearing it come from Eileen's spoken words hurt deeply. In some ways, I knew this decision was potentially coming as Eileen started to act differently toward me as our graduation date drew near. But then, she tactfully and politely started limiting our time spent together.

Looking back on this phase of my life, I realized that going steady, being popular, and gaining the approval and acceptance of others were gratifying. However, our romantic feelings and caring for

WHAT A TALE MY THOUGHTS WILL TELL: WORDS NOT TO BE FORGOTTEN

each other were bonding moments that provided another learning stepping stone in life, leading me to self-growth and the imagination of what type of man I might become. We both knew that moving on was best.

As you get older and more mature, you look forward to the summertime break. The thought of entering high school gave some stress to wondering about fitting in, entering a more intimidating institution, having more autonomy, and a whole new group of people making judgments. Mike was my best friend because we valued and respected each other's opinions and enjoyed many things in common. Mike always had a way of giving me a different perspective on things. Mike's reassuring and calming nature helped me find my way through life's obstacles and social situations. The friendship I shared with Mike could not be understated.

That summer, Mike and I spent a lot of time playing football in the street, learning new card games, or watching television in Mike's garage converted into a family room. The AFL Oakland Raiders had recently moved into their new stadium, the Oakland Alameda County Coliseum. Even though I was a San Francisco 49er fan, I did enjoy the wide-open, deep-passing offensive attack that General Manager Al Davis and Coach John Rauch brought into play.

My interest in professional football peaked after the first Super Bowl between the AFL Kansas City Chiefs against the NFL Green Bay Packers in 1967. The Vince-Lombardi-coached Packers won by a 35–10 score as the famed quarterback, Bart Starr, completed three touchdown passes in the second half. When asked to comment about the opponent they had just defeated, Vince Lombardi replied, "Even the best of the AFL, the Chiefs, doesn't compare with the top NFL teams." I thought those words were probably not appreciated by the fiercely competitive AFL players and coaches, guaranteeing that future Super Bowls games would be exciting to watch.

Mike and I loved to compete against each other as well. Mike had advanced analytical- and critical-thinking aptitudes. Mike's quick decision-making skills, combined with his examining situations logically for viable solutions, made it almost impossible to beat him by playing chess. However, once, Mike taught me how to play the card game Hearts. Playing this card game gave me a fair chance of competing against him. Hearts is a trick-taking card game for up to eight participants. While playing, you attempt to avoid winning heart-suited cards that count as one point each against your ending score. Most important was avoiding ending the game with the highest single point card, "The Black Lady" or Queen of Spades. That one card would count as thirteen points against your score. Playing hearts would become a favorite family pastime.

In the late 1960s, watching corny Japanese horror movies was popular. Watching the fake puppetry optical photography effects depicting birdlike fire-breathing monsters was enjoyable. They were classic movies that would make us laugh for hours because the storylines were predictable. The best science-fiction television series that Mike and I enjoyed together was *Star Trek*, starring William Shatner playing Captain Kirk and Leonard Nimoy as Mr. Spock, the half Vulcan, half human logical Science First Officer.

The TV series was ahead of its time as its cast included diversity by representing almost every cultural and ethnic group. In addition, the storylines and humanistic themes always gave us hope that a brighter future was ahead.

*****

Summer school programs were in full swing. The library, basketball gym, workout training room, and swimming pool were available at Arroyo High School. My routine would include playing three-on-three basketball games for a couple of hours before going to the library to watch 16-mm projector films for educational purposes. In addition, I enjoyed watching historical documentaries about World War II and science-related films. When Mike and Bob were not enjoying their private swim club, we would head over to Arroyo on most summer vacation days. Mike and Frank were the gym rats, enjoying the pickup basketball competition, often playing until the gym closed. Mike's brother, Bob, preferred training in the workout training room. One day, while watching a documentary about the

WHAT A TALE MY THOUGHTS WILL TELL: WORDS NOT TO BE FORGOTTEN

rise of Adolf Hitler, Coach Thornock walked by the windows of the film room, noticing me adjusting the projector.

Coach Thornock walked in and said, "Johnny, nice to see you! I got 16 mm Ted Williams and Willie Mays batting and fielding instruction films in my office. Would you like to watch them?"

Excitedly, I responded, "Sure thing, Coach, thanks!"

Within ten minutes, Coach was back with a stack of 16 mm reels. Coach said, "I want you to listen and observe the fundamentals taught and demonstrated in these films. Are you going to stop by tomorrow?"

I responded, "Yes, I usually get here around 11:00 a.m."

Coach replied, "Perfect, meet me at my office around that time, and we will go out to the field and practice these batting/fielding techniques tomorrow."

Again, I responded, "Thanks, Coach. I appreciate you wanting to work with me."

I would spend as much time with Coach Thornock as I could for the rest of the summer vacation. Before starting the practice, we would sit down on the dugout bench or outfield grass, and he would ask me to explain and describe what fundamentals I learned watching the batting instruction films. After stating what I thought I knew, Coach laughed and said, "Johnny, there are five keys to a good batting stance, Good plate coverage to hit an inside or outside pitch, balance, and aligning your batting stance to be perpendicular to the pitcher. You must have a comfortable foundation and vision so your eyes are on the pitcher. Additionally, align your feet, shoulders, and hips on a line perpendicular to the pitching rubber. Let's get some work in."

Looking over the practice field after an extended hitting and throwing workout, I asked Coach, "Why are you spending so much of your time with me, Coach?"

Coach Thornock said, "You have a natural talent for this game, kid. You are a good all-around athlete with great speed." He paused then continued, "Let's continue to work on the fundamentals of the game and see where it takes you."

During my hitting session, Coach Thornock noticed that my forearms were more massive than my biceps. Coach said, "You got Popeye forearms." He commented that my batting stance and muscular forearms generated a lot of bat speed. He would say, "You must be able to hit every pitch in the strike zone. Your forearms and strong hands give you that quick and powerful swing."

Coach Thornock would work on my swing by repeatedly having me choke up on the bat, taking two-handed and one-handed swings in a specific part of the strike zone. Coach would say, "There are nine sections to the strike zone. You have to be able to cover all of them. At times, you are losing balance by trying to pull everything with that Willie Mays swing. Make sure to shorter your stride while aiming your front foot towards the pitcher, not third base."

While working on throwing drills, Coach Thornock would say, "Always play catch with a purpose." Coach recommended, "Practice often by trying to hit certain target locations while playing catch or throwing balls at home."

When practicing at home, I would use a garbage-can lid for a target or throw a tennis ball against the garage door, practicing for hours to hit a specific area on these targets. Coach showed me how to shuffle my feet when coming up to throw, keeping my hands out in front of my body to gain momentum before releasing the ball. We worked on these drills at each practice session. He was the first coach that instructed me in these terms. I learned more from Coach Thornock than from any other coach in my life. He inspired and motivated me to reach my full potential. After a Ted Williams film-room batting review in the school library, we walked out to the practice field. Coach Thornock was always a little cranky, pushing me hard to reach my full potential.

After finishing a two-hour grueling workout, I said, "Coach, thanks for spending so much time with me."

Coach responded, "I love coaching you, kid."

Moving into my first year of high school during the 1967–1968 school year was a time of nervous introversion and awkward insecurities. I had grown to six feet, one inch tall and weighed 165 pounds. As I was maturing into manhood, acne and a slight overbite appeared. The onset of these abnormalities caused some anxiety and emotional self-consciousness resulting in becoming a homebody focusing on academics, reading books, and listening to music. I preferred the comfort zone and protective seclusion of staying home. Attracting girls was out of the question. I clearly remember how my acne impacted my self-esteem and self-consciousness about not being attractive. That inner voice of mine would say, "I should have listened to Mom's warning about shaving too early." As a result, I spent a lot of time at my neighborhood Rexall Drug Store, asking the pharmacist what works best on acne blemishes. I tried almost every possible remedy to eliminate the hindering skin condition, buying over-the-counter creams, using makeup to cover or camouflaging the pimples, and washing my face methodically twice a day.

Having an overbite was difficult as well. Knowing that my parents could not afford the cost of orthodontic correction, I worried about the possible ramifications of putting off braces for an extended period. After visiting my dentist, he reassured me that my overbite was slight with no jawbone irregularities. He said, "We will keep a watchful eye for any tooth movement or misalignment."

Thank God I was a good athlete because having an overbite and dealing with acne placed my social life on hold for the next two years. Even when I was invited to high school parties or dances that my best friends participated in, I had no desire to attend—too much beer drinking and marijuana toking. I was not too fond of the taste of beer and had no desire to experiment with drugs. Instead, I was more interested in watching the upheaval of social change on TV. Protestors and activists fought for equal rights and racial equality as conscientious objectors rebelled against the Vietnam War.

Being the most significant event of the 1960s and early 1970s, the tragic and controversial Vietnam War would cause the downfall of Lyndon Baines Johnson's presidency. Anti-war and civil rights protests raging in the Bay Area, particularly at the UC Berkeley campus where enlisted protesters rebelled by burning their draft cards remain unforgettable images. President Johnson continued to escalate the bombing campaigns. The commitment to drafting more American troops to help fight the war ballooned to well over one hundred thousand men inducted into US military services to help fight the war before 1967. During this time, Mohammad Ali refused his induction into the United States military forces as a conscientious objector saying, "Shoot them for what? They did not rob me of my nationality, rape, or kill my mother and father. Shoot them for what? How can I shoot them, poor people? Just take me to jail."

Watching the horrible scenes of the Vietnam War casualties and Walter Cronkite's commentary on television had me praying for the war to end. Thinking about the possibility of being drafted into a very unpopular war after completing my senior year remained on my mind as a distressing thought.

The historical landmark of the Haight-Asbury area of San Francisco near Golden Gate Park was the birthplace of the hippie counterculture movement called "The Summer of Love." The area became the living space of choice for thousands of flower children who descended upon San Francisco, creating a marijuana-smoked-filled environment of pleasure-seeking expressions of rebellion against that time's norms and values. It would become the home of colorful clothing stores, bars, thrift shops, bookstores, and creative musical artists like Jimmy Hendrix, Grateful Dead, and Janice Joplin. While all this free-love/free-spirited change was happening, I was intentionally kept busy by my parents. They would encourage my continued participation as an altar boy at St. Joachim's Church. They did everything in their power to attempt to protect me against what they viewed as an attack on traditional family values. My parents limited my extracurricular activities outside of school by requiring me to be home no later than the mandatory 9:00-p.m. curfew.

The transition from a Catholic middle school to a public high school initially gave me apprehension about fitting in and being liked. I noticed that most groups or cliques were single-gendered, assisting my transition as most of my friends were jocks who would participate in high school sports programs and create our peer group. Throughout my high school experience, I was fortunate to avoid rejection, teasing, bullying, and unwanted grapevine rumors. As some of my friends would have to grapple with insecurities and feelings about being judged and accepted, I noticed that their struggle with family relationships would often take a back seat to peer groups and romantic interests. I was the exact opposite. My family prioritized my independence during my first two years of high school. I concentrated on my academic performance by taking prerequisite college coursework and playing freshman/sophomore baseball and basketball while figuring out my career plan.

While playing in our second season of senior division baseball during the summer, we took second place in the standings, one game behind Cuna Trucking. Frank and I continued to play as we made the San Lorenzo Senior Division All-Star team. My buddy, Mike, missed making the All-Star team by one vote. We had a very talented team with Mickey Lopez as our starting pitcher. When not playing center field, I was placed in the pitching rotation. We won many single-elimination games, qualifying to play in the Western Regional Senior Division Finals' Division Two-Tournament championship held in Sacramento, California. We would be playing a team from Sunnyvale, who had won their Section Four title game. The winner of this game would grant entry into the Senior Division World Series held in Gary, Indiana.

Mickey incredibly pitched a no-hitter. However, he loaded the bases twice, throwing borderline pitches not called in his favor, walking in two runs. I was agitated as the home-plate umpire had difficulty tracking Mickey's curveball. I remember screaming at the home-plate umpire from center field, seeing that Mickey's curveballs were landing in the strike zone, "Hey, Blue, Stevie Wonder could see that was a strike!" After hearing and liking what I was saying, my mom yelled loudly and lambasted the home-plate umpire. My mom suddenly became a Mickey Lopez supporter. The Sunnyvale team pitcher was equally as challenging. We only got two hits for the whole game, with my teammate Ron Roberts and I getting singles. Finally, I got into scoring position, singling to left field and stealing second base. However, I was stranded at second base as the next batter struck out, eliminating us from the playoffs.

Over the next two years, I played one season of Babe Ruth baseball and one season on an American Legion team that Coach Thornock managed and recruited me to play. Coach was my inspirational and motivational mentor as he was preparing me to move up to the high school varsity team entering my junior year.

Before entering my junior year of high school, I scheduled an appointment with my school counselor two months before the end of my sophomore school year. Many students were taking aptitude tests, and I thought this would be a good idea to help me determine my career direction. I had a couple of questions: Will an aptitude test help identify individual strengths for college coursework and an appropriate major? Secondly, will it help me determine the proper course of study and type of occupations I would become more likely to succeed and enjoy?

My guidance counselor responded, "Absolutely. You will take cognitive, personality, situational judgment, and logical-reasoning tests. I will help you understand the results usually defined within three main areas, your natural abilities, personality assessment, and occupations you would find satisfying."

I responded, "Great, let's do it. I am struggling with determining what career path I should take."

I knew that I was an above-average athlete. But I also knew that one out of every two hundred players drafted into professional Major League Baseball would make it to the big show, meaning a 0.05 percent chance. Major League baseball players were not making huge salaries back then. The greatest player of all time, Willie Mays, was barely breaking the $100,000 salary mark in 1968. I dreamed about playing a "Kid's Game" for an occupation, knowing it would be a dream come true, but I had to be realistic. Everyone gets challenged at some point and time with some level of self-doubt. I was challenged by always reflecting inward, debating whether I had the God-given talent to be a professional athlete or should choose and focus on a different career path. I was an inwardly reflective and empathic kid.

My uncle Gil commented about my reserved nature to my father, "Still waters run deep."

It was a very insightful assessment. My passionate, subtle heart would challenge me throughout my life, often internalizing difficult emotional experiences, challenges, and decisions.

WHAT A TALE MY THOUGHTS WILL TELL: WORDS NOT TO BE FORGOTTEN

After completing the aptitude testing, my guidance counselor said, "John, we should get your test results back in four to six weeks."

My aptitude test results were fascinating. My counselor explained that my personality evaluation scored high in social influence, sensitivity, empathy, reasoning, rule-consciousness, and self-reliance. On the other hand, I scored low in dominance, abstractness, extroversion, and vigilance. My counselor said, "Your DISC personality type came back as an S/I, 'Steadiness/Influencer.' This reveals your strengths and best career choices would include business manager, counselor, sales, teacher, social worker, or academic advisor."

She explained that S/I personality attributes mean you are highly optimistic, trusting, deliberate, and empathetic. You are skilled at persuading others and emphasize cooperation, sincerity, and dependability. Accordingly, you would have a strong desire to help and motivate others.

The downside of this personality type is that you tend to avoid confrontation and can be sensitive to criticism. You are mainly driven by social interaction but also need space and time for *reflection*. I thought, *That is a pretty accurate description of how I feel about myself.* I thanked my guidance counselor for the information and review. It gave me a wide array of choices for my future professional plan, insights into who I am as a person, and that most personality styles are uniquely complementary. From a psychological viewpoint, I understood how personality aptitude strengths and weaknesses are related to a sense of self-discovery, motivation, and well-being. At the time, I did not know how the broad impacts of life experiences, life transitions, and family pressures can change personality trait values, thus affecting future choices, actions, and decisions.

Entering my junior year of high school in September of 1969, turning sixteen years old, I realized that I was soon on the path to becoming an adult. The importance of academics got prioritized by taking college transfer courses with the end goal of attending college. I also appreciated that I would close out my first decade of the 1960s. Reflecting, it was a time of turbulent change. Nineteen sixty-eight was probably the most stunningly dreadful year as the dominant opinion was that the Vietnam War could be lost after the

North Vietnamese Tet Offensive. Then two of the decade's most symbolic civil rights advocates, the Reverend Martin Luther King and Robert F. Kennedy, were assassinated back-to-back within three months, leading to riots in the streets. During the 1960s, we grew up with the Cold War's shadow, thinking that World War III was a distinct possibility advancing the fear that a nuclear holocaust could happen. It was a time when we were willing to question authority and demand social change.

Music followed this change as Diane Ross was given top billing by Motown Records executive Barry Gordy, resulting in my favorite musical group's eventual break up just before the end of the decade. Music would shift, becoming a manifestation symbol of society's counterculture and microcosm as the decade closed, with the Woodstock Rock Festival attracting over four hundred thousand participants. This decade's tension would turn my anxieties inward, suppressing my distress about disturbing events in silence without retreating into alcohol or drugs.

Growing up and having roots in the warm and friendly small town of San Lorenzo was a cherished refuge. The village of San Lorenzo wasn't cosmopolitan or high profile. It was relaxed and comfortable. The neighbors were kind and helpful. The apprehension and upheaval of the 1960s could be unremembered by having a pizza dinner with Mom and Dad at the Ye Olde Pizza Joynt on Hesperian Blvd. We loved listening to the Wurlitzer Theater Pipe Organ and its booming rendition of "Chattanooga Choo-Choo" or watching the midget race cars at the racing track directly behind Kennedy Park on Saturday afternoon. The San Lorenzo community seemed protected from all the chaos, walking around the duck pond or enjoying a featured movie like *The Nutty Professor*, starring Jerry Lewis, at the Lorenzo Theater. Goodness speckled the streets like the sycamore trees in bloom. My thoughts about the change and uncertainty of the 1960s would melt away, thinking, *I like this place. This is home.* I was hopeful, looking forward to what the seventies would bring. I had my driving license, my dad's Chevy station wagon to drive around, and a parental curfew that expanded to 11:00 p.m.

WHAT A TALE MY THOUGHTS WILL TELL: WORDS NOT TO BE FORGOTTEN

It's cringeworthy to admit that I lived like a hermit during my first two high school years. My best friend, Mike, was much more outgoing than me. He would attend high school parties and dances. Mike had a beautiful girlfriend at the time named Andrea. Mike loved Andrea as she was an angel-faced beauty queen with a sweet and pleasing personality. Mike would ask me several times to attend school parties and dances with him and Andrea, but I never felt the urge to go. Instead, I preferred to stay home in my bedroom reading books about UFOs, watching TV sports, or listening to music.

Additionally, I knew beer drinking and marijuana smoking would be prevalent, and peer pressure would be intense to partake in this indulgence at high school parties. On the other hand, high school dances were always chaperoned by a handful of teachers, and you got checked for alcohol and drugs before being allowed to enter. A few months into my junior year, I became more self-confident as my acne was under control. I remember becoming more interested and looking forward to joining Mike and Andrea to experience a high school dance.

Before I was ever going to attend a high school dance, I decided that I needed to learn a few rudimentary dance steps and routines instead of freestyle dancing awkwardly. To learn, I started watching *American Bandstand* religiously. Shaking a leg in the sixties and early seventies was often related to a song. In popular dances like the Loco-motion, the Shake, and the Swim, you could listen to the lyrics and take dance step instructions from the song. One of my favorite groups during this time was the Four Tops. When performing on *American Bandstand*, I noticed that Four Tops' dance steps were choreographed and simple. The movements were elementary, with your feet shoulder-width apart. You would start your dance moves by including head-and-arm movements (lifting and lowering), bending your knees in unison with the music's rhythm, including sliding left/right side steps. I would practice the dance routine repeatedly in front of a mirror in the privacy of my bedroom, listening to "It's the Same Old Song" or "I Can't Help Myself." After a few weeks of practice, I felt comfortable that I had enough dance moves in my repertoire not to be intimidated or self-conscious about the next school dance.

I never talked to Mike about my self-practice dancing sessions as he invited me to meet with him and Andrea on Friday night. Many baseball and basketball teammates enthusiastically welcomed me when I arrived. The theme was "A 50s and 60s Dance Party," with appropriate decorations and impressive blinking strobe lights. The high school cafeteria provided the dance location with either a disc jockey or a live band. This first high school dance that I attended had a DJ. I noticed that most people were standing around talking while waiting for someone to ask them to dance or sitting in chairs lined up against the wall. Most of the people dancing were either on a date or a couple.

The DJ played famous Billboard Top 20 music hits and requested titles that most kids wanted to hear. After about an hour, the DJ just happened to play the Four Tops song that I had practiced my dance routine to, "It's the Same Old Song." I didn't have the guts to ask a girl to dance, so I just went out to the dance floor and started dancing next to Mike and Andrea. Feeling confident and in rhythm with the music, I noticed that my hip movements, right and left limbs moving independently, and sidestep foot motion attracted some attention.

Then out of the corner of my eye, I noticed a girl approaching me. She was tall and had beautiful long brown hair that reached her waist. Looking at me with big brown eyes, she said, "Can I dance with you?"

I immediately responded, "Absolutely, nice to meet you. My name is John."

She replied, smiling, "My name is Debbie."

My heart skipped that familiar beat again. Debbie had alluring, good looks and was a good dancer. She seemed to enjoy dancing with me. After the song had ended, Debbie said "Thanks for the dance, John!" and walked away.

Mike noticed that I had just finished dancing and asked, "Who were you dancing with?"

I said, "I just got her first name, Debbie."

I found out later that Debbie's last name was Blanchard, and she was a freshman taking part with my sister, Mary, as a member of the Arroyo High School Yearbook Committee Journalism Staff.

WHAT A TALE MY THOUGHTS WILL TELL: WORDS NOT TO BE FORGOTTEN

I did well on all the standardized testing and preliminary SAT exam during my junior year, comfortably scoring high enough to be accepted into college. Before entering my senior year, I knew that after graduation, I would have to enter a two-year junior college if I didn't get a scholarship as my parents could not afford college tuition. My sister, Judy, decided to attend Chabot Junior College in Hayward, enrolling in their two-year AA degree LVN-RN nursing program. Judy had known what career path she wanted to pursue for a long time.

During my senior year, I was still undecided. At the end of my senior year, I worried about what lottery number I would draw from the Selective Service Military Draft as the Vietnam War was still raging. I decided to spend the summer vacation acquiring a part-time job and strengthening my physical fitness. My goal was to be in top physical condition for the forthcoming varsity basketball and baseball season. Thanks to my father, I could work out at home or school during the summer.

Dad spent the time and effort to record all the measurements and materials needed to build us an outdoor basketball plywood backboard, including pole extension attachments, a backboard template, and a rim that would securely fasten onto a wooden gable accent located just below a pitched section of the roof directly above the garage door. It was a significant project that looked professionally done upon completion, with the slightly slanted driveway serving as the playing surface. We were the only home in San Lorenzo to have a basketball backboard attached in that fashion. My father also got a hold of a friend's old workout/weight lifting bench, including barbells and loose metal weights so that I could work out in the garage.

The summer of 1970 started with my brother Frank getting a part-time job and being hired and trained as the head food preparer for the local Kentucky Fried Chicken fast-food restaurant. Frank was excited, saying to Mom, "The boss made me take a pledge. I had to place my hand on a Bible, promising never to give out *the secret eleven herbs and spice recipe*." Frank said the secret recipe was secured in a vault at KFC's headquarters in Louisville, Kentucky.

My mom laughed and told Frank, "Get me the recipe."

As the head cook, Frank sprinkled one four-ounce packet of ingredients (the secret recipe) onto the chicken during the preparation process using large stove-top pressure-cooking pots. Not sure if it included the secret formula, Frank brought home a few packets for Mom to use.

A couple of weeks later, Frank got me an interview opportunity with his boss for a part-time job opening as a dishwasher with some opening and closing side work tasks. I got the job, making $1.40 per hour as my starting wage.

After one week of working, I was not enjoying my job. As the primary dishwasher, you had to clean all dishware, glassware, and cooking pots by hand using a large sink station equipped with high-pressure faucets. We received aprons, hair caps, plastic scrubbers, and sponges for the cleaning accouterments. You had to stand for your entire four-hour shift except for one fifteen-minute break. Cleaning the large cooking pots was difficult as the aftermath of cooking the chicken would leave a crusty residue on the bottom and inner sides of the pressure cookers. Some pots were so bad that a single pressure cooker could take up to ten minutes to clean thoroughly and properly using a lot of elbow grease. As time went on, I was also responsible for restocking the freezer, bathroom cleaning duties, and emptying and disinfecting all trash receptacles. Every shift required two counter employees, two cooks, one dishwasher, and an assistant manager. The manager, Al, would come out of his office to resolve in-person customer service issues and relieve employee front counter breaks. In addition, Al hired an older gentleman named Pete who would come in every other day to help maintain the front lobby tables and floor cleanliness. It was a busy store.

During my second month of work, one day, Pete called in sick, leaving me with the additional tasks and pressure of finding the time to clean off lobby tables and mopping the main floor while maintaining my regular duty of washing cooking utensils. Working as fast as I could but still ensuring all pots were cleaned thoroughly, I started getting behind with dirty pressure cookers stacking up. My manager, Al, walked by and said, "John, you are not going to last here long. You are taking way too long to clean those pots."

WHAT A TALE MY THOUGHTS WILL TELL: WORDS NOT TO BE FORGOTTEN

That comment pissed me off. I thought to myself, *Get me some help then. I'm doing the best I can.* I was exhausted after the shift. When I got home, I told Mom what Manager Al said.

Mom asked, "Why didn't the manager get you some help?"

I responded, "He may have tried but couldn't find anyone else to come in. Those pressure-cooking pots are challenging and take time to clean correctly. I got backed up."

Mom then responded, "Take one of my steel-wool scrubbing pads. That should make cleaning those pots much easier and faster."

I thought, *What a great idea.* On my next shift, I kept the steel-wool scrubber in the front pocket of my apron, only pulling it out to clean the pots. It cut the time to clean the pots by more than half.

Manager Al noticed the improvement and said, "Nice job cleaning those pots, John!"

During the following work week, while Frank was busy cooking chicken and I was cleaning pots in record-breaking time, we heard a big commotion going on at the front counter. A customer was yelling at the top of his lungs as he slammed open the front entrance doors so forcefully they wouldn't close, letting in all the traffic noise from Hesperian Blvd. I heard the customer screaming, "Look at what your fucking chicken did to my front tooth!"

Even though Manager Al was in his back office with the door closed, he could hear the disturbance and ran out of his office to the front counter. After things calmed down, and the upset customer left. Al temporarily closed the store for an emergency employee team meeting. Al gathered us together in the back and said, "The upset customer that just left is threatening to sue my business. He claims that while eating a drumstick, he chipped his front tooth on this." Using his fingertips, Al held up and displayed a small piece of steel wool at eye level.

I thought to myself *Oh shit!* as my steel-wool scrubbing pad was dripping wet but concealed behind my apron pouch. Frank started laughing.

Al turned to Frank and asked, "Why are you laughing? This is a serious matter."

Frank, thinking fast, said quickly, "Did you see that customer's face? He was pissed." Frank knew I was using steel-wool pads to clean the pots.

Al paused and said, "Does anybody know how a piece of steel wool got into our chicken?"

Nobody said a word. After looking at each employee's eyeballs with a long stare, Al said, "Let's get back to work."

When I got home that night from work, I told my mom what had happened. She said, "Oh, shit."

The following week while driving to work, it was an uncharacteristically hot summer day in San Lorenzo, rising above ninety degrees. When I arrived, I discovered I would be on my own again. Pete had called in sick again. It was always warm in the store's back end once the chicken started cooking, but the heat was extremely uncomfortable this day. Then Manager Al came out of his office to announce he had to make a bank deposit.

I decided after he left that I would take my fifteen-minute break. I took my break time in the freezer to cool off. Sitting in the chair, I looked up at the chocolate milk cartons and various premade pies stacked perfectly on the specialized storage racks. They sure looked good. One of the employee rules was not to eat any of the inventory without the manager's approval.

I concluded at that moment, "To hell with the rules. I am going to have a slice of lemon pie and wash it down with some chocolate milk. Manager Al will never notice the difference."

That lemon pie was delicious. I grabbed a small carton of chocolate milk; after opening it, I guzzled it down, finishing it off within a few seconds. As I was wiping my mouth with my left hand and holding the empty chocolate milk carton in my right hand, the freezer door suddenly opened; it was Al.

Al looked at me with a demented expression and said two words, "You're fired!"

I said, "Serious? Hey, Al, guess what? I was thinking seriously about quitting anyway. This job sucks."

Losing my job at KFC gave me more time to enjoy my summer vacation before school started. My dad was cool about letting us use

WHAT A TALE MY THOUGHTS WILL TELL: WORDS NOT TO BE FORGOTTEN

his '68 Chevy Impala Station Wagon when he didn't need it. You could legally seat up to nine passengers. It was huge, comparable to the size of a boat at 17.9 feet in length. You could fit a queen-size mattress in the back end! My dad had the V8 Turbo 5.4 liter, 325 horsepower, gas-guzzling engine. Gas replenishment was no problem as the price for a gallon of gas in 1970 was only 0.36 cents.

Watching drive-in movies was a trendy pastime during the summer vacation break. It had a similar atmosphere to today's stadium pre-football tailgate parties. So one Saturday night, Frank asked Dad if he could use the Chevy wagon to take six of his buddies to see the movie *M*A*S*H**, starring Donald Sutherland, at the Alameda Island Drive-In.

"You can use the station wagon. But no shenanigans," Dad replied.

Frank asked me to go, but I wanted to stay home and watch a segment of *The Engelbert Humperdinck Show* on the ABC network, hoping that he would sing one of my favorites, "Winter World of Love." My common sense and foresight would prove to be a wise choice. Fortunately, I had a feeling Frank was up to no good.

About three hours later, Frank walked in through the front door with an anxious facial expression. I asked, "How was the movie?"

He walked right past me, with a fast and panicky stride heading toward the hallway leading to our bedroom. Following him, he finally responded to me by saying, "Yea."

Confused, I asked, "What do you mean 'Yea'?"

Frank shut the bedroom door in my face. As I reentered the living room, I noticed flashing red-and-blue lights coming through our front bay window. Dad and Mom said simultaneously, "What the hell?"

Before they could finish the phrase, the doorbell rang. My father answered the front door. Two of our finest from the Alameda County Sheriff's Department were on our front porch. It was around 11:45 p.m.

My mom finally got the whole phrase out, empathically asking, "What the hell is going on?"

Dad responded to Mom by saying, "Calm down, Dee Dee Baby Boo Boo's."

The two cops, looking through our front screen door, turned their heads, looked at each other, and started rolling their eyes. Finally, one of the police officers said, "Are you Garth Delmane Edwards, the registered owner of the 1968 Chevy Station wagon in your driveway?"

My dad responded, "Yes, what is going on, Officer?"

The policemen continued, "We got a formal disturbance of peace complaint from a citizen who wrote down the license number of your vehicle."

My dad asked, "What kind of disturbance?"

The police officer firmly stated, "The complainant and his wife said that six teenagers exposed themselves by 'pressing ham' against your station wagon's side windows while at a stoplight on Atlantic Ave. in Alameda."

My dad responded, "Serious?"

My mom interrupted and said, "What do you mean pressed ham, Officer? Garth, did Frankie take the ham out of the refrigerator to make sandwiches at the drive-in?"

The officers started laughing. Now, my father was rolling his eyes. Dad told Mom, "Pressing ham is another term for mooning somebody, Dee Dee. You know, when you pull your trousers and underpants down while bending over, overexposing your bare ass."

Mom said, "My little Frankie wouldn't do such a thing. It was probably Bob Grover who instigated this."

The officer asked, "Is Frankie here so we can get to the bottom of this complaint?"

Mom yelled, "Frankie, get the hell out here!"

Frank sat politely on the couch with an innocent look as the officers entered our living room. Frank began his story, "Right before the movie ended, we wanted to get a head start getting out of there because the place was packed. There had to be over three hundred cars at the movie! So I started the Chevy Wagon and turned on the headlights. We noticed the guy parked in the row directly in front of us was in a red Chevy C-10 pickup truck. He was making out with

WHAT A TALE MY THOUGHTS WILL TELL: WORDS NOT TO BE FORGOTTEN

his date. He flipped us off, giving us the middle finger while holding his hand outside his driver's window! He got pissed off because I turned on the headlights before the movie ended. I politely turned off the engine and my headlights right away, Officer. We decided to wait until the movie was over before leaving. Meanwhile, all the guys in the back end of the station wagon are calling the guy an asshole. Once the movie was over, we headed for the exit. Then it got backed up big-time. Bob Grover noticed that the red Chevy truck was behind us. The jerk intentionally turned his high beams on and off while revving his engine. Then sitting in the third-row seat, Bob says, 'Hey, Frank, that asshole is still following us.'

"I look in the rearview mirror, then suddenly, the jerk accelerates ahead of me and cuts me off, making a right turn onto Atlantic Ave. We pulled up next to him at a red stoplight. He immediately looked over at me and flipped me off again. Suddenly, the passenger lady rolls down the window and starts hysterically screaming and yelling at me! I turn around to look at the guys in the back seats. They laugh uncontrollably, pull their pants down, and smash their bare butts against the side windows. Immediately, this started a high-speed chase through the Alameda Posey Tube. Finally, we exited the tube and entered a residential section near downtown Oakland, making left and right turns through several neighborhood streets until we eventually lost him near Laney College. After dropping everyone off, I drove straight home. The guy was a real dickhead."

After Frank's explanation, Mom said, "I'm going to kick Bob's ass next time I see him, and, Frankie, knock off the foul language."

I observed the police officers as they started fidgeting and doing everything they could to remain professional and keep a straight face. Finally, one of them said, "Look, I have one question, Frankie, did any of your friends expose their genitals to the lady sitting in the passenger seat?"

Frank responded, "You mean their dicks?"

The police officers started laughing, saying, "Yes!"

Frank replied, "No, sir, Mr. Policeman."

Then my father responded, "Sounds like an innocent prank. Let's call it a form of artistic expression."

The policeman says, "I think we got enough here to finalize our report. Frankie, in the future, make sure to control your friends. You are responsible as the primary driver. Many people would consider your friends' actions as a provocative form of indecent exposure and a symbol of disrespect. Not a joke."

Before the officer's walked out the front door, Mom asked, "Would you, boys, like a ham sandwich for the road?"

Later, we discovered that Frank had instigated and encouraged the troublemaking incident. As a result, Frank got grounded for the remainder of the summer vacation.

WHAT A TALE MY THOUGHTS WILL TELL: WORDS NOT TO BE FORGOTTEN

I showed up for my senior year in the best shape of my life. I was six feet and two inches tall and gained fifteen pounds of muscle. My ankle weight exercises and workout sessions in the garage during the summer had paid off. Practicing in the gym, I was able to slam dunk the basketball for the first time. Projected as a starting forward, I was anxious for our season to start.

Before the regular season started, our team was expected to win the HAAL basketball division. However, we lost three players over disagreements with our coach. Consequently, this hurt our team's initial cohesion and continuity, disrupting rotations and weakening our bench. As a result, we lost three of our first four games. Unfortunately, one of those losses was a game on our home court against our main rival, the San Lorenzo Rebels.

The game against San Lorenzo High School was notable because my former eighth-grade girlfriend, Eileen, was a song girl for the Rebels basketball team. Eileen and I had only communicated a couple of times over the phone since we graduated from St. Joachim's. Then during pregame warm-ups, I noticed Eileen near the grandstands. I nodded, smiled, and waved at her. She acknowledged by waving back and mouthing the words, "Nice to see you."

It was a close defensive game until the early fourth quarter when we finally opened up an eleven-point advantage. Then San Lorenzo scored fifteen straight points, taking the lead with only two minutes left to play. The score changed three more times before the Rebels won the game on a buzzer-beating shot, winning 55–53. I was so upset and frustrated about the loss; I didn't want to talk to anybody. After the game, avoiding Eileen, I ran straight into the locker room, showered, and drove home. It would be our last contact.

Before Christmas and during New Year's breaks, we improved our record to 5–3 by beating Tennyson High School by twenty points, 78–58. After the game, my sister, Mary, told me there would be a New Year's Eve party tomorrow night at her journalism teacher's house.

Mary said, "You should come. Debbie Blanchard will be there."

I told Mary, "I probably won't go. I plan to watch Guy Lombardo's Big Band New Year's Eve celebration with Mom and Dad."

Mary responded, "Well, we can go together if you change your mind. Debbie likes you a lot."

The following night, New Year's Eve, Mary said right before leaving the house, "Have a good time watching Guy Lombardo. I will tell Debbie that you said hi."

I couldn't tell if she was being sarcastic. Later in the evening, around 11:00 p.m., I got a phone call; it was Mary. She said, "Somebody here wants to talk to you."

As I wait for several seconds, I heard, "John, this is Debbie. Do you remember when we danced together not too long ago?"

I responded, "Yes, I do. There are shortcuts to happiness, and dancing is one of them."

Debbie laughed. "You know, this party would be much more fun if you were here. Can you come over?"

Debbie would become my first mature love, my first intimate sexual relationship, and my high school heartthrob. There is always something special and unique about your first adolescent love. Debbie introduced me to the dream of love. Our relationship would grow into a tender-hearted connection. It would become the first interpersonal bond that would unfold into an intimate loving whirlwind romance. We fell in love so quickly, and nothing else before could compare. I wanted that feeling to last forever. I thought about Debbie as a potential partner for life. Debbie proudly wore my Arroyo Block Sweater when attending my varsity basketball games.

After watching me play from the stands, she said, "I love how you wiggle your hips and butt when you shoot a free throw."

I loved it when she would pick me up to drive me to school in her beige-colored Volkswagen Bug, making my mornings extra special.

The simple things of life were heightened. The simple act of helping her grandmother sell potted plants during weekends at the Alameda Flea market or conversing on her front porch about our future desires were precious memories.

I remember being surrounded by the smell of star jasmine plants hanging from a wooden arch bordering her home's front entrance. The pleasant and precious memory of Debbie extending an unexpected heartwarming touch by hugging my arm while placing her head on my shoulder remains a treasured recollection. Whenever I catch the scent of star jasmine, it brings me back to that moment, that enduring memory.

We ended our basketball season by winning seven of our last eight games, giving us a 12–4 record. Sadly, we didn't win the championship, but we did lead the HAAL as the highest-scoring team. All league honors went to our star guard, Mike Soto, who led the league and East Bay Area Division with a 28.9 scoring average. Center, Brad Tauscheck leading the HAAL in rebounds, made All-League honors. I ended my varsity basketball season with a 17.1 scoring average and earned an honorable mention all-league nomination.

At that point, my mindset was focused on transitioning to my final year of varsity baseball with my mentor, Coach Thornock. Additionally, I was looking forward to taking Debbie to the senior prom. Going into my varsity baseball season, my coach had me pre-ordained to play center field.

During preseason workouts, I went to Coach Thornock to talk to him about our starting lineup. I said, "Coach, I wanted to offer you the option to consider placing me at second base instead of center field. We have Craig Leipelt, Randy Barker, and Bob Grover who can play center or left field. Allowing one of them the opportunity to play would give us a much stronger hitting lineup and substitution options."

Coach responded, "Center field is your natural position. I appreciate your flexibility to help the team. I will consider it."

Before the season started, the annual ritual of team and individual photos began. Coach had me as the starting second baseman and leadoff hitter on opening day. I usually would bat third in the batting order, but Coach wanted to use my speed to steal bases.

Coach Thornock explained, "Johnny, you had the fastest timed speed from home to first base at 3.59 seconds. You will steal a lot of bases for me this year."

In front of my fellow teammates, Coach always called me by my last name, *Edwards*, but when talking to me privately, it was always

Johnny. I loved Coach Thornock as much as my father. He always made a point to boost my confidence through subtle compliments.

With a sixteen-game schedule ahead of us, we were forecasted to be in the hunt for the HAAL Baseball Championship, with Sunset and Marina High Schools as our primary competitors. We had exceptional talent throughout our lineup. I was eager to start, particularly with Debbie in the stands watching me play, and I anticipated a great season. Unfortunately, we got off to a terrible start, losing our first five games by one run. We ended the first half of the season with a 1–7 record, ending any realistic hope of having a successful season. However, I had a tremendous first-half batting of .353 overall with two home runs, placing me in the top position of the HAAL batting average statistics.

Finishing the first half always ushered in the annual San Lorenzo Lion's Club Easter Baseball Tournament. The tournament was founded and organized by Coach Thornock. For the first time, the sixteen-team bracket would include teams from the Diablo Valley Athletic League, Catholic Athletic League, and Mission Valley Athletic League. We played up to our full potential during this tournament, getting to the championship game against one of the top-ranked high school teams in the state—St. Elizabeth. They were heavy favorites to crush us.

With Debbie, family relatives, and my parents in the stands looking on, my inner voice said, *There is no way we are going home losers today.* I had a great game, getting a single-, double-, and ground-rule triple. I crushed a fastball on a hit-and-run play so far, and the baseball landed on the fly into the opposite junior varsity diamond's infield, driving in three runs. The ball traveled in the air at such a great distance that I could have run around the bases twice without being thrown out.

After the game, my dad told me, "That ball you hit took off like a rocket, gaining speed and height as it went."

An obscure ground rule stated that a ball hit into another field of play is automatically designated as a ground-rule triple. I finished the five-game tournament with a .375 batting average, four extra base hits, including two home runs and 10 RBIs. We trounced St.

WHAT A TALE MY THOUGHTS WILL TELL: WORDS NOT TO BE FORGOTTEN

Elizabeth by a final score of 15–7, and I was presented with the Most Valuable Player Award.

After the game, Coach Thornock and I walked together, pacing off three-foot strides to approximate how many feet in the air that triple had traveled. After counting 147 strides, we calculated an approximate distance of 441 feet! He told me, "I am happy to tell you that UC Davis NCAA Division 1 baseball Coach Phil Swimley was scouting you today. He is very interested in recruiting you to play for his Aggies next year. He will schedule a visit for you and your family to tour the campus. I will let you know when." Coach Thornock then put his arm around my shoulder and said "Great tournament, kid" handing me a large envelope.

I was so excited that I forgot to open the envelope for several days. Contained in that envelope was our team photograph with a written inscription from Coach on the back side stating, "You have the talent, Johnny, reach for the stars."

We had a two-week break before starting the second half of our season. My meeting with Phil Swimley was scheduled for the following weekend at 10:00 a.m. Visiting UC Davis and taking the tour with my parents was an impressive experience.

Upon meeting Coach Swimley, he said, "Welcome to Aggie ground."

Phil showed us classroom facilities, the student center, the bookstore, dorm rooms, the strength-training gym, and the baseball stadium. He ended the tour in the cafeteria for lunch. We discovered that UC Davis could offer partial financial assistance and a part-time job working for the campus bookstore. I also found out that Phil had played professional baseball for the New York Yankees organization and had been the head baseball coach at UC Davis since 1965. He was well-known for recruiting several players who eventually made the big leagues and signed professional baseball contracts. Mr. Swimley answered multiple questions from my parents.

He ended the tour by saying, "John, you have the type of baseball talent we look for here at UC Davis. I have been scouting your play for some time now. Your coach speaks very highly of you. I hope you enjoyed the tour and seriously consider our school to play baseball and receive a highly rated educational curriculum. Would you be able to let me know your decision before you graduate?"

I responded, "Absolutely. Thank you for showing us around the campus and spending the time to explain your baseball program."

On the drive home, I had several questions running through my mind, *What about Debbie? Can my parents afford the other out-of-pocket tuition expenses required? Will I get another college offer or be drafted by a professional baseball organization? Do I want to be away from home to attend college? Will I get drafted into the Vietnam War?*

While driving home, my mom said, "It is an excellent opportunity for you, Johnny. You could tell how much Mr. Swimley wants you to play for him. However, I would rather you get your college education first before accepting a professional draft choice offer. And I am not sure we can afford the cost of college housing."

My father added, "At least you have plenty of time to decide. Let's wait to see what other options might develop."

That comment from my father put my mind at ease. I needed the time before deciding and wanted to talk with Debbie about all this. I had just turned eighteen and had never spent much time away from home. Staying on campus away from home would be a financial burden for my parents, even with the part-time job and monetary assistance offered by UC Davis. I couldn't wait for the second half of our season to start.

The drive home seemed to take forever. UC Davis University was about one hundred miles from our home in San Lorenzo, a two-hour drive. We got back late in the afternoon. Debbie called later and asked if I wanted to come over for dinner and watch an *All in the Family* episode. I said, "Perfect. I need to discuss something with you."

Arriving at Debbie's house, I wanted to wait for the right moment to talk to her privately. That opportunity came much later in the evening after her parents went to bed. It was a beautiful warm summer evening as we sat next to each other on her front porch steps. After an affectionate hug and kiss, I said, "I love you, and I have so many things running through my mind. I want to share my concerns with you and get your opinion. After graduation, a military draft lottery may require me to enter the Vietnam War."

WHAT A TALE MY THOUGHTS WILL TELL: WORDS NOT TO BE FORGOTTEN

I continued, "Additionally, as you know, I just got back from UC Davis where Coach Swimley is recruiting me to play baseball for him next year. Thank God I have some time before making any decisions because I am not sure I want to move away from home to attend college. It probably would be best to go to Chabot Junior College in Hayward for my first two years and then transfer to a university. You have two more years before you graduate from Arroyo, so choosing this scenario would work for us. What do you think? We could attend college together."

Looking at Debbie's face, I noticed an expression of caring and apprehension. Before responding, she paused for quite a while. "John, I don't want to lose you, but this will have to be your decision, not mine. I don't want to influence you either way. No matter what, you have some time, and your options could change, take the time to consider all possibilities. Whatever you decide, I will support you."

I wasn't sure how to take that reply. I thought to myself, *That response is neither negative nor positive. It's neutral.* I was a little concerned about her answer. I was a young adult facing several choices and important decisions to make. Playing professional baseball has been a dream for as long as I can remember. I never anticipated that love for a woman would compel confusion within my thought process and effectuate a burdensome choice. At that moment, I remembered my school counselor's words about my personality type, "You fear judgment and don't want to upset others, leading to difficulty making choices or decisions." I knew that I had some time to weigh my options. I understood that my upcoming choices or decisions would impact my life as they were more complex.

We opened the second half of our varsity baseball season against our cross-town rival, San Lorenzo Rebels. I noticed for the first time Debbie was not in attendance. Terry Huckabee was the starting pitcher for the Rebels. I always owned him when playing Little League baseball, winning games against him by hitting home runs. I intended to swing as hard as possible at his first pitch to lead off the game. I got a fastball down the middle of the plate and led off the game by hitting a home run. Terry walked me in my next two at-bats by throwing curveballs outside the strike zone. We entered the last inning in a close game, being one run behind. Our first two batters struck out. Settling into the batter's box, I positioned myself closer to home plate. I wanted to reach his curveball if he threw it outside the strike zone. On the third pitch, I got a hanging curveball on the outside corner of the plate and went with the pitch hitting a single into right field. I then stole second base to get into scoring position. Terry looked at me and shook his head in frustration.

Terry struck out the next hitter to win the game. Then walking toward our dugout, Terry met me on the infield grass, giving me a hug and high five, saying, "Not this time, Edwards."

Leaving the dugout to jump on the bus taking us back to Arroyo, a guy came up to me, handing me a business card saying, "I am a scout representing the Pittsburg Pirates. You are having a great year. We will be scouting your play until the end of the season."

I showed Coach Thornock his business card on the bus during the ride home. My coach said, "Johnny, he has been watching you since your Babe Ruth and American Legion days. I didn't want to say anything to you because I didn't want to put unnecessary pressure on you. You are one of the best overall athletes I have ever coached. Let's finish out the year strong."

My father liked quoting Eleanor Roosevelt, saying, "If life were predictable, it would cease to be life." I had always related to and interpreted that quote from a historical event viewpoint. That was a narrow perspective on my part. I completely understand that life is a series of pivotal moments and transitions that can change and shape us as individuals. Unknowingly, I was about to face such an event.

Being a little late for baseball practice, I ran out of the basketball gymnasium toward the varsity baseball field. I noticed right away that something was different. I didn't see Coach in his usual position. Coach Thornock started every practice by having the players stand on the right-field foul line as a starting point to run forty-yard wind sprints forward and backward in a straight line. Instead, I saw most of my teammates sitting or milling around the third-base dugout. As I approached the dugout, I noticed that the junior varsity baseball coach, Bill Basacker, was waiting for me to arrive to hold a team meeting.

WHAT A TALE MY THOUGHTS WILL TELL: WORDS NOT TO BE FORGOTTEN

As I sat down, Coach Basacker said, "I am sorry to inform everybody that Coach Thornock was admitted into the hospital earlier this afternoon with a serious heart condition. Unfortunately, we do not know what his status is at this time. Therefore, I will probably have to coach you for the remainder of the season."

Shocked and overwhelmed, I couldn't control my emotions as tears started streaming down my face. Being so shaken, I do not remember how I got through baseball practice that day.

I was devastated. When I got home, I pulled out my rosary and prayed for Coach. The following day, my mom called the school office to tell them that I wouldn't be attending class. Mom went with me to St. Joachim's Church to light some candles and prayed for Coach. Later that day, we discovered that Coach Thornock had a "non-ST elevation myocardial infarction." In other words, a mild heart attack. He was in stable condition and would stay in the hospital until cleared by doctors. Regrettably, he would not return as our coach for the remainder of the season.

Feeling down and out, I called Debbie to pick up my spirits. Answering the phone, Debbie said, "I am glad you called. I was wondering if I could come over?"

I asked, "When did you want to come?"

She responded, "Is now okay?"

I said, "Sure."

Debbie had no idea about what happened to Coach Thornock. Waiting for her arrival, looking through our front window, I saw that Debbie had just pulled up in her Volkswagen Bug. I was so excited to see her. I ran outside to greet her. She said, "Jump in." She drove for two blocks and stopped at the Via Catherine entrance to San Lorenzo Park Community Center.

I said, "We could have walked here instead of driving your car?"

After exiting the car, Debbie said, "Let's go walk around the duck pond."

As we walked toward the duck pond, I was about to inform Debbie about Coach Thornock's serious health issue. However, I noticed that Debbie was not walking next to me, holding my hand, or saying a word. My instincts were advising me that something was wrong here. My heart and mind started racing. In my confusion, I forgot to tell her about Coach. I thought, *I haven't talked to Debbie for almost two weeks, and she did not attend my last baseball game. Something is not right. What is going on?* Debbie sat on one of the park benches bordering the duck pond's walking path.

Sitting next to her, I asked, "Is something wrong?"

Debbie said softly, "John, please don't be upset with me. I was thinking a lot about our conversation a couple of weeks ago about your options after graduation. I even talked to my parents about this. You will be graduating in two months. I still have two years left in high school. Then you will be attending college somewhere and meeting new people. I think the best thing for us to do is break up. I have your block sweater at the dry cleaners. I will drop it off to you after I get it returned. I am so sorry about this. I know you were not expecting this, and this is not easy for you or me. I never wanted to hurt you, but this is the right thing to do for both of us." Debbie stood up and walked away.

I remained seated in silence as her words broke my heart. I sat on that bench, bewildered, feeling light-headed for several minutes while staring at the ducks on the pond. I felt the same despair, abandonment, and desperation when I was three years old, accidentally locked up in that tiny apartment bedroom on School Street. I was dealing with two life-changing events happening back-to-back within a few hours. *How do I navigate through this heartache?*

At first, I sought solitude. I needed to be away from the influence of others. I felt a strong need to regroup privately, trying to make sense of the two devastating, life-changing events I had just experienced. I prayed and read Bible passages, attempting to organize my thoughts. I reflected on previous heartaches shared with Nancy and Eileen. The pain of this loss was overwhelming and intensely significant. I was in unfamiliar territory and needed to find a way out of the despair.

I reached out to my father. I told my father, "Dad, how do I make the sick-to-my-stomach emotional sadness disappear?"

Dad responded, "Son, life is not fair sometimes. Nobody can protect you from life's transitions. You have to feel the hurt before you can move on. Try thinking about it this way. If Debbie wanted to be with you, she would have done everything to stay. There will be another girl that unexpectedly comes into your life and changes everything. You will look back at this moment as an experience where you learned more about yourself."

My father's words were profound and thought-provoking. Nonetheless, I struggled for a long time before recovering from our breakup. All I could feel emotionally was turmoil and unrelenting sadness. The mental photographs of the special moments we shared were self-inflicted torture. I couldn't recognize happiness in anything. I decided not to finish the last seven games of the baseball season. Without Coach Thornock and Debbie, I lost my desire to play and compete. Anytime I saw Debbie at school, I felt a stab in my heart. I just wanted the school year to end. I kept thinking back to my father's words. Maybe my relationship with Debbie was destined to end. Therefore, I didn't fail. It served a purpose. I was still learning how to love. I was still learning what type of man I would become. I gave my love for the third time—each time, my heart broke. But somehow, I eventually found the courage to move on and continue my journey of self-discovery.

Before graduation, I took a job at Smorgy Joe's, an all-you-can-eat buffet, as a dishwasher/table waiter to save some money to take my friend, Debbie Fletcher, to the senior prom.

On August 5, 1971, my brother and I received Vietnam Draft Lottery number, 323. That year, the highest lottery number called into service was 95, accommodating the option to enlist or not serve. The Vietnam War was at the center of United States politics. Television brought the savagery and cruelty of the war into our living room. Disturbing images displayed a growing anti-war movement. My brother was going to enter his final year of high school. I was considering which college to attend. My father served in North Korea. We both reached out for Mom and Dad's advice.

My mother was blunt, "You, boys, are going to finish school. You are not going to Vietnam. I could not handle the possibility of my boys coming home in a body bag."

Dad said, "The Vietnam War has been considered by many as a mistake. I have witnessed the tragedy and brutality of war. A parents' most important role is to protect their children. You have the opportunity to finish school. Take it."

Mike was accepted into Cal State University, Hayward, and had decided to pursue his four-year degree in political science. My sister, Judy, completed her AA nursing program degree at Chabot College and was hired to work at St. Rose Hospital in Hayward. Because of financial constraints, I followed in Judy's footsteps. I decided to register into the Chabot Junior College business management AA degree program, allowing me to stay at home while attending college as Chabot's campus was only four miles from my house. Deciding to quit baseball eliminated any chance of being drafted by a professional baseball organization. I called Coach Swimley at UC Davis and thanked him for his sincere consideration and desire to join his baseball program. I explained that I had ultimately decided not to play baseball anymore. Instead, I was going to focus on my academics and seek a business management career.

As the summer started, I couldn't stop thinking about Debbie. I was still in the midst of the grieving process of losing her. I decided to cut off any contact, hoping it would diminish my attachment to her. Mike was always there to help talk me through my anxieties. His moral support and close personal friendship had a way of making me feel better.

WHAT A TALE MY THOUGHTS WILL TELL: WORDS NOT TO BE FORGOTTEN

"Look at it this way. You were worried about the Vietnam draft lottery, the affordability of moving away from home for college, debating if you wanted to continue playing baseball, and being separated from Debbie while attending school. All those agonizing concerns and choices are gone. Heartbreak doesn't last forever. You won't always feel this way," Mike advised.

His words provided a fresh perspective and a sense of relief. The following week, I got a phone call from Mike. "Do you want a full-time summer job?"

I said, "Sure, where?"

Mike told me that he got hired by Hunt-Wesson Foods Cannery in Hayward at $4.75 per hour. They guarantee forty hours per week with optional overtime pay. He said, "My friend, Barry Balk, his father is an operations manager at the cannery. They need workers for the summer tomato processing season. We can work together. Just go down to their employment office on A Street and apply. Barry's father will make sure we work on the same shift."

Accordingly, Mike and I started work the following Monday on the day shift. We were hired as utility workers that performed multiple supervisor-directed jobs. We would be loading fruit containers on pallets the next day, feeding the product into processing equipment. It was hard work, but it was a welcomed diversion and change of pace until college started.

Entering Chabot College, I was prepared for the divergence from a high school education and transitioning into college. My sister, Judy, forewarned me about college, saying, "In college, you are now considered old enough to take responsibility. College is voluntary, and you must manage your time effectively. You will experience large lecture halls instead of individual hands-on classroom instruction. It's up to you. You will pay the price or reap the reward from your decisions about study habits and note-taking. You are in control of your actions and decisions."

Having only a high school education would not open many doors to a rewarding career. However, that one precursor was a motivating and dominating factor. After summarizing my high school aptitudes and SAT results, I was confident that a business management course would provide numerous opportunities after graduation. I never looked back on my decision to quit my pursuit of playing professional baseball.

I cherished my two years of college at Chabot. The two years I spent at Chabot expanded my depth and breadth of knowledge and self-awareness. It represented my awakening to how social relationships and institutions enrich our lives. It allowed me to express my thoughts and ideas through essay writing, interpretation of abstract theories, and public speaking. Studying and interpreting the rich language and complex characters from the greatest prose writer in our history, Shakespeare, was intellectually and philosophically enjoyable. One of my favorite English literature readings was Victor Frankl's *Man's Search for Meaning*, which influenced my understanding that we are responsible for our destiny in life. However, my favorites were studying the social sciences of history, sociology, philosophy, and psychology.

My psychology teacher was so impressed with my essays that he implored me to seek a psychotherapy career. The study of Sigmund Freud, Carl Jung, Erik Erickson, and Abraham Maslow inspired my understanding of how social conditions, human development, and self-actualization influence our lives. Learning the theories of scientific time management by the founder Frederick Taylor or studying Peter Drucker, known as the father of modern management, prepared me well for my future management career. I was excited about transferring to St. Mary's College in Moraga to complete my four-year business management degree.

St. Mary's was a highly-rated private Catholic College. Once I learned that tuition costs in 1973 would be just over $3,000 per year to attend, I decided to get a full-time job to save up the money needed to continue my education as my parents could not afford the expense. In 1973, the economy stagnated, resulting from the OPEC Oil Embargo during the Richard Nixon administration. Long lines and waits at the gas station pump became a familiar sight with enforced gas rationing. Finding a full-time job proved to be more difficult. Networking or having an in-road through a family member, relative, or friend was helpful.

WHAT A TALE MY THOUGHTS WILL TELL: WORDS NOT TO BE FORGOTTEN

About three weeks into my search for a job, a good friend from high school, Rick Waters, told me he was leaving his warehouse manager position in one week at Blue Chip Stamps in downtown Oakland on Telegraph Avenue. He said, "It's a good job with decent pay. Make sure to apply in person. I already talked to Mr. Grissom about you. He said to stop in next Saturday morning around 10:00 a.m. for an interview."

During my interview, Mr. Grissom asked me several questions I had prepared for and anticipated. His last question was, "What questions do you have for me?"

I responded, "What date and time do I start?"

Mr. Grissom laughed and said, "Next Monday at 9:00 a.m."

I was very motivated to save money so I could continue my education. Working Monday through Friday at Blue Chip Stamps left the weekend open for a part-time job. I applied for a job at the Oakland Alameda County Coliseum during the home games for the Oakland A's and Raiders. It was a weekend customer service job helping manage and oversee concession distribution to fans and players. I was hired and worked both of these jobs until October 1975.

Over the next three years, it would become a time of understanding how to deal with new learning experiences and make adjustments to cope with life's curveball transitions being thrown at me. I was pulling away from the crossroads of adolescence, being responsible personally as an emerging adult while staying home and remaining tied to my parents and family. Family, music, sports, and solitude would continue to be my main diversions to relax my mind, be a source of pleasure, and boost my psychological well-being. At this time, my father would get a job promotion transferring him to Lockheed Missiles and Space Company in Sunnyvale, California.

Upon leaving the Alameda Naval Air Station, he helped manage the quality assurance program working on various classified national security programs, such as the nuclear-armed submarine Polaris and Poseidon ballistic missile projects. Even with this promotion and pay increase, my parents struggled financially to meet all their living expenses, causing an inability to save. Unknowing to me at the time, Dad would sign over his payroll checks to my mother without getting involved in the budgeting process or seeking financial advice. He loved and trusted her.

One day, before leaving for class, my mom approached me with an animated expression of overwhelming stress and panic, saying, "Johnny, I need to borrow some money from you to pay last month's and this month's mortgage payments. If I don't make these payments this week, the bank said they would start foreclosure proceedings. I don't want to lose our home."

My mother's alarm and anxiety immediately triggered my empathy and sensitivity to help her. "Whatever you need, Mom. I have money in my savings. How much do you need?"

When you are faced with uncontrollable circumstances, including the fear of losing your home, I thank God I was in a position to help my mother. I thought to myself, *This was an unavoidable consequence of life...a disruption to my plan.* An experience that would have a lasting impact and shape my outlook to recognize and realize that life doesn't always follow a predictable path. My life becoming a caretaker for my parents' home would shape a part of my identity. Helping my mother and meeting her needs revealed my humanity and empathy. *Sometimes it is nice to be needed*, I thought.

After giving my mother the funds needed to save our home, she replied, "Johnny, keep this between us. I don't want your father to know or worry about this."

Faced with my parents' difficult circumstances, potentially losing their home, bailing them out was a no-brainer. I never asked my mother any questions. I provided the money without giving it a second thought. Not just once but on two other occasions within these years. I just wanted my mother's stress and anxiety to go away. It was a complex and challenging experience to handle.

Learning about my parents' financial vulnerability, coupled with the fear of displacement, uncertainty, and potential economic hardship, was stressful. Typically, I would seek alone time during anxious times, listen to music, or watch sports to get away from others' influence. Having solitude allowed me to think independently and fulfill the desire to escape from worry.

WHAT A TALE MY THOUGHTS WILL TELL: WORDS NOT TO BE FORGOTTEN

Sports in the Bay Area were an exciting time in the early '70s. The 49ers, Giants, Raiders, Oakland A's, and Warriors were all competing for championships by winning their divisions and entering the playoffs. John Brodie, Willie Mays, Kenny Stabler, Reggie Jackson, and Rick Barry were great athletes that brought something special to uniting Bay Area communities. Flamboyant sports personalities followed the Bay Area at the forefront of the fashion movement of bell-bottom pants, tie-dye shirts, and platform boots in Oakland, such as Reggie Jackson, Catfish Hunter, Rollie Fingers, Ben Davidson, and John Madden being the most preeminent. Flashy uniforms, long hair, protruding sideburns, and handlebar mustaches reflected the fashion movement of the early '70s. The Oakland A's brought home three straight World Series championships (1971–73). Wearing their fabled Kelly green and gold double-knit pullover style jersey with white pants with elasticized multicolored waistbands, the players ushered in the most unusual and unique uniforms in Major League Baseball. Working for the Oakland Coliseum at this time was an advantage. I would have access to watch some of the championship games for free and experience "Charlie O," the mule, the famous mascot of the Oakland A's (named after the ostentatious owner Charlie Finley), running around the warning track before the start of games.

I was starting my second year of employment with Blue Chip Stamps and the Oakland Coliseum while finishing my two-year AA degree in business management. I was still living at home with my parents while attempting to save as much money as possible while forgoing my final two years of college. I purchased a brand-new Honda CB 350 motorcycle to save gas money, and even though I no longer had a curfew, my mom would always ask when I got home late, "You didn't do anything illegal tonight, did you?" She was well aware of the prevalence and popularity of the illicit drug cannabis.

During the 1970s, Congress passed legislation to decriminalize and reduce statutory criminal penalties for the use and possession of marijuana. I had no interest in experimenting with a drug with addictive risks and the potential long-term effects of becoming dependent, causing adverse health consequences. However, regarding risk-taking behavior, I did start experimenting with alcohol as my friends would frequent the local bars in town.

My friend, Mike, and some of his fun-loving buddies decided to move into an old two-story home off Hesperian Blvd. near the ancient burial grounds of the San Lorenzo Pioneer Cemetery. It became a wild party pad hosting several large parties on a Friday or Saturday night.

My ever-loving matchmaking sister, Mary, who attended a couple of these parties with her boyfriend, Bill, mentioned that a couple of her single attractive girlfriends would be attending another kegger party at Mike's house this Saturday.

I said to Mary, "Yea, I know about the party. I will be there. Who are your friends?"

Mary responded, "Donna Tusi and Mary Lou Voecks. Both are very attractive, but I think Donna is more your type. By the way, she's a swimsuit model." That comment from my sister shifted my attention and curiosity as I looked forward to the party.

I was not disappointed when Mary introduced me to Donna and Mary Lou. Both women were beautiful. As I chatted with them, I was immediately drawn to Donna. Donna had a rich beige-tone shade of flowing blond hair and detailed facial features. I scanned her perfectly shaped eyes with full lips and high cheekbones. She fashioned her tall, curvy, and slender supermodel body well. I was instantaneously attracted to her and had a strong desire to know her better.

Over time, Donna and I established a very close friendship. I would visit her at her tiny one-bedroom apartment, enjoying her freshly baked chocolate chip cookies, or she would stop by my parents' house to spend time together. I loved her unannounced stops at my house. She would always greet me with a beautiful smile and say, "What are you doing, Big A?" Donna had a feisty, determined personality, and she had no problem calling you out. Her assertive character trait was sexy, and she was a hell of a lot of fun. She reminded me a lot of my mother.

Mom loved Donna. She told me, "I want you to marry that girl someday."

WHAT A TALE MY THOUGHTS WILL TELL: WORDS NOT TO BE FORGOTTEN

My attraction to Donna eased the hurt still in my heart and mind from my breakup with Debbie. However, this unique woman who flirted with me and gave me the impression that she found me attractive had another close guy friend who was very interested in her as he would regularly visit her apartment. Donna talked about Frank often, and I could tell she had intimate feelings for him. My natural empathetic nature took over, and I became a sounding board, good listener, and rescuer for easing Donna's distress when she and Frank were in an argument or conflict.

I knew Frank and highly respected him as a good guy as we both had graduated from Arroyo High School. Everybody liked Frank. Therefore, I understood Donna's attraction to him. I had no intention of stealing her away from him.

A famous sixties song hit describes how I felt about Donna during this time. It's called "It Hurts to Be in Love" by Gene Pitney. The lyrics express my sentiment and love for her perfectly. I decided that though it hurt, I must pretend. The only way to stay close to her is to keep it to myself. As time passed and we went our separate ways, I will never forget dreaming of Donna at night, knowing that I never dared to say how much I loved her.

I would hook up with my best friend Mike now and then between his classes at Cal State Hayward. Being a political science major, he was engrossed in the ongoing involvement in Vietnam and the Watergate scandal. We would spend our time together sharing viewpoints about the Nixon administration's denied knowledge of a break-in into the Democratic Party campaign headquarters while listening to Crosby, Stills, Nash, and Young (CSNY) albums. Mike loved CSNY's intricate vocals and exceptional acoustic guitar harmonies that flawlessly reflected the time's counterculture mindset. Mike would say, *"I love how CSNY's music is associated with political causes."*

Crosby, Stills, Nash, and Young embarked on a Summer Tour in 1974. During this time, I met my new girlfriend, Sharon Lee, whom I met as a coworker at Blue Chip Stamps. We attended a "Day on the Green" CSNY concert together, promoted by Bill Graham. Sharon and I arrived near the gate entrance in the early morning hours with some friends. We were able to position ourselves very close to the stage. Over sixty thousand people attended as the air perfused with the smell of cannabis, beach balls flying everywhere, and incredible musical melodies. CSNY had a great show, opening with "Love the One You're With" and ending with "Carry On."

Sharon loved taking rides with me on my motorcycle as she frequently mentioned her feeling of energized freedom on the open road and a sense of calm. However, she was nervous about the possibility of an accident and being much-less protected. I decided it was about time to trade in my motorcycle and purchase a car with so much going on. I went shopping with my father and purchased a 1971 baby blue Opal GT at a Buick used car dealership in San Leandro. I paid cash for the vehicle from my savings. For me, the selling points were the unusual feature of the pop-up and down headlights controlled from a lever near the center console and the Opal GT's fastback design. Many automotive magazines cited that the Opal GT styling resembled a Chevy Corvette, promoting the nickname "Mini-Corvette." My father was not a big fan of the vehicle. Dad was a "Chevy Man" and wanted me to buy a used Chevy Camaro, but he was happy because he knew I wouldn't be bumming rides or using his car anymore.

Standing outside admiring the car, I said, "Dad, check this out."

I quickly jumped into the driver's seat, pushing the headlight lever and rotating the pop-up headlights in a counterclockwise direction, revealing and turning on the headlamps. I said, "What do you think? Pretty awesome, right, Dad?"

My dad rolled his eyes and said, "Let's go."

My first appointment in my new car was at the dentist's office. As I mentioned, my dentist kept an eye on my slight overbite, tooth movement, and jaw position. The problem was I hadn't seen him for about two years. After taking some x-rays, he said, "John, the good news is that you have no cavities. The bad news is your overbite has gotten worse, compressing your jaw joint into an unhealthy position. I recommend you make an appointment with an orthodontist to see if braces would be the best course of action."

Leaving the dentist's office, I knew that braces would be a significant expense I would have to pay for myself as my parents did not have any dental insurance. Therefore, I scheduled an appointment with an orthodontist recommended by my dentist about thirty miles from my home in Walnut Creek. After examining and reviewing x-rays, the orthodontist said braces were required to align my tooth crowding and jaw misalignment.

He said, "You should have had braces treatment several years ago. Unfortunately, you will need to wear them for two years." He continued, "You will require a full workup to correct all issues, including bracket adhesion, bands, spacers, arch wires, springs, and face-bow headgear."

I said, "Face-bow headgear?"

"Yes. Headgear is rare, but you will need the extra pressure to correct your overbite in your case. However, wearing the headgear every night when you go to bed will help tremendously," he responded.

I said, "I hear that you can pull in radio stations with that type of headgear, is that true?"

He smiled, saying, "See you in two weeks, John."

I agreed with a two-year payment plan requiring a $125 payment every month. If I didn't miss any appointments, I would get my braces taken off in the summer of 1975.

All of a sudden, sticking to a budget would become necessary. Tracking and calculating my orthodontic payment, auto insurance, gas, entertainment/going out to dinner expenses with Sharon, and helping my parents each month required me to keep an eye on my spending. I had a checking account, a savings account, and one credit card. I understood that I did not want to get into financial difficulty like my parents. Therefore, I managed my money carefully. I never overused my credit card for significant expenses, keeping my balance low while developing a credit rating. I adjusted my budget, adding whatever I had left to my college savings account. I eliminated wasteful spending. Creating a budget was easy; the hard part was sticking to it. Having a girlfriend and dating made adhering to a budget tough. I always worried about not leaving a negative impression of how expensive things were or what I could or couldn't afford. I never wanted Sharon to think she was a financial burden. Pleasing her was a more powerful influence.

Sharon was beautiful, intelligent, had a charming personality, and was an accomplished pianist. Often playing for me my favorite Jim Croce song, "I Have to Say I Love You in a Song," on her Steinway home piano. Sharon took the time to teach me more about her culture and traditions. I loved it when she prepared me *Popiah*, a traditional Chinese roll made of a crepe-like wrap filled with various meat fillings with thinly sliced cucumbers and other vegetables. We would spend time together attending cultural events in downtown Oakland Chinatown, like Chinese New Year, which gave me a sense of appreciation, belonging, and fulfillment about the importance of appreciating cultural diversity and different ways of being.

Back in the 1970s, people did not always view interracial relationships favorably. The presence of long-standing stereotypes and family traditions caused barriers and complications for our romance to flourish. Sharon's father never approved of our connection to one another. He objected to our interracial relationship but reluctantly allowed his daughter to make her own choices. I loved Sharon for her uniqueness and the delightful human being that she was. I never considered cultural differences as an obstacle. Sharon and I realized we would not change her father's opinions about race. We continued to live and enjoy one another as we realized that the process was somewhat burdensome but not impossible. I did, however, think to myself, *Is this going to be a love that will never advance, knowing that her father will never let a seriously committed relationship happen?*

After dating for over a year, I got a phone call from Sharon. Noticing the nervousness in her voice, she said, "John, I am two weeks overdue for my menstrual cycle. I am worried that I might be pregnant."

I asked, "Have you ever been two weeks late before?"

Sharon responded, "No, never."

"There are many possible reasons for a late period. Can't you go to your doctor or a clinic to confirm whether you are pregnant?" I said.

WHAT A TALE MY THOUGHTS WILL TELL: WORDS NOT TO BE FORGOTTEN

"Yes, I plan to do that," Sharon responded with some unease in her voice.

I acknowledged, "Great, don't worry. Everything will be okay. Let me know if you would like me to go with you."

After hanging up, I tried to hold my composure and reassure Sharon during our conversation, but the shadow of uncertainty and foreboding anxiety was worrisome. Neither one of us was mentally or financially ready for the responsibility of raising and supporting a child.

Arriving at work the following day, I noticed that Sharon was absent. I assumed that she was probably seeing a doctor. Three more days pass by. Sharon continued to call in sick and did not answer or return my phone calls. That sinking feeling of anxiety overwhelmed me as waiting for Sharon's pregnancy test results, and not talking with her became unbearable. I could only imagine that the worst scenario had come true.

Finally, the following day, Sharon returned my call. She said, "John, I am sorry I haven't called you back immediately. Please forgive me. I have been coping with some family issues. Mom took me to our family doctor and promised not to tell my father. So the good news is that the pregnancy test results returned negative. I am not pregnant and started my period yesterday. The bad news is that my father found out what was going on through an unwitting follow-up phone call from the doctor's office staff. My father is so angry that he is not allowing me to see you anymore and is demanding that I quit my job at Blue Chip Stamps."

I responded, "What? Are you going to abide by that demand? Do you still want to continue our relationship?"

Sharon paused for several seconds and replied, "I will miss you, John. But unfortunately, my father comes from dominant authoritarian culture and childhood, and he will not allow me to evade his wishes. I hope you understand. You will always stay in my heart. Goodbye."

Sharon hung up the phone, not waiting for my response. Finally, after several attempts to reach out to her with no reconnection, the words "You will always stay in my heart. Goodbye" have always remained in my heart. After that, I never communicated with or saw Sharon again.

The heartbreak always hurts—another blow and a deep scar on my young heart. I felt abandoned and helpless again. The cumulative hurt and memories from my previous heartaches and disappointments caused apprehension. This breakup reopened old wounds of not having control over the circumstances and the genesis of the root source of separation. When love doesn't happen the way we expect, it becomes frustrating. I was still learning to participate in a loving relationship with a woman. I realized the many moments and memories within my love experiences shaped me into the man to come. Living through heartache, I never questioned if love existed. Instead, I started wondering who would be the one to ignite the type of love that lasts forever.

Having some fortitude and resiliency pushed me toward putting myself first for once. I felt it was central to rekindling some level of self-confidence. A lot of my life experience and self-worth came from my thoughts that I was attractive, a good athlete, intelligent, and could be empathic and thoughtful. By focusing on these strengths, I decided to devote myself to a workout program to get back into participating in sports.

WHAT A TALE MY THOUGHTS WILL TELL: WORDS NOT TO BE FORGOTTEN

By this time, my best buddy, Mike, had graduated from Cal State Hayward University and was hired as a security officer at Yosemite National Park. Yosemite National Park was a three-hour drive from San Lorenzo, considerably reducing our time together.

Joining the US National Park Service and Curry Security Company, Mike enjoyed a compensation package that included low-cost housing and meals allowing him to reside on the park grounds. I visited Mike at the park now and then, but his brother, Bob, already a close friend, instantly became a companion and confidant. At the time, Bob worked full-time for Industrial Clean Air Company, specializing in providing filtration and ventilation systems in the Bay Area.

Over the next several years, we would become softball teammates, workout partners, and a night out on the town. Brother Frank, Bob, and I went out into our local community of San Lorenzo to find a softball team sponsor. We thought visiting local businesses in person would enhance the consideration and motivation for additional advertising exposure. The first family-owned business we talked to became our sponsor, Emery's Carpets. They provided commercial and residential carpeting services in San Lorenzo, Oakland, and Hayward. Ultimately, Mr. Emery decided to sponsor us for league and tournament play in our regional area to attract business.

Playing under the men's slow-pitch softball rules of the Amateur Softball Association (ASA), we comprised our team mostly of former Arroyo High School Varsity baseball players. We went on to win several league championships and tournaments. We were ultimately ranked by the ASA governing body as one of the top twenty men's slow-pitch softball teams in the State of California.

Bob and I would become creatures of habit, sharing a deliberate and scheduled regiment of working out/strength training at the local gym or in my garage. Our unwavering dedication to conditioning our bodies significantly improved our ability to build muscle and reduce body fat. Moreover, playing tournament softball together and working out became priorities. During an annual physical examination, my family doctor used a skinfold caliper as a measuring tool and took body circumference measurements, estimating my body fat percentage at 12 percent. My physician told me that a low body fat ratio or excellent fitness percentage typically registers within the 14 percent to 17 percent range. At twenty-two years old, I was six-foot-one inches in height and weighed 195 pounds of lean muscle. I was in the best shape of my life.

During the fall of 1975, Bob and I typically would complete four sets of eight repetitions per set of bench press with 225 pounds while working out. Bob could always beat me on a single repetition bench press competition, lifting over 350 pounds. My best was 325 lbs. During one of our workouts, Bob mentioned that United Parcel Service (UPS) in Oakland was hiring for their Christmas season rush.

Bob said, "I heard UPS pays well with good benefits as they have a unionized workforce. You must have a good driving record to be hired as a delivery driver. I have two speeding tickets on my record, so I have to wait, but you should check it out."

I responded, "You mean the brown uniformed drivers that deliver packages out of those brown delivery trucks in our neighborhood?"

"Yeah, Big Brown," Bob responded.

I was still working for Blue Chip Stamps at the time but was interested in checking out UPS once I discovered that I could more than double my hourly pay. Completing some research on UPS, I discovered that they were a well-established, privately held package delivery company founded by James E. Casey (known initially as American Messenger Company) in Seattle, Washington, in 1907. In 1975, UPS grew its business by leaps and bounds to meet the demand for its exceptional services. It became the first delivery company to serve every address in the continental United States, with international expansion plans to Canada on the drawing board. Most importantly, UPS had clear workplace policies that encouraged aggressive training programs with a promote-from-within culture.

As Bob mentioned, the Oakland-area UPS employees were represented by the Teamsters Union Local 70 through collective bargaining agreements ensuring worker rights and the industry's highest pay. Through my research, I recalled an interesting fact. In 1975, as Frank Fitzsimmons continued his reign as Teamster president, the search for the former Teamster boss Jimmy Hoffa intensified. Hoffa disappeared from a Detroit restaurant in July of the same year as he planned to seize the Teamsters' presidency again.

I called the Human Resource Department the next day. I got scheduled for an interview with an employment manager named Pat Stafford on Wednesday, November 12, 1975, at the primary distribution hub in Oakland for a seasonal package delivery driver opening.

Wanting to be a stand-out candidate, I wanted to discover more details about United Parcel Service through research to prepare me for my interview. Therefore, I studied the company's corporate hierarchy, mission statement, culture, and values. I examined the types of products and services UPS provided to determine the prototype applicant they desired. I found out that the job would demand little time for socializing as every motion is timed, measured, and concentrated on proven methods. The job's physical demands were substantial as moving hundreds of packages daily, weighing up to seventy pounds at the time (UPS weight limit today is 150 lbs.), necessitated strength and endurance.

Having hobbies that promote physical fitness was a plus as possessing a college degree was not required. Having already completed a two-year college AA degree in business management and attaining the best physical condition I'd ever been in, I felt well-prepared and confident. After an initial interview, which was more of an informational session and application process, I was called back for a second interview the following day. UPS hired me on November 21, 1975, and asked me to report to the Oakland Center. I called Bob to let him know I got the job and thanked him for the referral. It would be the start of a thirty-three-year career as I would become known as "A UPSer." I made a wise decision to pick an excellent road to start on. And the even better decision was to stay on it.

Being a UPS package car delivery driver came with fringe benefits other than excellent pay, generous paid vacation/sick leave time, health insurance, pension, and a college-tuition assistance program. UPS drivers receive a lot of autonomy while being under ridged monitoring by management on the back side. After delivering different routes daily, I realized that I was furnishing an essential service that supported a moving economy by transferring vital goods and services to businesses, residential consumers, and institutions. The job provided a strong sense of worth as adoring customers venerated you with respect, attachment, and reliance on your performance efficiency, reinforcing your feeling of belonging to something that mattered. I loved the job.

UPS was growing internationally, offering services in Canada and Germany. Internal communications revealed plans that UPS would expand services throughout Europe and the Pacific Rim in the coming years. New technologies and support systems would allow diversification into overnight delivery options. It was an exciting decade for United Parcel Service as tremendous growth provided opportunities. My college studies concerned the fundamental business management principles of organizing, analyzing, and planning. The theory of industrial efficiency promulgated by Frederick Winslow Taylor, an American mechanical engineer, is considered the father of scientific management, providing a framework of understanding and knowledge. I appreciated the organization's pursuit of the four essential pillars of guidance that had made UPS so successful in its first seventy years of existence. Those four cornerstone pillars included an unyielding dedication and priority to achieve: world-class customer service, training, safety, and measured efficiency.

During the summer of the same year, a sign-up sheet (bid list) was posted for a regular delivery route opening in Berkeley. I was near the middle of the center seniority list as a Teamster union member. I signed the listing without much hope of winning the regular route. Remarkably, no one else signed the sheet. Therefore, I was awarded my first designated delivery area. My operations manager at the time, Tom Huff, said, "Dammit, Edwards. I did not think you would get that route. I am losing my best driver with multiple route knowledge flexibility."

I appreciated Tom's compliment and responded, "Sorry, Boss. But I look forward to meeting and greeting the same customers daily. So if you need me in a pinch, ask."

Shortly after getting assigned my delivery area, my orthodontist removed my braces. I immediately scheduled an appointment with my local barber, Rick, to create a new look. Rick said, "John, has anyone ever told you that you look like Bruce Jenner?"

I said, "No, but many people tell me I look like Jimmy Connors, the tennis player."

Bruce Jenner, a former Olympic decathlete champion (1976), became a poster boy displaying his long and carefully cropped locks. Rick said, "Yeah, Jimmy Connor's hairstyle is similar to Bruce's. It would look good on you." Hence, it became my new hairstyle over the next several years.

A new smile and haircut can do wonders for your self-confidence. My self-image was at its highest level during this time. The perception and evaluation that confident people become more attractive, unlocking opportunities with the opposite sex, are accurate. Making hundreds of polite meet and greets on the job, an active socializing nightlife, and maintaining energetic physical conditioning, competitive sports modus operandi, I noticed much more undivided attention and inviting body language/flirting from the opposite sex. The appeal and charisma of the UPS driver were the real deal. Infatuation and crushes on a good-looking uniformed man delivering your specific package were part of the mainstream charisma. Delicately negotiating indirect and direct dating enticements was commonplace on my daily route. My saving grace was the UPS package delivery job requires moving at a consistent swift pace to get the job done. There is only time for courteous short-term verbal exchanges as your self-esteem flourishes.

Bob and I shared a large group of friends, which multiplied as we enjoyed social interaction and support from mutual companions, softball teammates, and acquaintances. Our core group did everything together, and everyone had a nickname. Bob inherited his nickname "Bobby Bench Press" because nobody could out-bench press him. Chuck "Starsky and Hutch" Barrett got his name tag because he owned a 1968 Oldsmobile Cutlass, custom-painted bright red with white "Vector" stripes that matched the famous 1976 Grand Torino used in the famed plain-clothes investigator's TV show, *Starsky and Hutch*. Ken "Wild Turkey" Weaver's nickname became famous because of his classic 1977 Lincoln Continental pulling up onto the curb in front of your house, blaring Bill Withers music before a night out. Before you got in the car, he would always have the same routine of taking a drag from his Marlboro cigarette after gulping a swig from his Kentucky straight bourbon whiskey "Wild Turkey" flask. He was quite the character. Rob "Lester" Caisse coined his byname for dressing up as the famous black saxophone player Lester Young for a Halloween party. And Seth "Okie" Williams received his nickname because his grandfather was a migrant farmworker from Oklahoma. Finally, they called me "Johnny Angel" because I naturally attracted girls. Whether it was a bar, nightclub, or restaurant, we always seemed to gather twenty or more friends enjoying the nightlife.

We had a favorite watering hole and nightspot that we frequented often. The bar was called "Joe's Sneaky Tiki" in San Leandro. A Hawaiian bar specializing in tropical cocktails. The Blue Hawaii mixture, my favorite, included rum, pineapple juice, Blue Curacao liqueur, and sweet-and-sour mix. Unfortunately, after having a few too many during a memorable night out at the Tiki, it caused me to experience my first unpleasant hangover while playing pool with Bob and Rob, who drove me home to sleep it off.

The 1977 Christmas holiday release of the movie *Saturday Night Fever* triggered disco, a cultural dance and musical movement. Several popular recordings from groups and solo artists, such as the Bee Gees, Village People, and Donna Summer, were played in dance clubs everywhere. Consequently, it was a time of distinctive fashion styles featuring bell-bottom polyester pants, puka shell necklaces, platform shoes, and wide-open butterfly-collared shiny polyester shirts with wild patterns.

Our large group of friends would dance the night away on a Friday or Saturday night at a nightclub called "The Cardinal Lounge" in San Leandro while following our favorite disco band group, Clean Air, who performed there often. Being twenty-four years old at the time, I took pleasure in the companionship and company of several female friendships without making any serious relationship commitments. I was still living at my parents' home, enjoying my freedom, independence, and ability to save a lot of money.

WHAT A TALE MY THOUGHTS WILL TELL: WORDS NOT TO BE FORGOTTEN

Brother Frank, at the time, was working as an account executive for Kragen Auto Parts Supply Company while living in Union City with his girlfriend, Terri. Frank decided to pursue a sales manager career after completing one year of college. My sisters, Judy and Mary, had married their longtime boyfriends, John Thurston and Bill Creese. Judy and John purchased a home in Hayward so Judy could enjoy a close commute to her work at St. Rose Hospital. Mary moved to Federal Way, Washington, as Bill's job transferred and relocated him. While my youngest sister, Susan, was still living at home with me and working for Mervyn's Corporate Office as a purchasing agent for the children's shoe department. Dad had recently retired from Lockheed Aero Space Division in Sunnyvale as Mom was adjusting to a reduced "empty nest stage" as several of her beloved children had left home.

Financially, my parents were in a much-improved position. Dad decided to work full-time for St. Bede's Church in Hayward as their on-site handyman while collecting a government pension and Social Security. Susan and I supplemented our parent's household income by contributing monthly room-and-board payments.

With a large sum of money in my savings account, I surprised my parents by offering to pay for interior painting, new furniture/light fixtures, carpet, wall art, and accent pieces for their home. My father had decided to retire after a thirty-two-year career. Never being able to afford nice furnishings, I wanted to provide this gift so my father and mother could retire in comfort. Graciously accepting my offering, Mom decided upon a rustic country decor to create a warm and cozy style for her home.

It was a meaningful experience helping my mother decide upon the color palettes, accent considerations, and distinctive furniture pieces to consider. I will never forget the delight and joy of her tender facial expression and appreciation. Putting their needs before mine brought me a lot of self-satisfaction and happiness. It was my way of expressing my love for my parents. We used Emery's Carpet for the flooring and carpet needs. When the interior design renovations were completed, my parents' living space was transformed into a model home. Giving without expectation is extremely rewarding.

During this time, my good friend, Rob, was coping with a difficult transition in his life. His parents pressured him to move out of their home as Rob was coming and going as he pleased without demonstrating any desire or motivation to become self-supporting. His parents would become furious when Rob would barge into the house at 2:00 a.m. smelling like alcohol. Rob had two favorite alcoholic beverages. He loved his Stinger cocktails of cognac and crème de menthe on ice. However, when taking multiple drinking "shots" with the group, Rob always preferred Green Chartreuse 110 proof rum with a 60.0-percent alcohol by volume percentage. Rob enjoyed showing us the alcohol potency by lighting a match over the top of the drink and setting it on fire. I thought to myself, *If you can light an alcoholic beverage on fire, that cannot be good for your health.*

Rob was famous for calling us pussies for not joining him to drink the firewater. One night at the Cardinal Lounge, Rob preordered shots for the whole group, including Bob, Seth, Chuck, Ken, and myself, as the waitress lined up the 110 rum-filled shot glasses on our table. It was customary for one guy to make a toast before the group downed the shots in unison. Rob said, "Too good-looking women!"

As Rob and Ken gulped their shots down quickly, Bob, Seth, Chuck, and I threw our heads backward as if we guzzled the firewater but threw the drink over our right shoulders and then slammed the shot glasses on the table for emphasis without Rob and Ken realizing the difference. Rob would then say, "You guys want another round?"

We all responded simultaneously with force, "No, we're good."

On more than one occasion, I had to help Rob get home after a night of heavy drinking. Rob then confided to me a couple of weeks later that he had experienced troubling abdominal pain symptoms, fatigue, and bruising on his stomach. Concerned, he contacted his family doctor, who completed a physical exam, MRI scan, and blood work profile. After the results returned, Rob's physician gave him a grave warning, "Rob, you have advanced liver disease. Scar tissue is starting to take over your liver. If you don't stop drinking, you will enter late-stage liver disease that will end your life." Rob was only twenty-seven years old at the time.

WHAT A TALE MY THOUGHTS WILL TELL: WORDS NOT TO BE FORGOTTEN

After Rob revealed this to me, I stood in shocked silence. I couldn't respond as I felt a compelling sense of dread, concern, and empathy that overpowered me. We all loved Rob. He was always the life of the party. Rob knew how to make an entrance and create an environment where the people around him would have a good time. Rob was an accomplished welder by trade, an excellent baseball player, and a talented dune-buggy race car driver. He was a passionate "kind-of-crazy" guy who believed in working hard, playing hard, and enjoying life. In some respects, Rob was larger than life to all of us. However, his most virtuous trait was his trustworthiness as a person who was there for you in times of need.

Rob exercised good judgment and decided to quit drinking. Consequently, he felt compelled to move out of his parent's home to reduce anxiety as his mother and father continued to badger him about doing something with his life. Temporarily, he lived out of his 1965 Chevy C10 camper shell pickup truck until he could find an apartment or home to rent. Rob had a twelve-volt automobile power adapter which allowed him to shave, warm food on a small cooking stove, and pump air into an air mattress. Rob would use cardboard boxes to store his personal belongings in the bed of his truck. At this time, Bob and Chuck lived together in a two-bedroom suite at the Lakeside Apartments complex in San Leandro. To help Rob, Bob and Chuck would allow Rob to sleep on their couch or shower at their residence three times a week.

Having a lot of sensitivity and empathy about Rob's situation, I decided to provide a bit of uplifting kindness to his current life dilemma. I offered to pay for some new clothes and shoes to cheer him up and elevate his confidence.

We had plans to hook up with our friends for a night of dancing at the Cardinal Lounge. Rob took me up on my offer as we headed to the Mervyn's and Grutman's Clothing Stores in the San Lorenzo Village shopping center.

Rob picked out a blue-colored three-piece leisure suit, two bell-bottom angel flight slacks, horseshoe buckle belts, a few silk nylon/polyester dress shirts, socks, and a couple of pairs of platform boots. Later that night, Rob gave me a ride in his pickup truck, fashioning some new clothes as we headed toward the nightclub. He looked good and seemed to be high-spirited.

Going to the Lounge was an opportunity to observe Rob's commitment to sobriety and self-control. Rob passed the test with flying colors as he drank Coca-Cola throughout the night. Rob's ego and confidence seemed restored as he danced the night away with a girl named Kay. They appeared to like each other's company and ended the night by exchanging phone numbers.

Leaving the club, we headed to Carrow's restaurant for a late-night bite to eat. Seth called out "shotgun," claiming the front seat with Rob. Rob said, "Hey, John, you will have to jump into the back of the truck." There was a small unstable aluminum folding chair in the back of the camper shell, among many cardboard boxes and camping equipment. Rob's pickup truck was in bad shape as a burning smell filled the camper shell.

When Rob accelerated, the vehicle would produce a noisy tapping sound coming from the engine bay. As Rob continued down the street, the exhaust became excessively loud and started making a popping noise. I shouted, "This truck is a piece of shit! It's got a leaking or cracked exhaust manifold."

Suddenly, at a high rate of speed, the truck starts swerving to the left and right. As I attempted to stand up, trying to regain my balance and brace myself for the next zigzag, Rob hit the brakes, hurling me toward the exit door of the camper shell. I thought, *Oh my god. I'm going to be launched out the door and onto the street.* Falling on my backside and sliding at high velocity toward the camper door, my feet pushed up against a cardboard box full of clothes, making a thumping impact forcing the camper shell door to open, propelling the corrugated container of clothes into the air and onto the street. Luckily, my extended arms on the sides of the door frame prevented my body from falling out onto the road.

I start yelling "Stop the truck! Pull over!" repeatedly. Finally, after going another couple of blocks, Rob slows down and pulls into an empty Mervyn's parking lot, coming to a stop.

Being disheveled and flustered, I tried to compose myself while standing outside underneath the glow of a flickering parking lot light, thinking to myself, *I could have been killed.* I bend over and put my hands on my knees, trying to keep from hyperventilating as I rationalize the type of anxiety and fear I just encountered. Stunned, I saw Rob and Seth standing over me with broad grins. They asked, "Johnny Boy, are you okay?"

I scowled as I stood up, straightening my posture, asking, "What the hell just happened? Did you lose control of the truck?"

Rob and Seth laughed hysterically, saying, "No, man, we were just fucking with you!"

Shaking my head, I said, "You, dumbasses, got me good. I owe you one."

I never said a word to Rob that I had accidentally kicked some of his personal belongings out the door of his pickup truck. Then, out of the blue, our buddy Chuck came pulling into Mervyn's parking lot in his *Starsky and Hutch* motorcar. Chuck rolled down his side window and said, "Bro, I found this box of clothes spread all over Hesperian Blvd. Look at this nice blue three-piece leisure suit."

As Chuck held it up, Rob took a glance and yelled, "Dude, that's my stuff! What the hell?" Rob turned his head and looked at me with a quintessential death stare.

I yelled, "That box of clothes saved my life. We're even!"

Later, we discovered that Chuck was ten minutes behind us, heading toward Carrows to join us for breakfast. This incident became a legendary saga that would be retold for years.

Living a life of personal freedom, social engagement, and self-sufficiency was enjoyable, meaningful, and fulfilling. My inner voice would tell me, *You are living your best life.* No part of my daily existence was unfailing or unfulfilling. It was a time to joyfully pursue my passions, learn new things, and expand new skills. It was the most contented time of my life. I was gratified for my blessings and for what I was becoming. I celebrated my traits of being a compassionate, giving, respectful, and empathetic man, trying to improve no matter the circumstance. After a few disheartening broken relationships, I realized it is our choice to feel happy or unhappy. At the young age of twenty-five, I realized that it's not the problematic transitions or conditions of life that prove to be a roadblock to happiness but my own choice of attitude, behavior, and thoughts that confront life's burdensome adjustments.

Being a bit materialistic, I purchased a 1978 Chevy Camaro Sport Coupe. My father said, "Now that is a vehicle I can appreciate. Good choice."

I could have paid cash for the vehicle, but I decided to finance it. I loved the car as it had a reputation for a stylish two-door coupe design and eating Mustangs as its main competitor. My other objective was establishing an impeccable credit rating as I knew that potential larger purchases would require excellent financial standing in my future. However, my choice of purchasing a shiny new thing did add to my enjoyment and happiness even if it lasted only for a short period after making that decision. Becoming a minimalist would not be in my future until much later in my lifetime.

While the dealership was preparing my new vehicle, I was waiting in line at the bank to take out some cash for the down payment. Patiently waiting for my turn, I felt a tap on my right shoulder. As I turned around, the man standing behind me said, "Hello, my name is Victor Hamilton. What is your name?"

I responded, "John, John Edwards."

Victor went on to say, "Nice to meet you. Is it all right if I ask you a question?" Nodding in agreement, Victor continued, "Have you ever considered being a fashion model for local advertisement campaigns or magazine publications?"

Taken by surprise with a curious expression on my face, I said, "No. Why do you ask?"

Victor responded, "I work as a scout and fashion photographer for a primary modeling agency. You have the type of look we actively seek. You are handsome, tall, well-proportioned, and have distinctive facial features. Would you be interested in developing a modeling pictorial portfolio?"

In the late 1970s, modeling was a female-dominated career. Unlike today, male models back then had the perception of being models of a femininity stereotype related to that career choice. In addition, fashion modeling was mainly considered a hometown part-time job without substantial pay. Not being interested, having already completed three years of a meaningful career with United Parcel Service, I answered Victor by saying, "Thank you for the offer, but I wouldn't be interested in a modeling portfolio."

Victor handed me his business card and said, "If you change your mind, give me a call."

Instead of being flattered and building my self-esteem or confidence after the modeling offer, I remarkably thought to myself in a reflective vain. I wondered, *What woman will enter my life in the future? Who will fall in love with me and become the love of my life?* As my moral character traits and values were established, I started soul-searching more seriously about seeking a lifetime partner. Having experienced painful breakups and heartaches, I had not committed to a deep romantic bond for three years, with Sharon as my last significant relationship. I wanted to find a partner that would be attentive to building trust, respect, and commitment to having our best interests at heart. I yearned for someone who could adore me for being myself rather than displeasure for what was missing. I left it up to intuitive thinking, fate, and spontaneous activities. I promoted and upheld positive emotions as I waited for a lifetime companion to come into my life.

A few weeks later, my friend, Rob, called asking if I wanted to go to an Italian Restaurant in Concord called Michael Anthony's. Naturally, I asked, "Why Michael Anthony's?" Concord was a forty-minute drive from San Lorenzo.

Rob said, "Our favorite band, Clean Air, will be playing there this coming Friday and Saturday night instead of the Cardinal Lounge."

Michael Anthony's was an upscale eating place and nightclub. The restaurant's design included a large bar, an open lobby area, and a comfortable dining room accommodating three hundred guests. The ambiance had the feel of simple elegance with soft lighting, white linen, wood architecture, and walls with mural paintings. Michael Anthony's was well-known as a "romantic dating hot spot," featuring live music and dancing.

Rob said, "Can you pick me up around 8:00 p.m. Saturday? The band won't start playing until 9:00 p.m."

Thinking this would be an excellent opportunity to put some highway miles on my new car, I responded to Rob, "You got it, buddy. See you then."

Rob and I were running late. As we pulled into the restaurant's parking lot, we noticed a relatively long line of people waiting to gain entrance. We paid a five-dollar cover charge to get a standing-room-only option to enter. As we entered, the atmosphere was electric as Clean Air was playing a disco song standard, "Le Freak" by CHIC. We found a spot to stand directly across from the bar next to a four-foot-tall raised block-work partition wall with a framed wood countertop to rest drinks and have a bird's eye view of the dance floor and band.

Small round tables and chairs outlined the dance floor perimeter to serve four people per table. Rob started a conversation with a table of four attractive girls on the opposite side of the partition where we were standing. Rob, never lacking confidence, had an endearing extroverted way about him that invited entertaining conversation as introductions commenced.

I loved going out with Rob because I was more on the shy/quiet side with a thoughtful, considerate nature, not seeking validation from others. Rob always took care of my insecurities by pulling me into the conversation as we exchanged introductions. Rob ended up being very busy for most of the night as he would offer the recently introduced woman free drinks if they danced with him.

I could tell that one of the girls, Charlotte, was interested in me as she kept staring directly at me with bedroom eyes. Suddenly, she approached me to break the ice by asking, "Do you like to dance, John?"

I looked into her green eyes and said, "Sure, just waiting for the right song. Would you like to dance when one of my favorite songs is played?"

Charlotte responded, "I thought you would never ask. Of course."

We exchanged smiles as Rob returned from the dance floor. As Rob consumed a few nonalcoholic Arnold Palmer beverages, he inadvertently knocked over my drink onto the tiled floor, breaking the glass into several small pieces. It caused a modest disturbance as a waitress quickly cleaned up the mess. As I was trying to help, I looked up and noticed a stunningly good-looking woman sitting at a table near the left-hand corner of the stage, right next to the band. As I made eye contact with her, she smiled adorably. She captured my full attention. I couldn't take my eyes off her as her beauty defied words. My immediate thought was, *Was she smiling at me?* She was enjoying the band with six other people (four males and two females) using two tables pushed together. I assumed that one of the guys had to be her boyfriend.

After the commotion settled down and the waitress cleaned up the mess, I said to Rob, "Check it out. Look at that sensational beauty sitting near the band."

Rob turned his head toward my scanning eyes and said, "Man, where have you been? I noticed her an hour ago. She is a total smoke show and a good dancer."

I asked Rob, "I can't tell if that guy sitting across from her might be her boyfriend."

Rob answered, "No way, that dude is more interested in the dude sitting next to him. I noticed them holding hands."

I told Rob, "As I was helping the waitress clean up the broken glass, I looked up and noticed her. We made eye contact, and she smiled at me."

Rob nodded, acknowledging my comment as the band announced they would take a twenty-minute break. Taking a sip from my drink, Rob abruptly grabbed my arm and said, "Look, that seriously hot girl is walking this way."

I noticed an older woman was walking with her as they seemed to be heading toward the lady's restroom, taking their walk path in our direction. Before they approached both, Rob and I rotated simultaneously, turning our backs to the stage to ensure eye-to-eye contact as they passed. The older lady scurried quickly ahead of her, walking past us without turning or making eye contact. As I made eye contact with the stunningly beautiful woman walking directly toward us through the smoke-filled room, her beauty in my mind was so spellbinding as to be unattainable.

She abruptly stopped. Her smile indicated interest. While looking directly at both of us, she said, "Hi, how is life treating you?"

Rob, not hesitating, immediately responded, "How are you doing? Are you having a good time tonight?"

I didn't say a word, frozen in open-mouthed awe. She followed the older lady without responding to Rob's question as I observed her sexy walk.

I told Rob, "Dude, she was saying hi to me."

Pausing with a smile, Rob passionately said, "No way, man, she was talking to me."

I said, "Well, we will find out once she returns from the restroom."

At least thirty minutes passed. Waiting impatiently, we both assumed they probably had left for the evening. Then unexpectedly, I noticed that they were approaching. My heart started beating at a faster pace. Wanting to make eye contact again, I smiled as she came closer. She walked up to me, stopped within an arm's length without looking at Rob, and said, "My name is Robbin. I just had to say hi to you. What is your name?"

I responded, "John. It's a pleasure to meet you. You are amazing."

Robbin hesitated for a moment as a beautiful smile seemed to radiate happiness. Finally, she said "Don't be a stranger tonight" as she turned and walked back to her table.

I thought, *Come on, man, don't let her get away without saying anything.* I reached out and grabbed her wrist gently. As she turned her head, I said, "Would it be all right with you if we could share a dance before the end of the night?"

With the most alluring and soulful brown eyes filling my heart with the sun's warmth, Robbin sweetly said, "I will wait, just for you."

As song after song played, I couldn't drum up the courage to ask Robbin to dance as her beauty took my breath away and caused me to react with self-doubt and nervousness.

Rob said, "When will you grow a pair and ask Robbin to dance?"

Clean Air started playing one of my favorite songs, "More Than a Woman" by the Bee Gees. I noticed Robbin walking out onto the dance floor with one of her friends. I had promised Charlotte a dance, so I asked her. I was a good disco two-step dancer incorporating single or double-handed swing spins and wrap-style moves with synchronous timing. Charlotte was a terrific dancer following me, perfectly integrating big hip swings, body bumps, and independent right-and-left leg/foot movements with asymmetric arm variations. It was so much fun dancing with her, but my mind was on Robbin. I thanked Charlotte for the dance and returned to my standing place. The band played a couple more songs, and then Clean Air announced the last call and dance.

My heart sank. I had to ask Robbin to dance. The last song was a slow dance tune by Roberta Flack and Donny Hathaway, "The Closer I Get to You."

Not sure if Robbin would accept an intimate slow dance with me, I walked over to her table, gracefully reached out my open hand, and asked her, "May I have this last dance with you?"

Robbin held my hand and said, "I was hoping you hadn't forgotten about me."

As Robbin put her hands on my shoulders, I placed my hands against her hips as we slowly moved closer together, swaying back and forth with the music. Our foot movement was minimal as we would slowly turn with Robbin resting her head on my left shoulder. I tenderly sang some of the song's lyrics in her ear, saying, "The closer I get to you, a feeling comes over me. Pulling closer, sweet as gravity."

As my heart was pounding against her chest, the song ended. It was a precious moment as I did not want the melody to end. Once we moved our bodies apart, we held hands with outstretched arms. I said, "Do you have time to go outside and talk before leaving?"

Robbin said, "Sure."

Under the lighting of a full moon, external landscape spotlights, and the wind of the air slightly blowing through Robbin's hair, feelings of happiness and loving anticipation were all around me as we rested up against a patio railing outside the restaurant. I said, "Thank you for dancing with me. I appreciate sharing that moment with you."

As Robbin responded, I wasn't listening, mesmerized by her exotic beauty. Appreciating her eye shape, full lips, skin color, and hair texture indicated she might be of different ethnicity and cultural tradition. Additionally, Robbin's symmetrical facial features were perfect. My mind pondered, *Is this what love at first sight feels like?*

Then I heard "John, are you with me?" as I broke out of my hypnotic state.

"Yes, wherever you're going, I'm going your way," I answered. A lyric I remembered from one of my favorite songs, "Moon River" by Andy Williams.

Robbin laughed and said, "I have to get going. My friends are waiting for me."

Not wanting her to go, I quickly asked, "Can I give you a call?"

Robbin paused and said "I don't normally give out my phone number. It's 925-689-6144" as she quickly walked away.

As I returned to my car, I repeated the phone number, not wanting to forget it. As soon as I got into my car for the ride home with Rob, I wrote down her phone number on a yellow Post-it note that I quickly grabbed from my glove box. Then I folded it in half and placed it securely in my wallet.

Before starting the car, I looked over at Rob and said, "I told you she was saying hi to me."

Rob contemplated his response for a moment and then said, "Impressive. You are one hell of a lucky man. She is a stone fox!"

I responded, "Yes. We are two drifters off to see the world. There's such a lot of world to see. We're after the same rainbow's end, waiting, round the bend, my huckleberry friend." (Song lyrics I had memorized from "Moon River.")

Waiting several seconds for Rob's response, he finally answered, "Shut the hell up."

On Sunday, I was in a state of blissful happiness. Robbin was on my mind all day as I listened to my favorite prerecorded cassette tape love songs on my Sony Walkman. First, I said a prayer, thanking God for blessing me with the opportunity to meet and have such a beautiful woman cross my path. Then being of the Catholic faith,

I grabbed my Catholic Daily Prayer Book and improvised on the devotion for Confidence in Prayer.

My prayer went like this:

> *Heavenly Father, your Son taught us to pray with confidence when he said, "Ask, and you will receive, seek, and you will find."*
> *My Father, I believe in your love for me.*
> *You will give me what is good when I ask in humble confidence.*
> *I thank you for your kind providence in granting me a meeting with Robbin with all my heart.*
> *I pray that you will give me all the graces I need to love.*
> *Glory be to the Father, the Son, and the Holy Spirit.*
> *Amen.*

I was anxious to call Robbin, but I did not want to seem too presumptuous or overly captivated by making a phone call the next day. Therefore, I waited to make that call begrudgingly. I planned to call Robbin Wednesday night to ask her out on a dinner date on Saturday night. I then called Bob to confirm our customary workout plan in my garage. Bob and I weight lifted every Sunday, Wednesday, and Friday night for a couple of hours. Bob said he would be there, and I was looking forward to giving him the details of last night's incident. Bob was an exceptional listener and always provided straightforward advice and guidance. My main question for Bob would be, "Is love at first sight possible? Or are my feelings based superficially on the excitement of an instant attraction?"

Once Bob arrived, I recounted the blow-by-blow sequence of circumstances that allowed and led to my fortuitous encounter with Robbin. I was still on cloud nine as Bob noticed my body language, enthusiasm, and heartfelt emotional elation as I described meeting Robbin and that I had plans to call her on Wednesday night before our workout.

Bob said, "I have never seen you as excited and impassioned about a girl."

I emotionally responded to Bob, "I believe in my heart that she is the one!"

Bob asked, "You mean your future kindred soul partner for life?"

"YES! That's why I have a couple of questions for you," I replied. "Do you think love at first sight is possible, or do you think my strong feelings for Robbin are simply based on the excitement of an instant attraction?"

Being his introspective self, Bob said, "Most relationships start by finding someone who we find attractive. At first sight, falling in love could not happen without you being attracted to Robbin in the first place. Therefore, whether it's love at first sight or an instant attraction, both play a role in your genuine interest in getting to know Robbin better. Relationships take time. Give yourself the time to answer those questions."

About one hour before Bob came over for our Wednesday night workout, I called Robbin from my parents' bedroom for privacy. The phone conversation went like this:

"May I speak with Robbin?"

"This is Robbin."

"Hi, Robbin! This is John."

Long pause. *"You remembered my phone number?"*

"Yes, I have an excellent memory."

"Look, like I told you, I don't usually give out my phone number. Thanks for calling. It was nice meeting you, but I have to go."

I heard a click and then nothing but a dial tone. I was devastated. Robbin's voice over the phone announced loud and clear that she was not interested and did not want to continue the conversation. I sat on the edge of my parents' bed with my hands on my knees, looking at the wall with a sad blank stare, contemplating my disappointment for several minutes. Then the doorbell rang. Bob had arrived for our workout.

Bob recognized that I appeared upset about something and wasn't my usual self during our workout. So Bob asked, "Is anything wrong?"

WHAT A TALE MY THOUGHTS WILL TELL: WORDS NOT TO BE FORGOTTEN

I said, "I called Robbin. Unfortunately, the call did not go as I had anticipated."

After giving Bob a word-by-word replay of my and Robbin's phone dialogue, Bob said, "Are you going to give up that easily? Robbin said it was nice meeting you. Don't give up that easily, John. You probably just called her at a bad time. Promise me that you will call her back."

I nodded my head in a half-hearted acknowledging way.

Later that evening, I sat on my parents' bed staring at the phone, trying to get up the guts to call Robbin back. I must have picked up the pink-colored handset ten times to only place it back in its place without pressing any Touch-Tone push-button numbers. Then suddenly, my thoughts were filled by having confidence after saying a prayer, giving me the spirit to make the call.

"May I speak with Robbin?"

"Yes, John, this is Robbin."

"I wanted to call you back to make sure you wouldn't regret passing on a fantastic opportunity."

"And what might that fantastic opportunity be?"

"Having an opportunity to get to know me better!"

Approving laughter. *"Okay, I'm listening."*

"I had a dream last night that you asked me out. Would you like to have dinner with me Saturday?"

Uncontrolled laughter. *"I would love to!"*

As we spent more time together, we bloomed into a long-lasting relationship. It was a whirlwind romance that we cherished and enjoyed to the fullest. During the initial stage of our dating period, I found out that your mother's full name was Robbin June Lockhart and that she was born in Vallejo but had lived most of her life in Concord. She was a second-year San Jose State University student living in a multistoried dormitory near the campus. I remember asking Robbin, "Who was that older lady you were with when we first met at Michael Anthony's?"

Robbin responded, "Oh, that was my mother."

Then, I asked, "What is your mother's name?"

"June Lockhart," Robbin replied.

I chuckled and said, "The same name as the famous TV actress of *Lassie, Lost in Space,* and *Petticoat Junction* fame?"

Robbin smiled and said, "YEP."

Robbin told me that her mother was born in Iraq and that her father, Walt, was much older than her mother.

Our attraction and fascination with one another were undeniable. I remember the sensations of love being powerful. We had many similarities. We both were good athletes and loved music, dancing, dining, movies, outdoor activities/camping, and many friends. On top of all that, Robbin loved baseball and was an advanced water and snow skier. Robbin's Episcopalian faith/spirituality was very similar to my Catholicism, and she came from a solid supporting family foundation as I did. I realized Robbin's stunning looks come from her varied Iraqi and English heritage. We shared the interchange of values and attitudes. We seemed to be very compatible and spent a lot of time together. My thoughts were, *This is too good to be true.*

Before our third date, Robbin called me and said, "I have planned a surprise excursion for you. Can you drive to San Jose and pick me up at the dorm this Saturday morning around 10:00 a.m.?"

The drive from San Lorenzo to San Jose was easily a forty-five-minute drive. I was so excited to see Robbin. I made that drive down Highway 880 in thirty minutes, breaking the entire route's speed limit without getting a ticket. Robbin was getting around those days in a 1971 Oldsmobile Cutlass Supreme that was in the repair shop for strange vibrations, leaks, odd noises, and poor performance more often than not. She loved my new Camaro. As Robbin jumped into the passenger seat, we spent the first ten minutes kissing and hugging each other before starting the car to hit the road. Robbin was navigating us to our surprise destination as I followed her directions. Within minutes, we pull into the San Jose Airport, driving into a parking section of the airfield property, about one-half mile from the main terminal. We walked through a building marked "Trade Winds Aviation." Robbin flashed a badge to the counter attendant and escorted me through a doorway that led us outside to a lineup of parked Cessna 152 aircraft.

Robbin said, "Jump in."

WHAT A TALE MY THOUGHTS WILL TELL: WORDS NOT TO BE FORGOTTEN

Then standing in bewildering amazement, I said, "You have a pilot's license?"

I had never flown in a small aircraft and was very apprehensive and nervous. I thought about the time I feared heights when Eileen had asked me to go on the Ferris wheel ride with her at the St. Joachim festival. Not wanting to show any perception of emotional uneasiness, I opened the door and buckled into the front passenger seat.

In total control, Robbin made preparations for takeoff, easing my anxiety somewhat as I said a silent prayer to quiet the fear in my heart. As Robbin accelerated the plane down the runway, eventually gaining elevation, the view was unique and different than flying in a large commercial aircraft. Robbin used hand-and-foot controls to practice soft banking maneuvers and turns as we reached a cruising altitude. My trust in her ability was not wavering as Robbin explained to expect more vibration and engine/wind noise than you would experience in a car.

The views were breathtaking as Robbin took a flight path heading us toward Vacaville as we viewed natural landscapes, home neighborhoods, and gardens. Robbin landed the plane at the public-use Nut Tree Airport. We spent the early afternoon eating and enjoying the various souvenir shops and train stations. On the flight home, Robbin took me on a beautiful sun-setting ride over San Francisco, Santa Cruz Beach Boardwalk, and Monterey Bay's coast. After we landed and came to a stop, I felt a deep sigh of relief as I got out of the plane and placed my feet on solid ground. I embraced Robbin for several minutes without letting go. Her instincts understood my sentiments, and she sweetly hugged her arms around me, holding me tight.

I whispered in Robbin's ear, "This is where you belong, in my arms."

Our shared experience was an unforgettable encounter that would become a moment in time, an embodied part of my life that will remain a heartfelt memory forever. I was falling wide-eyed in love. I asked myself, *Is this the love I have been waiting for my whole life?* It was a tender, naturally evolving relationship, turning my world around. Our beginning was an emotional and sweet adventure that involved the most profound wonders of falling in love. My thoughts were, *This love I feel is unique and different. Robbin makes me care with a different emotional passion. She is the love of my life. I want to be her hero.*

Within minutes after the plane landed, I knew my life would change.

We became inseparable and devoted to pursuing one another—romancing, intimate conversations, sharing our lives, evaluating compatibility, lovemaking, and unhurried commitment during our courtship. We took full advantage of everything San Jose had to offer. We would often go for walks in Alum Rock Municipal Park. It was a spacious park with incredible views of the San Jose skyline with stone and rock bridges leading to long-secluded trails. During our weekends, we would frequent Japantown or the Pruneyard Shopping Center, enjoying the variety of shops, multiple dining options, and movie theaters. One of our favorite pastimes was drinking hot chocolate in bed at her dorm apartment while listening to love songs by the famous American soft rock band Bread. I took great pleasure in showering her with expensive gifts, dining, and going to breakfast at Hobee's. I remember how hard it was waiting to see Robbin at the time. I often asked her, "When will I see you again?" and thought to myself, *I don't want to wait forever* as I would drive back home to San Lorenzo.

As days passed between not seeing her, something started happening to me. Almost every minute of every day, my thoughts were about Robbin. Day and night, I would think about her exotic beauty, her delightful smile, her laughter, and our deep-seated conversations. I prayed to God, hoping Robbin felt the same way about me. That night, I went to bed, listening to music, reflecting on my past relationships, and harkening back to the captivating wonder and beautiful innocence of my young love with Nancy. I thought about how my middle school romance with Eileen helped me realize who I was becoming. And how my high school and college heartbreaks with Debbie, Sharon, and Donna provided the stepping stones and stirring life experiences that would allow me the opportunity to learn more about myself. Before falling asleep, a favorite song of mine came on the radio, "More Than a Woman" by the Bee Gees. The lyrics of the music touched my emotions as they described my love for Robbin.

> *But now you take my breath away*
> *Suddenly you're in my life*
> *Part of everything I do*
> *You got me working day and night*
> *Just tryin' to keep a hold on you*
> *Here in your arms, I found my paradise*
> *My only chance for happiness*
> *And if I lose you now, I think I will die*
> *Oh, say you'll always be my baby*
> *We can make it shine*
> *We can take forever, just a minute at a time*
> *More than a woman*
> *More than a woman to me*

Before falling asleep, I remember affectionately saying to myself about Robbin, *I have never known a love like this before. She is more than a woman to me.*

During the first six months with Robbin, the feelings of intense emotion, romance, and pleasure were uncharted territory for me. Having endured the previous rejections, I was clear-minded but apprehensive about the possibility that disenchantment could happen again. When driving from San Lorenzo to San Jose to be with Robbin, I repeatedly played a favorite song of mine on the cassette player. The lyrics from Dave Mason's "Will You Still Love Me Tomorrow" mimicked my emotional thinking. Is this a lasting treasure or just a moment's pleasure? Will my heart be broken when the night meets the morning sun? Yet my main hope was that we shared so many things in common that our relationship had the potential to be life-changing. Each day, our feelings for one another and our emotional connection became more substantial.

Working for United Parcel Service, I took full advantage of a generous vacation, sick leave, and floating holiday benefits package to be with Robbin more often during weekdays, extending my weekends off. Taking a day off here and there allowed Robbin and me to strengthen our bond. Robbin and I believed that stable family connections and friendships were essential for our relationship to remain strong. We both discussed and agreed that the time was right to introduce family members and friends. Meeting Robbin's parents for the first time was a big step and very exciting as she invited me over for dinner. Knowing that fathers are pretty protective of their daughters, it was crucial to leave a good impression. Meeting parents can be a nerve-racking experience, but Robbin gave me a heads-up about her parents making this transition less stressful.

Before meeting Robbin's parents, my main goal was to dress modestly and remain sensitive and polite. Robbin told me beforehand that her mother was born in Iraq, inspiring me to learn a few native Arabic responses. Consequently, I memorized "Hello," "Thank you," "Excuse me," and "Goodbye" in Arabic, thinking this would leave a lasting positive impression if an opportunity presented itself, along with bringing a gift of a favorite Arab pastry called, *baklava*.

During our drive to her parents' house for dinner, Robbin mentioned, "Oh, by the way, my aunt Eve and uncle Sam flew in from New Jersey and are going to join us for dinner as well."

Being more invested in this relationship than in past ones placed an uneasy feeling of pressure, knowing that a larger group of family members would be present. To ease my mind, I asked Robbin, "Tell me about your aunt and uncle."

Robbin responded, "You will love my mother's sister, Aunt Eve. She is the sweetest person on earth. My uncle Sam is a traditional Arab born near Bagdad, Iraq. Family and honor are paramount to him as he celebrates his heritage. Therefore, being invited to my parents' home would be seen in his eyes as a great honor." Robbin continued, "Whenever my uncle Sam greets me, he says in Arabic, '*Asalaamu Alaikum*,' meaning 'peace be with you.' So if my uncle greets you this way, say in response, '*Wa Alaikum Salaam*,' which means 'and peace be unto you.'"

Once we arrived, Robbin and I stood next to each other on the porch as she reached out to ring the doorbell. The door opened slowly,

WHAT A TALE MY THOUGHTS WILL TELL: WORDS NOT TO BE FORGOTTEN

finally revealing a stocky man of relatively short stature dressed in a traditional Arab ankle-length, long-sleeve white robe with a rainbow-colored scarf/tunic covering his head, complimenting his dark complexion.

"*Asalaamu Alaikum!*" he exclaims with enthusiasm.

Robbin and I responded in unison, "*Wa Alaikum Salaam.*" This was my first meeting with Uncle Sam.

After greeting Robbin with an affectionate hug and kiss on both of her cheeks, Sam reached out with his right hand to shake my hand. The handshake lasted a long time as Sam finished his greeting by kissing my right hand and then placing his right hand over his heart. I later learned from Robbin that Sam placing his right hand over his heart was his way of showing me respect. This warmhearted greeting made meeting the rest of Robbin's family free from worries.

Sitting at the dinner table with Robbin's parents and family members, we enjoyed a delicious native Iraqi cuisine called *fasoulia*, a white bean stew with lamb and vegetables served over rice. We had a casual and enlightening conversation about how Robbin and I met, our family bonds, and Iraqi culture as I remained polite, sensitive, and affectionate to Robbin. Then after taking a bite of baklava, the buttery pastry made with a sweet sugary syrup that I brought as a welcoming gift, Uncle Sam forcefully and loudly sneeze-farted. At first, remaining quiet, everybody's eyes widened, trying to play it cool as if nothing had happened. Then sitting directly across from Sam at the dinner table, I noticed a slight smirk on his face as if he was trying not to laugh. About twenty seconds had passed, and the worst part happened. The smell started to creep over the dinner table.

I said in Arabic, "*Muedharat*" (which means "Excuse me, beg your pardon").

Everybody laughed. Sam responded in Arabic, saying, "*Barakallafik Shukran.*"

Robbin's mother, June, and Aunt Eve had approving ear-to-ear smiles, understanding what Sam had said. June later told me that Sam said, "God Bless you, much gratitude."

Taking the blame for Sam's fart left the lasting impression I was hoping to establish. Fortunately, being blessed, Sam became a loving kindred friend of mine for many years to come.

Over the next few months, my family, weekend camping trips, and mutual friends were introduced. We celebrated Robbin's twentieth birthday at the 94th Aero Squadron Restaurant, which looked like a WWI French countryside cottage near the San Jose Airport. They had the best prime rib in town and views overlooking the airport runways. While eating there, you could pick up headsets at your table and listen to the air traffic controllers as planes would take off and land. I met Robbin's best friend, Kim, who flew up from San Diego; Wally, an old family friend; and Robbin's ex-boyfriend, Mike. A few days before her birthday, I purchased a heavy embroidery patterned long black lace dress with intricate beading for her birthday gift. The dress accentuated Robbin's beauty with a feminine focal point. I was almost brought to tears by how stunningly beautiful she looked fashioning it.

As I got to know Robbin better, I discovered her uniqueness. I knew nobody quite like her. Besides being an accomplished Cessna pilot, she was a skilled ski-boat driver and an expert fisherwoman and knew how to change the brakes, fix a flat tire, or replace an alternator on her car. Robbin learned these life skill sets from her father as he wanted to prepare his daughter for the real world and how to survive independently. We would spend weekend camping trips with her parents and friends, enjoying Salt Springs Reservoir in the El Dorado Forest near Jackson or waterskiing at Lake McClure in Merced County. Using her mathematical/mechanical aptitudes, Robbin could assemble and completely set up her tent in ten minutes. In contrast, I would read instructions, figure out how to connect tent poles, and struggle to position my tent in the right direction sixty minutes later. During this time, I knew I wanted a more serious commitment to our relationship and thought about our long-term future.

After six months of dating, Robbin and I continued to see each other in a positive light. We were delighted with each other and did not pay any attention to alternate partners. We took a longer-range view of things and made decisions based on what was best for our relationship. Knowing we were sharing something special, I asked Robbin to join me for a romantic dinner at the Grandview

WHAT A TALE MY THOUGHTS WILL TELL: WORDS NOT TO BE FORGOTTEN

Restaurant on top of Mt. Hamilton in San Jose, a classically elegant restaurant with exceptional views of the Santa Clara Valley. We had a window table that offered an exquisite ambiance and intimacy. We looked at each other across the table. Before our dinner was served, I spontaneously reached out to hold Robbin's hand to express my deep affection for her. I paused for several moments without saying a word as her eyes embodied an aura of tenderness. For a moment, it was as if we were alone in that exquisite restaurant.

I finally responded to her, saying for the first time, "I love you." As my heart lunged into my throat, awaiting her response, I thought, *What if her reply isn't mutual?*

But then, as gently as a falling snowflake, Robbin responded "I love you too" as she tightened her grip on my hand. It was a magical moment and evening that will reside in my heart and memory forever.

I did not take saying the words "I love you" nonchalantly. Being more reserved and only calling upon those words sparingly, I wanted it to be an intimate moment free from any constraint. Robbin and I had built a bond of connection, mutual commitment, and trust over time. I knew that once we were willing to be exclusive to one another, the depth of our relationship was moving in the direction of love. After exchanging those memorable words, I removed myself from a casually intertwined loving connection into embracing something natural and formal. The essence of our passion was beginning.

Over the next several months, falling in love gave way to being in love. Our physical attraction, sexual intimacy, and shared interests eventually gave way to the importance of compatibility, communication, and how we related. We learned to accept our imperfections, validate our feelings, and understand each other's needs. I knew that my commitment to Robbin was strong. I wanted to be her hero and be there through sickness and in health. Creating a meaningful friendship and supportive outcome beneath my passion for romance and love was essential. I felt the full range of joy, contentment, and pride. I had never known such happiness. Robbin was the love of my life. I had found my forever person.

I was in my fourth year as a package car driver for UPS. At twenty-six years of age, after getting yearly phased-in UPS/Teamster's labor contract hourly wage increases, my yearly income matched my father's. Knowing that UPS was experiencing tremendous growth, had a promotion from within policy, and had a college-tuition reimbursement program, I fully intended to stay with the organization. In essence, taking a longer view of my potential career and earning future, I told Robbin of my plans to pursue a management profession with UPS and eventually finish my four-year college degree while working. If a good opportunity in management came along, I said I would seriously consider it. None of this came as a bombshell revelation to her. On the contrary, she supported me and said to do whatever made me happy.

After one year and three months of dating, Robbin and I were married at St. Michael and All Angels Episcopal Church in Concord on April 22, 1979, with more than two hundred of our friends, coworkers, and family members in attendance. We enjoyed our honeymoon at one of the ten most beautiful places in America and the largest freshwater lake in California, Lake Tahoe.

As newlyweds, we felt that renting an apartment would provide the best option to start our lives together. So we moved into a brand-new complex in Fremont called The Treetop Apartments. Our new home was located on Fremont and Stevenson Boulevard, close to Central Park and Lake Elizabeth. Our new one-bedroom apartment was an architectural treasure, making the living space feel larger with vaulted ceilings and a sizable patio sun deck, creating a welcoming and luxurious design. While homeownership was a future goal, renting an apartment provided the financial flexibility and urban lifestyle we sought before starting our own family. It was an exciting time as companies like Atari, Apple, and Oracle were founded and flourished in Silicon Valley, which became widely accepted as the technology/computer industry center in 1979.

Taking advantage of the rise of Silicon Valley innovation, Robbin decided to take a secretarial position for a start-up technology firm in Palo Alto after completing two years of college. We enjoyed our jobs and tried to figure out how to live with one another as partners

WHAT A TALE MY THOUGHTS WILL TELL: WORDS NOT TO BE FORGOTTEN

without developing bad habits. I often thought about how I could provide and promote a romantic and happy marriage. I wanted to be a good partner. Therefore, I always tried to create a warm and cozy environment for our home. Knowing that Robbin liked aged furniture pieces, comfy couches, and homey country antique interior design decorating style, I integrated a combination of candlelight, plants, fresh flowers, comfortable pillows, photo collages, and throw blankets into our apartment. I wanted Robbin to feel good about the space where we spent most of our time together.

Additionally, since Robbin had more nurturing instincts and manual skills to cook meals, I took on the responsibility of household chores, like washing dishes, laundry, and home maintenance. Often, I would randomly leave sticky love notes in strategic places like her car, bathroom mirror, or kitchen counter to express and write down some thoughtful words about my appreciation and love for her. Having expectations that Robbin might reciprocate her feelings in this way for me, I found it a little concerning that this type of affectionate display was not forthcoming. I rationalized that no two people are alike in showing their love. I let the thought of unease go away.

When you start, it doesn't take long to understand married life's realities. There was an anticlimax moment after the excitement of planning our wedding, getting married, and honeymoon. Robbin and I now had to consider working around our potential careers, how we would decide to combine finances, and how to manage the shared get-togethers of both families. I firmly believe that marriage is a partnership. Whatever is mine is yours. That included the business of making decisions about money and financial planning. Since Robbin's mother was a manager for Bank of America, we decided to start a joint checking and savings account with her bank. Knowing that money problems can be a disruptive force in a marriage and not wanting to cause any conflict, I trusted and allowed Robbin to take control of our financial planning and paying bills. As a result, we were debt-free and natural savers more than big spenders looking to get off to a good start.

Robbin and I were a young married couple. I had just turned twenty-six, and Robbin was twenty-one. In the 1970s, the appropriate or median age for marriage was 22.5 years for men and 20.5 years for women. Today, the recommended age to get married is between the ages of twenty-eight to thirty-two, which presents the least likelihood of divorce in the first five years. According to the "Goldilocks theory," people at this age are not too old or too young. A lingering concern was that Robbin and I sacrificed completing our secondary education to get married. We reasoned that we could be married and still achieve our final two years of a college education. However, I knew this could be demanding and stressful for our marriage and coping skills. Then during our second month of marriage, I remember Robbin coming home from work telling me, "My boss thinks I got married too young."

I hesitated momentarily before responding to Robbin's remark, thinking about the best way to respond. Finally, I asked, "What do you think about your manager's opinion?"

Robbin said, "He feels that I should have completed my education before getting married…it's just his opinion."

Feeling a little uncomfortable about our discussion and that Robbin did not answer my question thoroughly, I considered asking "Does his opinion matter to you?" but I decided not to ask that question and just let it be by ignoring the topic and changing the subject.

Over the next few months, I noticed that Robbin started coming home late from work as she began to partake in office parties or social get-togethers with her coworkers and boss. One of the social outings included a hot-tub party with associates from work. I thought to myself, *We just started our marriage partnership, is there something about our interpersonal relationship that is keeping her from wanting to come home and spend time with me?* I reasoned that my best strategy was to be upfront about my feelings and talk with Robbin without making any hasty conclusions.

I started by saying, "It makes me sad that you are coming home late from work so often. I miss your company and want to be the reason why you would want to rush home from work. Is there a reason you spend so much time away from home?"

WHAT A TALE MY THOUGHTS WILL TELL: WORDS NOT TO BE FORGOTTEN

Robbin said that her work commitments required her to stay late periodically, and when offered a drink or to party with coworkers after work, she felt obligated to participate. She reassured me that I had no reason to be concerned. I certainly did not want to nag about this issue, so I decided to skip the drama and move on. All I wanted was the type of love that brings peace to your mind.

I was still in the "honeymoon stage." My love for Robbin was in a period of euphoria. I couldn't wait to get home from work to be with my new wife. My attraction and desire were at their highest point, particularly during my favorite time of the year, the picturesque fall months of October and November. I never saw any flaws with Robbin. My body would physically respond whenever she was near me. I had an intense sense of longing as my sexual energy ran high. Any touch or look from Robbin was filled with desire. Then suddenly and unexpectedly, with a lack of attention, Robbin emotionally and physically distanced herself from me one night in bed. Feeling frustrated and rejected, I did not say anything. I rationalized that she must have been too tired or distracted by something. However, I couldn't help but think, *Is my marriage already in trouble?* Thus, this was my first experience with Robbin where our sexual desire did not match. I did not want to be insensitive to this issue or single-minded about one incident, but it did have a lingering impact on my psyche.

Consequently, I internalized the hurt without communicating my distress. Then over the next few weeks, I could not help but notice that our sexual activity had diminished. I remember trying to walk around naked more often or work out with weights in front of Robbin with only a tight pair of shorts on, attempting to stimulate her sexual desire. It had no effect. I started thinking that maybe there was a physical problem affecting Robbin's sexuality or that she might indulge her sexual desires elsewhere. Robbin knew that my love for her was unconditional. My emotional temperature toward her was always warm and loving. I was a romantic at heart. She had to feel my love for her was compelling. Not wanting to have an awkward conversation about our lack of intimacy, I thought deeply about how to approach the subject. I decided to ask her if something was wrong the next time it happened.

As the Thanksgiving holiday approached, Robbin and I decided to split and spend our first Thanksgiving together with our families. We attended the early afternoon with her family and the late evening with mine. During our drive to her parents' house, Robbin informed me that she had given her boss a two-week notice that she would be quitting her job at the technology firm. She explained that she wanted a commute closer to home and a less stressful job that provided more fun. This decision was a welcoming option. It certainly eased my mind about no longer dealing with her outspoken boss or late-night after-work gatherings.

Robbin said, "I love crafts, so I was thinking about getting a job with King Norman's Toys and Crafts Store here in Fremont. I could work full or part-time." Robbin could visualize my enthusiastic approval without me saying a word. She then added, "What do you think about having a baby? I know that I will be ovulating soon."

My thoughts went immediately to the fact that having a child and parenthood is a big decision. I was thinking, *Am I ready for this?* Before I could develop any ambivalent feelings about her question or respond, Robbin said, "I know that everything changes once you have a child. However, we are both young and will relate better with our children as they grow towards adulthood because of our youth."

I responded, "Are you ready to make that kind of sacrifice? We have been married for only seven months."

Robbin pleaded, "Pull the car over!" As I pulled the car to a safe stop off the highway, Robbin said with a light of love in her eyes, "I want to make a baby with you. I'm ready to start a family." She added, "Do you have any worries about having children?"

After thinking about it and pausing for several seconds, I finally responded enthusiastically, "Let's get started!"

We immediately embraced, and my concerns about our infrequent intimacy exited my mind.

Over the next couple of months, our conversations were immersed in the excitement about getting ready, making preparations, and comparing ideas on raising a child. Neither one of us ever considered what life would be like without children. However, I did have some lingering questions that I never communicated to Robbin. I remember contemplating, *How will having a child challenge our relationship and finances? Are we ready for this?* and *Was having a child so early a reason for Robbin to mitigate our relationship?* Looking back on it now, I unquestionably should have discussed my viewpoints about the strength of our relationship and taken the time to work out any potential challenges. But as usual, I discounted and made allowances without communicating. Instead, I focused on the here and now, not the future.

As the new year was upon us, January was always a notable month because it was the anniversary of Robbin's birth. So we decided to celebrate Robbin's twenty-second birthday by going out for dinner with her family. During dessert, Robbin said, "I have a significant announcement to make!" Abruptly, Robbin moves her chair backward, stands up, and lifts her blouse below her bra line, exposing her tummy. Written on her stomach with a black body marker were the words "Hi, Daddy, I can't wait to meet you!" Just below the words was a drawing of three stick figures holding hands.

Suddenly, time stood still. It was a moment of ecstasy filled with many emotions. Excitement, joy, disbelief, and happiness united before the revelation sunk in. I will never forget my exhilarated and beautiful emotional state. My face clearly showed my delight and radiance.

Robbin then declared, "You're going to be a Daddy!"

The months following were the happiest of my life and marriage to Robbin. I did my best to live up to Robbin's expectations of an expectant father. I started reading pregnancy handbooks, attending Lamaze classes, and seeking spiritual guidance from Father Mac. Additionally, Robbin and I discussed the American dream of homeownership. We both had saved up a reasonable sum of money. With the help of Robbin's mother adding to our down payment, we qualified and purchased our first three-bedroom, two-bath home in the community of West Pittsburg, moving within a ten-minute drive from Robbin's parents' residence one month before Johnny's birth.

Then in the early morning hours of August 13, 1980, Robbin's water broke. Standing stunned and motionless, Robbin implored, "Get me to the hospital!"

I stumbled around like a chicken with his head cut off. I automatically went into fight-and-flight mode. Finally, Robbin perceived my stress level and said, "Calm down, John, everything will be okay."

I grabbed the prepackaged baby bag as I helped Robbin out the door. After several hours of labor and courageously attempted natural childbirth, Robbin required a cesarean section. Moments later, I was introduced to Johnny Campbell Edwards, nine pounds and twelve ounces of the miracle of life.

I thought about the short two-and-a-half decades I had been on the earth as I looked into the questioning eyes of my new son. I felt blessed during that moment and thought about the evolution of how my parents had raised me. I was full of anticipation about how to go about parenting my son to his full potential. I hadn't developed any parenting skills besides my parents' role models. Therefore, I instinctively knew that raising a child would not be easy. I was on the path of learning as I went. I thought desperately about providing a better future for my child. I understood parenting in masculine terms. My instincts thrust me into the importance of playing the role of a provider, protector, and disciplinarian. I wanted to protect my child from outside influences by being a monitor and teacher of acceptable values. I firmly believed that regular church attendance and engagement in organized sports would benefit my son's development. However, I placed the most importance on being a provider. To provide for my family was viewed as a foremost duty of responsibility, identity, and manhood.

I immediately started thinking about assuming more responsibility at work through UPS's promotion-from-within management program even though I knew that this decision would require more extended hours and potential travel/relocation requirements. However, the advantages were a higher salary and taking part in UPS's Management Incentive Program. Only management personnel were eligible or could participate in a MIP award. The award was determined by multiplying your annualized salary by a MIP factor.

WHAT A TALE MY THOUGHTS WILL TELL: WORDS NOT TO BE FORGOTTEN

This calculation regulated the amount of free UPS stock shares you were awarded yearly. The objective of the Management Incentive Program was to align incentive pay with annual performance.

Later after researching the program, I told Robbin, "Did you know that UPS retires more millionaires than any company in the world?"

Robbin eagerly responded, "Sounds good to me!"

Understanding that promotions don't happen overnight, I started my plan to have initial conversations with my sponsor about my interest. Tom Huff, my former operations manager, who I admired and developed a mentorship with, supported my aspirations. Tom would informally coach me during our meetings and role-play potential interview questions.

Additionally, Tom was well-respected and became an influential advocate on my behalf, introducing me to several other high-ranking executives. Finally, Robbin and I discussed the advantages and disadvantages of a potential career path change in the future. She supported my decision wholeheartedly as long as I waited until Johnny entered preschool.

After a couple of crazy but joyful months, the realities and demands of young parenthood took hold. Robbin decided not to return to work while I returned to my full-time package-delivery job. We were very fortunate to have tremendous help from Robbin's mother. However, with Robbin not working, I quickly realized that baby's come with a hefty price tag. I remember us spending nearly $1,000 in the first month on child-related expenses. Overtime hours were always available at UPS as my forty-hour workweek now surged to a fifty-hour workweek to help ease the squeeze on our budget. Always being excited to come home and be with my baby boy, I did notice that exhaustion entered the circumstances. After Robbin would describe her day of alternating the mothering chores of breastfeeding, changing diapers, monitoring 24-7, bath time, storytelling, and not getting much rest, I never felt comfortable explaining my fatigue.

As this cycle constantly repeated, I was off doing important things like providing for my family. I noticed that Robbin would get frustrated if I did not live up to my fair share of child-care tasks. I recall my mother-in-law approaching me, annoyed and requesting, "John, my daughter did not sign up for a part-time husband. She needs your help. She cannot take care of this child alone!" I did not respond to this comment. I stood there in complete stunned silence as June walked away. Her criticism hurt me deeply, again internalizing my emotions. In retrospect, I thought I was providing practical support and a helping hand to Robbin, knowing she was withstanding the burden of all this. A change had to happen, as I am sure Grandma June was voicing her daughter's sentiments. I saw myself as a supporting spouse. I told Robbin that I would try to do better. I started taking over the night-shift responsibilities of getting up and calming Johnny if he woke up crying, allowing Robbin to get more rest. Often, I found myself prone on the family room rug with my son lying on my chest, falling asleep to the beat of my heart.

Over the next two years, making time for ourselves was challenging. There was a lot of change with so much going on. We kept very busy with child care and home renovations during this time. Both Robbin and I took pride in and enjoyed landscaping. We worked together to create and design a beautiful natural Japanese garden landscape arrangement for the front yard with river rock stones emulating a running stream underneath a wooden bridge. We combined the elements of color and texture with mixed hosta perennial plants, a miniature Japanese green leaf maple tree, and ferns attempting to produce a tranquil retreat view. We built a rustic wooded country log fence providing a standard dividing line from our next-door neighbor's home, and we had the greenest lawn in the neighborhood.

We had a large backyard with a sizable redwood deck and weed-infested patchy lawn. Before taking on the considerable task of a makeover, we both agreed that we would need to purchase a truck and rent a tiller, post-hole digger, and deck sander. The backyard renovation required specialized equipment to help dig, cut, and move the earth. We purchased a low-mileage 1975 caramel-colored Ford F-150 and a brand-new Pilgrim Cabover Camper for our annual camping trips to Trinity Lake and Salt Springs Reservoir. Our landscape design included building a fiberglass patio cover, laying

WHAT A TALE MY THOUGHTS WILL TELL: WORDS NOT TO BE FORGOTTEN

new sod, bordering the redwood deck with two long wooden box planters, structured shrub/tree plantings, and potted plants. We also purchased and installed a Lifetime Kids Swing Set.

Unfortunately, I was somewhat hopeless when it came to carpentry or building skills. Therefore, we requested help from Robbin's father, Walt, who had experience in various construction frameworks and knowledge of building structures, ceilings, and floors. I was Walt's gopher as I learned the intricate steps of constructing a patio cover. The beauty of the finished project was stunning. The patio was functional, pleasant, and relaxing. It appeared as if we were living in a lush garden. The view perfectly complemented our home.

As Robbin and I were still adjusting to life with a soon-to-be two-year-old, I felt like finding alone time for ourselves was impossible. Every moment of our lives seemed related to raising our son, working, home maintenance, attending church, and family gatherings. My only reprieve from this daily lifestyle was my seasonal weekend softball team tournaments playing with many of my high school buddies. Robbin never seemed interested when I tried to prioritize and schedule some romantic alone time. It felt like we were living separate lives. There never seemed to be any effort on Robbin's part wanting to nurture our relationship. I started questioning, *Do we have anything in common anymore? Does Robbin still love me?*

My need to connect and bond through touch and intimacy was disregarded. We evolved into a ho-hum sex life. Lovemaking dropped to the bottom of the to-do list. We were lucky to have sex once per month. The decline seemed to be particularly steep. I never felt comfortable talking about this enduring loss of affection and deep, wounding hurt that I experienced. I excused my feelings about the normal state of affairs that many couples admit to a dampening sex life after having children. The priority of parenting overrides everything else as the most rewarding part of life. I strongly believed that we were equal partners in marriage and I was devoted to Robbin. Marriage was sacred and forever in my mind. I prayed about these worries instead of communicating them to Robbin, hoping that things would change for the better in time.

As I gave our future more thought, one thing became clear. Robbin and I would need to communicate how to adjust our sexual expectations. We needed to reconnect emotionally and physically. Realizing that there was no magic bullet to fix Robbin's libido problem, I often debated alternatives. I considered talking to Robbin about hiring a nanny or asking her mother to come over once a week to allow us to take a two-hour vacation. However, I did notice that Robbin's sexual desire was more sensitive after social engagements with family members or friends.

Meanwhile, Robbin and I decided to attend an invite at my parent's house for a Saturday night family get-together to enjoy a Banchero's Spaghetti Feed and Hearts card game. It was a warm and beautiful August night. As usual, I won the Hearts game, and Robbin thoroughly enjoyed herself. She loved listening to my brother Frank's funny stories about fond childhood memories. During the drive home going north on Highway 580, Robbin implored me to pull over at the next turn-off.

I asked, "Why do you want me to pull over?"

Robbin unexpectantly exclaims, "I want to make love to you. I want to conceive a daughter!"

Suddenly, I am going 85 mph instead of the posted speed limit of 55 mph. I pulled off the freeway at the Keller Ave turnoff and desperately started looking for a quiet secluded place to park the car. Robbin taking this kind of initiative was operating way outside her routine. The unexpected gesture certainly kick-started my juices and sent my desire into overdrive. The spontaneity and the thought of having car sex in a risky spot were incredibly exciting. I thought, *Maybe this is Robbin's way to reignite our sex life?* We pulled into a perfect location, a quiet, moonlit, abandoned residential parking lot. We quickly jumped into the back seat of the Camaro.

In the middle of foreplay, Robbin requested to be in the missionary position. Robbin says, "John, make sure not to penetrate too deeply."

I mused, "No problem there, it's not like I am well-endowed like porn star John Holmes."

WHAT A TALE MY THOUGHTS WILL TELL: WORDS NOT TO BE FORGOTTEN

I found out later from Robbin's research that the missionary position and shallow penetration prevent boy sperm from reaching and fertilizing the egg. And on May 15, 1982, not quite two years after Johnny's birth, we welcomed Jessica Robbin into her mother's arms. Jessica was a drop-dead gorgeous, doll-like, blue-eyed beauty with thick blond curls that melted your heart. I gently bent over to kiss her cheek, marveling at her perfection.

Having a second child was a bit overwhelming for the first year. We were busier, and our organized schedules and finances were limited. But once Johnny turned three years old, our confidence increased in our maturing child-raising abilities, knowledge, and experience. To ease our financial stress, my desire to get promoted and provide a better life for my family superseded any other personal motivation outside of the home in my life. It was my number-one priority. Even when my and Robbin's intimate sex life took another nosedive but hadn't stopped entirely, I didn't even give it a second thought. I was preoccupied with producing a fantastic work ethic beyond the call of duty by volunteering to help the package operations team complete service commitments. Additionally, I built relationships across departments by networking and gaining access to knowledge about the company's strategic plan and projected expansion.

Robbin and I led a life with greater meaning the following year. Robbin was settling into motherhood. Even during the craziest and most hectic moments, Robbin seemed to center her parenthood role with an enhanced purpose. Robbin's warmth and love for her children resonated as she provided positive reinforcement, loving involvement, and fulfilling their needs. Watching Robbin build and nurture an emotional and affectionate closeness with our children had me yearning for the same type of attention, comfort, and friendship from her.

Robbin started preparing Johnny for entry into preschool as Jessica had just celebrated her second birthday. Robbin would use pretend play during playtime with Johnny to mimic what school would be like, acting out different classroom routines. Robbin would tell Johnny how much she loved school and reassure him that she would be there to pick him up at the end of the day. Subsequently, I was significantly absorbed in starting a new management career path, giving me a focal point of purpose, personal growth, and involvement. I signaled to my mentor, Tom, that I was ready to move into a leadership position and wanted to enter the initial stages of the management promotion process. The first step was meeting formally with my manager and submitting my "letter of interest" to the district manager.

After completing this task, requirements included passing a written test to qualify. After passing the test, I achieved placement in a pool with other eligible candidates. The candidate who gets promoted was determined by years of service, level of education, and an internal need to fill a management opening. If one or more positions are available, you get scheduled to undertake an intense panel interview with multiple operations and staff managers. Then the most-qualified candidate gets selected for promotion. This process continues every year if a candidate fails selection. Finally, I was considered a suitable candidate and placed on the waiting list for an interview.

During the following months, I continually put myself before influential managers, before or after work, introducing myself and expressing my interest in a management career. I placed a lot of importance on maintaining job security, monetary reward, and professional prestige. Looking back, providing my children with emotional, spiritual, and intellectual nurturing took a back seat. Even though I was physically present, I disengaged by being emotionally detached from my children. The day-to-day burden of parenting fell into Robbin's capable hands. Being a good provider became my overriding purpose as our credit card balances grew and money was incessantly tight.

My kids would ask me, "When are you coming home, Daddy?"

I would respond casually, "As soon as I finish my work."

In some respects, work became a distraction from facing or confronting my heart's numbing internal wounds from an emotionally distant spouse.

Then a bump in the road happens. While working my delivery route, I approached a residential delivery stop. I parked my

WHAT A TALE MY THOUGHTS WILL TELL: WORDS NOT TO BE FORGOTTEN

UPS package car in front of a magnificent Victorian-styled home characterized by intricately designed woodwork and gothic-pitched roof structures to make a four-parcel delivery. The house had a sizable ascending staircase that led to a large wraparound front porch. Trying to save time and avoid two trips, I stacked all four packages in my arms, weighing close to one hundred pounds. Walking up the staircase deliberately with the packages partially blocking my view, I finally took the last step reaching the porch landing. Before getting to the front door, my left foot accidentally bumped up against a flower pot, causing me to lose my balance and jerk forward. The weight of the packages caused me to use my back muscles and twist my torso to the left as I tried to avoid dropping the customer's boxes. I felt a pop in my lower back. When I tried to straighten up, I could tell I might have injured myself.

Over the next few days, I experienced radiating numbness and tingling in my lower back and left leg while still working my delivery route. I couldn't sleep at home because of irritating lower back, buttocks, and left leg pain. Sucking it up, I continued to work, enduring throbbing discomfort. I didn't want to take any time off. I felt that missing work could jeopardize my chances for promotion. Then while checking in my paperwork at the end of my day, I felt a sharp-knife stabbing pain in my left leg that caused dizziness, making the room spin. My boss noticed my sudden instability as I fainted and temporarily lost consciousness. The next thing I knew, my manager drove me to a DWC (Division of Workers' Compensation) medical evaluator. His diagnosis was a probable bulging disc.

While getting paid for being injured on the job, I underwent one month of physical therapy treatments, including passive (heat/ice treatments) and active (stretching exercise) therapies. Nothing helped. The pain kept getting worse. Finally, a high-resolution MRI was scheduled, finding that I had a fragmented herniated disc in the L-5 region. The herniated disc tissue was inflaming and compressing a nearby nerve root.

After consulting with several orthopedic physicians and one neurologist about the possible outcomes of undergoing surgery, I opted to undergo a relatively new procedure called microdiscectomy performed by a spine/neurosurgeon. The process was less intrusive, guaranteeing a safe and more rapid recovery.

Robbin's hospital visits were brief and limited during my one-week hospital stay and six-week post-surgical recovery. And once I returned home to heal, she was gone more often than usual. Robbin was disinterested and unavailable. Because of my limited capacity to move my body normally and required bed rest, Robbin made arrangements, asking her mother to help with the kids. As a result, Robbin and the kids often slept overnight at Grandma June's while I did my best to care for myself.

Having plenty of time to dwell on the complexities of our young marriage, I couldn't help considering that our connection with one another was waning. I thought, *We fell in love so easily. Why is our loving relationship so hard now? It hurts to be in love this way.* I never had any unrealistic expectations that everything would always feel perfect with no surprises or wanting to sustain a story-book love. Regardless, I thought it felt like love if you are loved. Our bond felt like we had lost something. Yet Robbin never expressed any dissolutions about our connection verbally. Her actions and body language said it all. I truly longed to build and foster a marital friendship that augmented our loving commitment to each other. I wanted to feel secure and supported. I wanted to be Robbin's top priority, her best friend, as we shared and faced life's struggles together.

I remember attempting to revitalize our relationship by playing the classic 1980 romantic movie *Somewhere in Time* with Christopher Reeves and Jane Seymour whenever I got a chance. My thinking and hope were that this hauntingly beautiful love story and heavenly musical score by John Barry could somehow inspire Robbin to renew our intimacy, tenderness, and delight for one another. Consequentially, I wanted the movie and musical score to do the talking for me. The movie's significance was that it portrayed the type of loving commitment and dedication my heart longed for in a marital relationship. I yearned for the kind of loving support that Elise McKenna (Jane Seymour) expressed for Richard Collier (Christopher Reeves) when she revealed to her meddling manager, William Fawcett Robinson (Christopher Plummer), "I love him, and he makes me very happy."

WHAT A TALE MY THOUGHTS WILL TELL: WORDS NOT TO BE FORGOTTEN

Yet with each passing day, I continued to retreat into silence, not communicating my fears to Robbin. In some respects, it was a paralyzing emotion as I worried about being vulnerable, rejected, or getting heartbroken. Additionally, being strong and not showing emotion was a deep-seated trait influencing my inclination not to appear weak or thin-skinned. However, I never thought of leaving the relationship because I was convinced that no relationship is perfect. Be that as it may, I knew being a polarized retreater was not working. I had to talk with Robbin.

Bleak as things seemed, after my lower back healed, I welcomed the usual routine of having my family home, returning to work, and playing tournament softball again. Still, questions about our relationship were very much lingering on my mind. Then while trying to figure out what approach I would use to communicate my tormented feelings to Robbin, the reality of my fears slapped me in the face. On a Saturday afternoon, while under the hood of our F-150 truck, changing the oil, I saw the shadow of a figure moving toward me.

Looking up, I saw Robbin silently standing motionless and expressionless, observing me before I made one last torque with my oil-filter tightening wrench. The look of resignation on her face startled me as I hit my head on the hood cover.

I asked, "Is everything okay?"

Appearing distant and impersonal, Robbin said, "No." She said, "I have been thinking a great deal lately about our relationship, and I think it might be best to separate for a while. I need some space. I want you to leave today until I can sort things out in my mind."

Shocked, I bitterly asked, "Are you asking for a divorce?"

Robbin replied, "No, I don't think so. I am not sure what I want except that I need time. I think it would be best to live separately right now."

Panic started to consume me. My intuition told me there was no talking her out of this. Not reasoning, feeling aggrieved and exasperated, all my deeply rooted anxieties boiled over. I became irate. I glared at Robbin and yelled, "If that is what you want, I am out of here!"

I quickly packed some clothes and other essentials into a suitcase. I grabbed the Camaro keys and stormed out of the house without speaking to Robbin. Robbin rushed out of the house, trying to get my attention before I drove off. I ignored her as I backed out of the driveway and left some burnt rubber on the roadway as I started my one-hour drive to my brother's house in Union City. I desperately needed an objective point of view.

During the ride, my preloaded cassette player started playing Dave Mason's version of "Will You Still Love Me Tomorrow." As the song lyrics played, my rage eased as I broke down and started sobbing while listening to the words. They were apropos: "You say that I am the only one. But will my heart be broken when the night meets the morning sun? I'd like to know that your love is a love I can be sure of. So tell me now, and I won't ask again. Will you still love me tomorrow?"

After arriving at Frank's and retelling him what happened, not surprisingly, he was stunned. However, he actively listened with empathy and asked several questions attempting to understand and uncover the root cause of Robbin's request. Resulting in an intense four-hour discussion as I reviewed my and Robbin's recent marriage history.

Frank finally advised, "It sounds like a communication breakdown, and Robbin has been planning this for some time. Do you want to reconcile your relationship?"

Having calmed down, I thought deliberately about Frank's question. Thinking about separation or the finality of divorce, I realized that was not a decision I was ready to make. It was then that I knew that I wanted Robbin back. I had to save my marriage. I have two young children to support, and I don't want to break up the family. So I said, "I have to ask Robbin for a second chance."

Frank emphatically responded, "There's only one thing you can count on. Staying here overnight will not settle anything. You need to return home and reveal your true feelings to Robbin. I will go with you."

It was 11:30 p.m. when we started driving back to my house.

WHAT A TALE MY THOUGHTS WILL TELL: WORDS NOT TO BE FORGOTTEN

As we pulled up in front of my house, we noticed a black Toyota Tacoma truck parked in the driveway. Frank immediately asks, "Who's truck is that?"

I did not recognize the truck as owned by any of my friends or family members, so I told Frank uneasily, "Dude, I have no idea."

Once at the front door, we noticed no light coming through the front window, and we could not hear or detect any sounds inside the house. As I was getting ready to open the front door, Frank held me back with his right arm and suggested, "Don't open the door. Let's go to your back patio and see if anything is happening."

Frank knew my house well and understood that our family room was adjacent to the sliding patio door leading to the backyard. So we quietly opened the side gate and headed toward the redwood deck. Standing on the grass next to the deck, we carefully stepped over the wooden box planter as we tiptoed slowly across the deck, doing our best not to make any noise and trying to prevent the deck joists or slats from squeaking. We instantly noticed a flickering light blinking through the sliding patio door blinds as we approached closer to the back door. Bending down on one knee, we recognized that the blinking light was coming from the TV set. Listening attentively, we overheard and realized somebody was watching the movie *American Gigolo*, starring Richard Gere. We could make out the scene of the film where Richard Gere, who was playing the role of Julian, a male escort, was choosing what to wear, getting dressed in his bedroom while singing along to the Smokey Robinson and the Miracles song, "The Love I Saw in You Was Just a Mirage." The veracity and coincidence of that movie and song lyrics playing were unforgettably cruel and relevant.

Then we heard Robbin's voice commenting as a male voice uttered a response. Suddenly, my heartbeat started racing, feeling frozen; I couldn't move. Frank and I stared at each other with mouths and eyes wide open. Shocked, Frank and I whispered to each other in unison, "What the fuck?"

At that moment, the lights in the family room went dark. Frank said, "We will wait for about ten minutes and then walk through the front door!"

I clumsily reached for my house keys in my jeans pocket as we approached the front door. I initially had trouble fitting the key into the dead-bolt lock with a trembling hand. Turning the key to the left, we opened the door little by little to reduce noise. As we stepped into the entryway, I noticed a pair of men's tennis shoes leaning against the baseboard. They weren't mine. As we turned left into the kitchen, we heard muffled sounds from the family room. Standing dead in our tracks, motionless and silent, Frank flipped on the kitchen light. At first glance, I noticed two empty wine glasses on the kitchen counter. Then, turning my head to the left, seemingly in slow motion, I had trouble believing my eyes as I saw some young kid having sex with my wife on the couch in the family room.

I yelled, "Who the hell is this guy?"

Disarranged and confused, the kid jumped off Robbin and awkwardly stumbled forward as he grabbed his truck keys off a nearby end table and sprinted toward the front door without wearing a stitch of clothing. Meanwhile, Frank was holding me back, bear-hugging me so I didn't beat the living daylight out of him.

We glance over at Robbin. The expression on her face was one of total shock and bewilderment as she sat upright on the couch, totally naked, not saying a word, not knowing how to react. I told Frank "Quit eyeballing my wife!" as I threw Robbin a dishtowel from the kitchen to cover up.

After the chaos and turmoil had settled down, I tried to process what had just happened. My disbelief turned to anger as multiple thoughts started hammering my mind.

Robbin was still speechless as Frank asked her, "Why? How could you do this?"

Frank's words triggered Robbin's emotions as she placed her hands over her face while shedding tears. At that moment, I did not recognize my wife anymore and thought about our children. Standing there in stunned dismay, with my jaw tightening, I bitterly shouted, "Are the kids in their bedrooms?"

No response from Robbin. She was temporarily disconnected from reality and staggered by our presence, so she couldn't answer our questions. With my mind clouded with anguish and not wanting to fake my emotions, I finally asked, "Is there anything you want to say to save our marriage?"

No response. I promptly tell Frank, "We are out of here!"

As Frank and I exited through the front door, we heard Robbin said quietly, "I am so sorry."

After having difficulty sleeping that night at my brother's home, I remembered rolling out of bed during the predawn early morning hour. While looking into the bathroom mirror, I heard the bedroom's clock radio turn on at its designated time, playing the song "Don't Know Much" by Barry Mann. While gazing at my face, I saw that my young years were already showing signs of age. My eyes reflected the pain of being beaten and battered. I felt in my heart that my dreams no longer seemed to matter as I cried out my sorrow. So many questions were still left unanswered, so much I've never broken through. My emotions mimicked the lyrics of the song.

The trauma from infidelity was devastating. I was disheartened with feelings of rage, humiliation, and betrayal. I had to cope with intrusive images and flashbacks from the visual portrayal my eyes witnessed. Kisses and body parts were being given to another man. My heightened anxiety triggered sudden mood swings, powerful soul-searching thoughts, and aching sadness. I had difficulty sleeping and concentrating. I knew that the consuming grief and visual representation I felt from my wife's unfaithfulness would last a lifetime. I looked over my life and did not know where it was going.

My soul was searching for salvation. Having experienced adultery for the first time, I didn't know much, but I knew I still loved Robbin. And that was all I needed to know. I also realized that my emotional wounds would take time and need healing. However, I decided that my marriage was still worth fighting for and deserving of the challenge ahead. Then suddenly and unexpectedly, the front doorbell rang.

As I approached the front door, I overheard Frank rising out of bed and asking his wife, Connie, "Who the hell is ringing our doorbell at 7:00 a.m.?"

As I looked through the door-viewer peephole, I saw Robbin and her mother standing on the front porch. Frank looked at me and asked, "Who is it?"

With a facial expression of fear and surprise, I whispered, "It's Robbin and June."

Frank then looked through the peephole and, in a normal tone of voice, turned toward me and said, "Don't answer the door."

Robbin and June, apparently overhearing Frank's suggestion, started pleading as they banged on the front door, "John, we just want to talk. Please open the door."

At that moment, I was experiencing an emotional overload. I was entirely submerged in my thoughts and emotions, feeling frozen. Not sure what to do, I acted on my gut instincts and shouted through the closed door, "I am not ready to talk. I will call you in a couple of days."

Looking through the peephole, I saw Robbin and her mother debating something. A few moments passed, and they seemed to agree that I was not going to answer the door and finally decided to leave.

Over the next few days, I struggled to determine how to restore my marriage or how I would communicate or ask questions about what happened in our lives or in our relationship that caused this to happen. Robbin's infidelity was an offense against my manhood. It struck a blow to the core of my identity. I needed to know what went wrong. Otherwise, I had no chance to change things. I decided that I would approach this painful hurt with patience and vulnerability. I knew it would take time to rebuild the broken trust if Robbin wanted to take on the challenge of repairing our marriage. So I made the phone call.

During a brief conversation, Robbin requested that we meet at her mother's home. When I arrived, I was extremely nervous and full of anxiety. When our eyes made contact, Robbin appeared weary and mentally exhausted. As if she was sapped of any emotion or spirit. Conversely, my eyes indicated hopefulness and consolation. As she began the discussion, I was somewhat astonished by her remorsefulness and contrition. She took personal responsibility for her actions.

WHAT A TALE MY THOUGHTS WILL TELL: WORDS NOT TO BE FORGOTTEN

However, she did draw lines under some events, not wanting to talk about them.

In contrast, during our discussion, I was reluctant to ask questions anticipating that her answers might be too painful. Robbin attempted to compartmentalize her cheating by saying, "It didn't mean anything."

It certainly meant something to me as the betrayed husband. Robbin's psychological ability to be unfaithful for sexual gratification was wearisome. Ultimately, we agreed to remain together and seek relationship counseling. I was hopeful that counseling could help us overcome the pain and anger to build a new and improved marriage.

Wanting our relationship to survive infidelity, I was anxious to start our sessions with a marriage counselor to help navigate the healing process. I needed to find a way to confront the heartbreaking and devastating visual representation my eyes witnessed. I desired coping strategies to deal with the potential psychological effects of walking in on a cheating spouse. In many respects, I understood that I had lost my marriage in the way that I once knew it. While moving forward together, attempting to understand how to overcome the damage imposed on our marriage, I knew our relationship would never be the same. There was no way to change the past.

We found a marriage counselor that was well-regarded and recommended by our parish priest. She was empathic, understanding, and a skillful reflective listener. Her professional skills facilitated an open discussion where Robbin and I progressed into an active listening process. I later discovered that our marriage counselor employed a therapy technique called emotionally focused therapy. The goal of this approach focused on making us aware of or identifying dysfunctional behaviors that interfere with the connection of secure relationship commitments, predominantly emphasizing forgiving, letting go, and moving on to assisting recovery. Unfortunately, instead of getting answers or finding out what caused Robbin's motivation and rationale to engage in an extramarital affair, the therapeutic approach uncovered a traumatic repressed memory from her childhood.

I was stunned into subdued silence as Robbin suddenly became profoundly disturbed and started crying as she had difficulty vocalizing the words. I suspected that she was going to convey something to do with her past, something that hurt her delicate youthful heart. Something that she had built walls around. With her face void of happiness, Robbin said, "My father sexually abused me."

My first thoughts beyond the shocking nature of her statement and my initial empathetic responses were, *This could explain a lot about Robbin's choice to commit adultery and our limited physical intimacy.*

I went into full sensitivity mode. I realized then that I would be supportive, compassionate, and patient in helping Robbin through her pain. I conceded that having a complete relationship with a whole and emotionally healthy spouse was more important than my individual needs. Standing by my woman was another way of saying to Robbin, "I love you unconditionally, without reservation." Understanding that being an incest victim in childhood could be associated with long-term disruptions in forming and maintaining normal sexual responsiveness. I decided to continue participating, reassuring, and supporting her through this challenging situation. I justified in my mind that it could only help recover the partnership bonds of our marriage and demonstrate my devotion to the marriage vows I took in the name of God.

To achieve optimal outcomes to confront her physical and emotional trauma as a victim of incest, Robbin wanted to eventually seek a professional psychotherapy psychologist who specialized in an integrative approach model of combining marital distress, child-parent relationship, and treatment for childhood-incest survivor therapies. Because of the complexity and multiformity of Robbin's revelation, our marriage counselor wanted to conduct sessions with Robbin alone for the next few months. Many factors played a role in Robbin's recovery. She had to deal with the isolation and indigence resulting from her repressed memory and cope with family disruption as she disclosed her incestuous relationship to her mother.

When Robbin discussed her recall and reconstruction of the event with her mother, she could only remember peripheral details or aspects of the experience that evoked emotional significance. For example, I recollect Robbin stating, "My recovered memory

WHAT A TALE MY THOUGHTS WILL TELL: WORDS NOT TO BE FORGOTTEN

always includes my father's hairy chest rubbing against my face." Additionally, Robbin mentioned that the incestuous relationship with her father stopped just before she commenced puberty.

Even though Robbin's sincerity and powerful emotional plea for understanding came across as rational and authentic, June seemed ambivalent. She believed that her daughter possibly had mistaken or might be confused about who perpetrated the abuse. It appeared that June was in denial and struggled with the magnitude of the disclosure, causing difficulty comprehending what happened. June may have talked to her daughter privately about this disclosure. However, I never heard June utter another word about the matter again.

Another critical factor, I was never made aware of whether Robbin or June ever confronted Walt or had a conversation with him about the abuse. Robbin's interaction with her parents during her therapeutic sessions could only be described as routine.

Life went on as usual. Family celebrations, friends visiting, and planned family vacations continued as expected. I can only assume that June and Robbin decided that adherence to privacy was the best way to protect. My primary role was to support my wife, be a good listener, and validate her experience by reinforcing that what happened mattered.

As 1985 approached, Robbin asked me to rejoin her for joint marriage counseling sessions. I became a willing participant because I wanted answers to why Robbin betrayed me and needed guidance about dealing with the visual representation of her infidelity that lingered in my mind. In addition, I sincerely wanted to work on improving our marriage and understand how Robbin could recover from sexual abuse. Furthermore, by joining Robbin, I thought my willingness or high tolerance to handle bad behavior could influence the success of the therapeutic sessions and equal a happier relationship.

Robbin and I were fortunate that my UPS benefits package paid in full for family and individual emotional health-care therapy services. Robbin had completed a lot of the complex emotional work. It was now appropriate for me to reenter this stage of her recovery. I was impressed and put at ease with the direction and components of the therapeutic approach as the marriage counselor broke down a road map to recovery. She clarified our roles, outlined how treatment works, and what progress to expect. Even though I initially struggled with passivity and the reluctance to be emotionally vulnerable, attempting to fortify my masculinity, the threat of losing my relationship was a wake-up call driving me to participate openly.

I remember feeling attacked during many sessions as Robbin would describe the ups and downs of our relationship and how our defined parenting roles within our marriage were out of balance. Robbin often expressed that she was troubled by how little spare time I devoted to my children.

I learned early on that no matter how difficult it was to listen to Robbin's objections, I had to be an active listener and validate her messages to reassure her that I got the message. For example, I remember Robbin once commenting, "Cat's in the cradle," inferring that I accomplished parenting necessities but didn't partake in quality time with my children. Thus, Robbin warned, as the famous recurring verse of the popular Harry Chapin's song has the son saying, "I'm going to be like you, Dad, you know I'm going to be like you."

Once I could express my feelings respectfully and calmly, I would explain that I felt stretched too thin. By the end of the day, I felt spent with little energy or adequate time left to invest in family time. I remember the therapist responding to my reasoning somewhat along these lines, "John, what you are saying is that your parenting style evolved naturally over time into a 'YOU' basket, meaning Robbin assumed the majority burden of child care responsibility. You have a full-time job. Robbin is a stay-at-home mom. Does this make you feel discharged from any child-related responsibility?"

I answered, "No, not necessarily. I think my focus on being a 'good provider' for my family often supersedes as a priority and causes me to sidestep my 'involved father' role. Being stretched too thin is not a good excuse."

Therefore, I did reassure Robbin that I heard her message and that I would work on becoming a more nurturing father and role model. Once we identified negative patterns in our relationship that interfered with trust, family cohesion, and intimacy, Robbin and I had to learn how to make our connection more secure by learning how to be more vulnerable with one another. Learning and understanding our negative cycles was only the first phase. We both knew our counseling work was not complete. We needed more time to understand the depth of our interactions fully. As it would turn out, we would have to manage another transitory moment in our lives that interrupted the continuation of our marriage counseling sessions.

One day, during the summer months of 1985, an opportunity to advance my career at UPS emerged. My mentor, Tom Huff, informed me that I was one of the multiple candidates selected to interview before a panel of various division managers to fill an entry-level supervisory management position within the Business Development Department as an account executive. The interview was scheduled for Monday the following week. I was very excited about the opportunity to progress in my position within the organization, exposing me to new and challenging learning situations. Internal management promotion's clear advantages included a substantial annual salary, gaining a higher title, career advancement, a college-tuition reimbursement program, and stock ownership.

Before talking to Robbin, I made a list of pros and cons. Besides the pros I mentioned, being considered a valuable candidate meant that my company felt I was ready to take the next step. Being offered career elevation was hugely flattering. However, I would be expected to take on additional responsibilities and be willing to travel or relocate with the promotion. Furthermore, the chance for advancement happened at a particularly stressful time in my personal life.

I went to Robbin and made my pitch. "Think of it as an opportunity of a lifetime. Being promoted from within an organization means more money and increased respect compared to managers hired from the outside. The opportunities are unlimited," I said.

Robbin thought for a moment and said, "You did tell me that UPS retires more millionaires than any company in the world, right?"

I replied with enthusiasm, "Yes! So what do you think?"

She kissed me on the cheek. "This has been your dream and something you have talked about often and wanted to do, so you should give it your best shot. Just promise me that you will always make time for your family if selected."

It was an exciting but stressful time as our relationship seemed to be going in a much better direction while managing a couple of demanding events together.

The structure, questions, and formal format presentation of the UPS interview panel were impressive and relatively intimidating. Opening comments from each division manager stressed the value of UPS promotion from within policy. They cited the criterion each candidate had to achieve before being selected or considered for promotion.

Frequently mentioned and categorized was an employee's attitude toward work. For example, the decision makers described a candidate's work ethic as critical in identifying eagerness, ability, initiative, and dedication. Their premise was that an individual's attributes could predict job performance objectively. Additionally, the panel conveyed the importance of how promotion played along with acceptance and loyalty to corporate values.

My strategies to develop mentors on my behalf to improve visibility and engage in critical business activities were beneficial because I was considered a high-potential candidate. If I won, I believed my hopes and dreams for a better marriage would manifest and change our lives. After sitting tight for a few days for the formal announcement, I waited with bated breath. I was ultimately selected to fill the management opening.

Tom Huff explained, "Your first promotion is a developmental position. An account executive role will prepare you for key positions in the future. Congratulations!"

Before passing on the good news to Robbin, I remembered the moment six years earlier when we first met, remembering my anxiety-inducing apprehension as we took flight together in her Cessna 152 aircraft. Robbin's radiant self-confidence and beauty that day were captivating. I knew then how special she was and how much in awe I was of her aviation accomplishment. She was more than a woman to me. She was a woman I was falling in love with, and I understood how blessed I had been to meet her. I hope Robbin views my promotion as pleasing and becomes an ardent supporter of my accomplishment.

Robbin's reaction to the news was heartwarming. Robbin and I kissed as she pulled away gently. She looked into my eyes as she smiled and nodded her head approvingly. "I know," she said. I placed my hands on her shoulders and squeezed them affectionately. She continued, "I know you will be successful. Thank you for being a caring and trustworthy partner."

Hellen Keller was once quoted saying, "The best and most beautiful things in the world cannot be seen or ever heard but must be felt with the heart." Robbin's words were significantly touching. Her words symbolized in my heart and mind that everything was okay, that love and forgiveness can make anything possible. As a result, my lingering skepticism and negative thoughts were starting to diminish.

Knowing that career paths can be an effective long-term tool for achieving positive employee development and motivation outcomes, UPS provided a New-Management-Employee Orientation Dinner for young married couples. The get-together would help navigate corporate policies, job-rotation expectations, travel, potential relocations, and work-life balance. Robbin and I enjoyed an intimate dinner at a stylish restaurant that emanated elegance and class in Walnut Creek. Tom and my new boss, Jim Sherman, a UPS veteran of twenty-five years, spoke of how the company was experiencing incredible growth, hailing that my unique opportunity was "an opportunity for a lifetime." They reflected upon how the company culture and success were built consequently to the efficiency and dedication of its employees.

The following day at the office, Robbin was the talk of the building that morning. Several male associates came up to me and said, "Edwards, I hear you have a drop-dead gorgeous wife!" Not surprisingly, I found out later that Tom had shared his opinion about my wife's good looks. As a result, Robbin could play an integral role in moving my career.

The foundation of my thinking was not how Robbin's attractiveness could help me but how her involvement and support of my professional pursuit would be essential.

Being promoted to my first management position was undoubtedly an exciting time. The increased visibility and responsibilities offered stimulating challenges as well as stressors. As a first-time manager, training would be a key to my success.

Within the first month of my new assignment, I flew to the small rural town of Atchison, Kansas, the birthplace of the famous female aviator Amelia Earhart. I would complete a three-week UPS business development training "boot camp" workshop at Benedictine

WHAT A TALE MY THOUGHTS WILL TELL: WORDS NOT TO BE FORGOTTEN

College. When I mention the phrase "boot camp" describing a UPS training workshop, it is because one of the corporation's main objectives was to emphasize the indoctrination process of management students to the "UPS way."

The UPS way was to bleed brown with loyalty to the organization through dedication, productivity, and attention to detail. In many respects, the instructors utilized psychological training to shape participants into an esprit de corps, inspiring devotion, leadership skills, functional methods expertise, shared goals, and discipline as core success values.

To ensure organizational buy-in, UPS recruited thirty newly promoted employees from almost every geographical region of the United States. Our class comprised twenty male and ten female participants housed in strategically separated dorm complexes on campus. I recall the dynamic impact of how the shared experiences of colleagues and the creation of an organizational structure allowed our small group to create an atmosphere of team spirit and camaraderie.

The instructors emphasized the importance of representing your district admirably. It was a pass-or-fail workshop. To kick off the workshop and create an atmosphere of fellowship and expected loyalty, the head instructor had each participant provide an introduction explaining who you are, what you do, and something exciting others need to know about you. I couldn't wait to talk about my beautiful wife and children.

It was interesting how the esprit de corps generated awareness of belonging, human interaction, and connection that evolved into a unique closeness among associates. We were part of a particular group of individuals sharing personal views and were not afraid to show vulnerability. I remember Daneen, a female classmate from Cleveland, Ohio, who resembled film and TV actress Jane Seymour. Daneen and I partnered during interactive training modules, including role-playing scenarios and guided group exercises. We quickly transitioned from acquaintances to a strong bond of friendship, increasing my sense of closeness and companionship.

Daneen would initiate conversation, always seemed very interested in what I had to say, and did her best to keep our conversations going by complimenting me often. Her nonverbal body language signaled interest through playful touching, eye contact, and approving, warm and inviting smiles. The clues were obvious; Daneen was attracted to me, and I felt gratified by this unexpected favorable attention. It was flattering.

As training sessions continued, I had a fire in my belly to be the best. I have always been competitive with a passion for winning. As our instructors passed out written assignments, I had a high sense of urgency to excel and accomplish the tasks. I knew we would have to recite the seven stages of the sales cycle word for word in addition to play-acting the role of a salesperson, overcoming customer objections in front of the class. I was prepared for a late night of study. My thoughts and cramming were interrupted by a knocking on my dorm room window at around 11:00 p.m. It was a smiling Daneen.

She said, "We need to practice our role-play, and I need your help with the sales cycle. Do you have time?"

I poked my head in an awkward position, nodding, and jokingly shrugged my shoulders, hesitating before saying, "Sure."

We studied and quizzed each other into the early morning hours, refusing to sleep and having enough time to get ready before our 8:00-a.m. session.

When my turn came to recite and carry out my role as a salesperson while handling objections from my partner associate, Daneen, I wanted to control my environment by presenting a positive appearance and assertiveness, demonstrating refined sales processes. My natural sales skill, ability, and preparation paid off. My performance stood in sharp contrast to other associates. I received approval and recognition from my instructors and classmates as having the potential to be a rising star. It was heady stuff.

The positive reinforcement and recognition were inspiring and alluring. When I think back now on my feeling of exhilaration—the sheer boldness—of self-confidence motivated me wanting to make a dramatic and lasting impression on the organization. The magnitude of the desired stimulus cannot be understated. The power of positive reinforcement was a natural bolstering of attitude that made me feel good about myself. I was ambitious but realistic. I knew this

WHAT A TALE MY THOUGHTS WILL TELL: WORDS NOT TO BE FORGOTTEN

was only the beginning of a long road of executive grooming. As I gave this feeling more thought, I grasped that this kind of supportive fortification from my spouse was lacking during most of my six-year marriage relationship. Looking back, I can now understand how my desire to look for and achieve positive things on the job influenced my compulsion to work excessively. Subsequently, I asked myself, *Am I happier at work than home?*

Going from being with my work colleagues eight hours a day, seven days a week, for almost a month made it hard to say goodbye. We shared our life experiences and the finest characteristics of our identities. Strong feelings of kinship evolved. Saying goodbye was bittersweet.

At the airport, before departing on our flights home, Daneen said, "I feel blessed to have met you, John. Saying goodbye to you is hard."

As Daneen reached out with her hand, I quickly hugged her. As we separated, I said, "Be well, do good work, and remember, good friends never say goodbye."

As she walked away, she blew me a kiss and responded, "Until we meet again."

Flying back to the Bay Area, I couldn't shake the thought of what type of reception I would receive from my wife, having been away for three weeks. Would Robbin be animated with the expression and body language of love? Would she be delighted and eager to show how much she missed me? I did not know. However, I knew that my soul was still craving trouble-free salvation. I wanted to feel emotionally safe.

After landing and walking through the passenger boarding bridge, I knew beforehand that Robbin would be waiting for me in the airport reception concourse. I instantly caught sight of Robbin as her beauty stood out from the crowd. Her joyful and engaging smile exuded genuine pleasure that I had returned home. It was touching. Robbin was elegantly dressed in an ankle-length high-waisted flowing black silk maxi skirt with a white long-sleeve laced blouse embroidered with a colorful canopy design of vine stems with fruit. Her choice of dress was attentive and thoughtful—the outfit was a gift from me during our dating phase before marriage. As we embraced, I detected a radiance of tenderness from her eye contact. Then we shared an emotional kiss.

I never felt comfortable asking my wife if she missed me or still loved me. Asking those questions would place me in a position of vulnerability that I did not want to accept. Infidelity powerfully undermines the foundation of trust and creates psychological uncertainties.

I relied on three simple words from your mother to ease my fears, "I love you." Those words always provided comfort as I interpreted them to mean that I am offering you my commitment.

Then while driving home from the airport, your mother touched my shoulder and whispered "I love you," melting my uncertainties away. It felt good to be home.

I received a nice raise in salary, and our improved finances not only reduced some stress but allowed your mother and I to purchase a much larger new home in 1986. We paid $174,000 for a three-bedroom, two-bath, 1,750-square-foot home in an upscale neighborhood in Martinez, with 20 percent down (thanks to some help from my mother-in-law, June). My sole income comfortably supported our monthly mortgage payment as your mother controlled our finances. It is interesting to note as I was writing this memoir in 2022, our former primary family residence is now valued at over one million dollars.

Over the next several years, your early school years spent at Valhalla Elementary and Valley View Middle School, your mother and I settled back into a better-functioning marriage, working together to achieve harmony and good family values. These were the most pleasing and fulfilling years of our marriage. You will have the memory of many of the following experiences and events I will write down from this point on. Your memories matter because, without them, you cannot learn. The continuity of what was and what you will believe has a consequence.

As you entered structured classroom environments, Jessica, first grade, and Johnny, third grade, your mother wanted to transition from marriage counseling to family therapy. Marriage counseling was somewhat beneficial in helping us to understand what was hurting each other and ways that we could create healthy patterns to gain trust back. In addition, I recognized that our marriage therapy sessions provided the tools to help our communication process.

It was up to us now. But for my trust to be wholly salvaged, we both understood that rebuilding trust would take some time. Consequently, Robbin believed and suggested that transitioning from marriage counseling to child-parent family psychotherapy could help us learn new ways to work with our children to improve relationship and parenting skills. I agreed.

Your mother and I researched a lot before deciding upon a psychotherapist. We knew that our range of issues would require a specialist experienced with an integrative therapeutic approach. Our choice was Adrianne Casadaban, PhD, in Lafayette. Over the next two years, as a family, we experienced joint and individual sessions. Adrianne's humanistic, nonjudgmental, straightforward, and empathetic structural therapeutic approach helped us tremendously. What I remember most about her was how confident/analytical and patient she was in providing clear guidance and assistance with a challenging issue. She had a way of making me feel comfortable and trusting enough to be open with her.

During my last scheduled individual session, we discussed comfort measures to deal with my continual spouse-cheating nightmares. I remember her saying, "John, I want you to know that I admire and respect you very much for putting forth all the hard work to save your marriage and family unity. Listening, viewing, and accepting negative feelings is never easy. More than 50 percent of unfaithful wives are no longer married to their husbands. Most men would have left. Your post-traumatic nightmares will diminish over time. Best of luck to you and your family."

I responded, "I will put a lot of faith in the Bible verse. There is no fear in love. Thank you for helping us."

Meanwhile, we became devoted participants in Sunday service at St. Michaels and All Angels Episcopal Church. To worship and grow in faith, along with the opportunity for our children to come into contact with others who shared Christian values, was necessary.

In addition, the church was a safe place to find fellowship, peace of mind, and support.

Robbin and I both believed that connecting with God through prayer and creating a sense of community for our children could benefit them and help our marriage. In my prayers, I remembered Robbin's words of caution, "Cat's in the cradle."

Over the next three years, it helped that my career path was stable, experienced lateral job assignments within the same facility, the UPS Oakland Hub, to showcase my management skills in new ways. A forty-five- to fifty-hour workweek was reasonable enough for me to make a conscious effort to improve family involvement time and to show my family members how deeply I cared for them. I did my best to balance my work duties with my home responsibilities.

Trying to eliminate inconsistencies, I was reasonably diligent in making time for the little things. I made time for birthdays, holidays, family gatherings, parent/teacher conferences, family vacation trips, reading bedtime stories, bicycle teaching lessons, helping with homework, and normal day-to-day activities. I remember trying to set a goal of having at least three family dinners together each week.

Being a better role model became a priority. I found these early years of parenthood gratifying, with many hilarious, joyful, and precious moments captured through the new VHS camcorder technology introduced in 1983. For example, Jessica's innocent face was caught on the camcorder, expressing her cherished and delightful chant while opening a Christmas present, "It's just what I wanted. It's just what I needed."

While attending my daughter's soccer games or my son's T-ball and Minor League baseball games, I relived my childhood memories through my kids. My brother, Frank, and I even found the time to volunteer and coach Johnny's sixth-grade basketball team. I will never forget when Johnny won a close game for us in the final seconds by making a crossover dribble maneuver to get by his opponent, scoring the winning layup. In the team huddle after the game, my pumped-up son exclaimed, "Dad, Uncle Frank, did you see how I put that guy on skates!"

WHAT A TALE MY THOUGHTS WILL TELL: WORDS NOT TO BE FORGOTTEN

During the 1980s, this was basketball slang for getting past a defender by making him fall. During these priceless and shared moments, I thought about how content I felt about my decision to stay married to your mother. You figure out that nothing brings out the joy of parenthood more pointedly than the love shared through childrearing family togetherness.

I appreciate that your mother decided to be a stay-at-home mom during these years. Consequentially, I did not take for granted that she sacrificed her career ambitions and placed her family first. Your mother was always good at building a social network of friends and acquaintances to share experiences and come up with solutions for each other's problems. Your mother's love for you was deep and powerful. She not only wanted to share cherished moments with you, but her main priority was your well-being and safety inside and outside our home.

Robbin, always the more outgoing of the two of us, quickly befriended relationships with our neighbors as a practical choice to protect and watch over our property in case we encountered an emergency. As you know, we developed very close friendships and community involvement with the Ranahan family across the street and the Smiths around the corner from our home. All of us had children in the same age categories. Our engaged closeness with them through the years increased our enjoyment and quality of life. I don't think it was a coincidence that you had unblemished academic and school behavior track records throughout your elementary school years.

On the job front, my new boss, Lenny Weaver, called me into his office for my 1989 annual performance review. Lenny offered constructive feedback about my strengths and weaknesses. I remember Lenny saying, "Your performance and professional development have prepared you for future promotion opportunities. However, you must know that racial diversity promotion has become a priority within our organization. As society diversifies, our workforce and the people who move up need to be diverse."

I asked Lenny, "What would you recommend that I do to set myself apart from other candidates?"

"Your educational profile indicates that you have completed two years of college," he said. "I recommend taking advantage of our college-tuition reimbursement program, returning to school, and getting your four-year degree."

I asked myself, *So why did another potential life disruptor appear when my marriage returned to normalcy?*

That night, while driving home in commute traffic, with some trepidation, I pondered over the question of how I could balance going back to school while raising a family and continue building upon my healing marriage. Increasing my career options and advancement opportunities to provide a better life for my family was always my stated priority and goal. Your mother and I had both discussed returning to school at some point to finish our degree work before we married. Therefore, I approached this significant undertaking, an eighteen- to twenty-four-month commitment, by asking for support.

Doubts came naturally to me, not knowing exactly how Robbin might react to this request. Surprisingly, it wasn't a question about me going back to finish college for her. Instead, she was most concerned with its effect on "fatherly involvement" with the children. She reminded me that I played an irreplaceable role in healthy child development.

"If you can promise me that you will maintain quality time with your kids, I'll back you up and support you one hundred percent," she said.

Anticipating this potential response, I reassured your mother that my boss told me he would adjust my work schedule to accommodate family/work-life balance. Shaking her head, your mom looked out our arched front window. We both understood that I was asking for another interruption to our family routine. Nevertheless, it was something that I wanted that she seemed to accept half-heartedly.

"After you finish, I want to enroll in Cal State University Continuing Education Program. Then, it will be my turn. Is that okay?"

"Absolutely," I said.

WHAT A TALE MY THOUGHTS WILL TELL: WORDS NOT TO BE FORGOTTEN

A few months later, I received a confirmation letter from St. Mary's College of California that I had qualified and been accepted into their School of Extended Education Business Management Program. Because of St. Mary's Extended Education Program's highly regarded and prestigious reputation, I felt honored to have been accepted as typically over 450 applicants file for admission every fall term with only seventy spots available. I took great joy because I would only have to pay for miscellaneous registration, parking, and book fees. The UPS tuition reimbursement program covered all other costs amounting to a twenty-thousand-dollar bill for the two-year program.

The business management curriculum was time-compressed and intensive. Accordingly, courses of study require maximum learning effort because of minimal time constraints. The coursework was designed to provide students with a working knowledge of business management functions and principles, including studies in financial management, economics, business math/statistics, strategic planning, fundamentals of leadership, and project management.

Additionally, each student had to complete a thesis to fulfill the bachelor's degree requirement. The life-experience topics for the dissertation had to be approved by the Faculty Advisory Committee. Writing a thesis composition was going to be time-consuming as there was a ten-thousand- to twenty-thousand-word requirement. Thank God I could elicit help from our one-year-old IBM PS/2 home computer with Windows 2.0 Microsoft Word-processing software.

I am sure you still remember your dear old dad typing away, surrounded by crumpled paper, research books, and scholarly publications sprawled all over the living-room carpet. As I worked hard composing answers to elaborate class-writing assignments, with classical piano music melodically playing in the background, the words came quickly. But simultaneously, it required considerable effort to maintain and fulfill my promise to your mother not to fall short of quality time with you.

To help sustain the harmony of family togetherness, Robbin and I agreed that converting our living room into a billiard game room would maintain and support collaboration. Our elongated rectangular living room space was a perfect choice for a pool table as it mirrored the shape of the game table. We purchased an antiqued-designed Talon pool table. It was embossed with egg-and-dart molding that adorned the oak cabinet, blending gracefully into the claw and ball legs. Our new pool table was a handsome addition and a blend of craftsmanship with antique styling. It was a fantastic idea as we all spent countless hours of family companionship.

As the end of 1990 was approaching, with only six months left to achieve my bachelor's degree in business management, I was exhaustively preoccupied with writing my thesis while listening to the TV news coverage of Iraqi President Saddam Hussein's invasion of Kuwait as the UN Security Council passed a resolution demanding Iraqi withdrawal. As the US rushed troops to Saudi Arabia to defend it against an expected Iraqi attack, I remember working into the late-night hours under the faint illumination of an old-fashioned banker's desk lamp as its half-cylinder green shade would cast my shadow across the opposite wall contemplating my family's future as well as the world's fate.

More importantly, my mother-in-law, June, your grandmother, now affectionately known as "Mama June," was talking about retiring from Bank of America or, at the very least, to start reducing her hours at work. Her willingness to help look after you or help with your homework was a blessing and made everyone's life easier. Being mostly homebodies, your mother was busy developing Jessica's modeling portfolio showcasing and highlighting your natural beauty during the week. Soon after, you were off doing photoshoots for JC Penney's and Macy's at the beautiful coastline destinations of Monterey, Stinson Beach, and Half Moon Bay.

During the spring weekends, we spent most of our time watching Johnny playing shortstop in the Concord American Little League or traveling to various destinations to attend my tournament softball games. During the summer months, we enjoyed our newly purchased Malibu inboard/outboard ski boat waterskiing and tubing on the Sacramento-San Joaquin River Delta or our annual one-week camping vacations to Trinity Lake. In addition, we often shared dinners with my family, including a traditional competitive household group playing the card game of Hearts. Or we enjoyed a game of Bunco with our close-knit inner circle of friends—Dennis, Marlene, Bob, Patty (whose kids were the same ages as ours)—and Rob and Christie, our treasured friends that we met at St. Michaels and All Angels Church.

The most remarkable moments and loving remembrances that Robbin and I shared, meaningfully etched in my mind, were during this period of our marriage. My thoughts contemplated then that our marriage had withstood the test of time.

As a couple, we were working together to make things better. Robbin and I had been tested with enormous adversities and life-changing transitions, but we seemed to have won half the battle. We had weathered the storm. Learning to live with each other's flaws, forgiveness, and sharing our love again made our marriage exceptional and memorable during this phase. The original promise of our wedding vows was solid. Love was received and satisfying. God was good.

It inspired my hope and recall of a quote I once read in a romantic novel, "Grow old with me. Let us share what we see. You and I as we are."

Soon after graduating from St. Mary's University, intriguing and more stimulating job assignments requiring a higher level of responsibility started being delegated my way. The UPS East Bay District was large and expanding, spanning from Napa to Bakersfield. However, in the mid-1980s, UPS's overnight air-business segment struggled to keep up with a formidable competitor, FedEx. While FedEx embraced technology as a competitive advantage, my organization continued to time-study package-delivery processes to reduce physical motions in handling or delivering packages. However, UPS did recognize that the internet and integrated global communication technologies would be the main engines driving the future of expansion and international business development.

UPS decided to invest heavily in advanced computing and communications technology during this time. Tremendous growth required state-of-the-art data networks, landlines, telefacsimiles, and phone-switching system equipment/technologies to be installed into existing and newly constructed UPS facilities.

Thus, I was promoted from account executive to district telecommunications coordinator. As a phone system/equipment administrator, I oversaw our district telephone network operations. My duties included submitting RFPs (requests for proposals), providing a standard base to evaluate competitive alternatives for new PBX phone systems/services, providing outside maintenance support, providing knowledge transfer to associates, and monitoring the accuracy of billing statements. After spending one month of schooling from the previous district coordinator, I was off traveling again to the UPS Corporate Offices in Atlanta, Georgia, for a two-week telecommunications training workshop.

I was informed upfront that my new job assignment would require business travel away from home. As a result, several phone system upgrades were needed, including our Visalia Billing Office, Cordelia Package Center, and Fresno Package Sorting Hub. In addition, groundbreaking ceremonies were planned to construct a brand-new package center facility in Bakersfield. Each site would take four to twelve weeks to complete depending upon the project's complexity.

For the most part, I found my advanced position intoxicating and exhilarating. I put in ten-hour days, five days a week while sleeping in a Holiday Inn or a Hilton Embassy Suites hotel.

Business traveling became one of the favorite parts of my work. In some respects, I would describe it as an adrenaline rush to experience new things, people, insights, and discoveries. As an introvert, I never minded having space or alone time. Because my first ten years of marriage were full of life-changing hectic events, I became comfortable with the distraction and prospect of having periodic solitude. I enjoyed being alone. My traveling nonworking hours were unhurried and entirely mine. It was refreshing and liberating.

While away from home on business, I found myself being more easygoing, less temperamental, and apprehensive with the decrease in the intensity of family life. These good feelings were influencing my subconscious. Looking back, this was the starting point of my devotion to work and enjoyment of being on the road. My fixation was not compulsive by nature. It was about passionate internal energy when performing challenging work tasks and traveling.

The repetitive nature of my long three- to four-hour drives home from Visalia, Fresno, and Bakersfield on Highway 99 North became routine. Always anxious to return home and rejoin my family, I tended to exceed the speed limit while driving past the fruit tree orchards of the San Joaquin Valley. Those long journeys prompted the mental catalyst for self-evaluation and an appreciation for the beauty of the sights, smells, and sounds surrounding me. Conversations with myself made me curious about why I cherished the occasional state of being alone. It crossed my mind that I had chosen to be surrounded by loving family members and friends. Unlike my brother, Frank, who couldn't wait to move out from our parent's home to blaze his path, I stayed until the day I got married, preferring to be a reliable form of support for my parents. Although this was a fleeting thought and rationalization of intention at the time, it was a notion of consideration that I didn't dwell on.

Despite my crazy schedule, your exuberant and elated happiness that Daddy had returned home always put me in a heartening and joyful mood. On the other hand, your mother's welcome would be considered low-spirited and understated. Your mother rarely shared her feelings with me. Even though she supported my career ambitions and business trips away from home, I sensed an undercurrent of unease in her. It was subtle but consistent and made me wonder if there was a shift in feelings.

Anticipating that my absence would cause her outward body language and energy to mirror happiness to make me feel special, instead, it was uninspiring and disappointing. I remember a feeling of angst. However, I saw no reason or point to adding tension to my marriage by having an honest discussion about my inner feelings. There wasn't much I could do to change our current circumstances. Therefore, I avoided confrontation. My desire to succeed at work was a top priority. Not so much for personal growth or self-fulfillment but out of regard for the benefit of my family. Deeply ingrained in my belief was that work was a duty on the part of man—an obligation. In hindsight, avoiding confrontation protected me from facing the painful nature of the foreseeable truth. What I couldn't fully appreciate at the time was how my absenteeism from family life contributed to your mother's loneliness.

Returning home from my business trips, I was always happy to be home but felt a bit adrift by ordinary family life compared to my work's adrenaline rush. To seek a perception of normalcy, I would be brought back to a routine by attending one of Johnny's Saturday afternoon Major League baseball games or joining Jessica for one of her weekend modeling photo shoots in Bodega Bay. More importantly, after being away for several weeks, I could see how fast my children were growing. As you were leaving from grade-schoolers to preteens, I noticed the changes in your physical appearance and how diverse your interests and favorite activities became. During these times, even though I believed in the importance of pursuing a successful business career, I couldn't help but think about what I was missing. Looking back, I wish I had spent more purposeful time cultivating our relationship. I often thought about or questioned myself if I was placing too much of the burden of parenthood onto Robbin's perseverance. However, the steady, loving presence of your grandma, Mama June, always lightened some of the guilt I felt.

My mother-in-law was a godsend regarding her willingness to always step in and provide warmhearted support. Her influence set an example for healthy family values. For us, she became an essential role model as she helped shape your views of the world around you. I always respected your mother's relationship with her mother, and there was no doubt that Mama June wanted to be a close participating member of our family and a generous contributor.

Before you were born, as a young married couple, it was commonplace for your grandmother to lend us money, shower us with gifts, or help with errands. We shared a joint bank account with her, and she was given the key to our home. In later years, even when we did not ask for assistance, I am sure you remember Mama June popping in unannounced, arriving at our house with a home-cooked meal or a bag full of groceries.

Can you think of a time when your grandmother was not invited on our trips or vacations to Rio Vista/Sacramento Delta Waterway,

WHAT A TALE MY THOUGHTS WILL TELL: WORDS NOT TO BE FORGOTTEN

Trinity Lake, or Salt Springs Reservoir? Can you remember when Mama June was not encouraged to attend any party or social event we hosted in our home? Over time, I couldn't help but feel that her unconstrained assistance and involvement in our lives were becoming overbearing and infringing on our autonomy and independence. I was placed in the challenging and unenviable position of considering a potentially conflicting discussion with my spouse or mother-in-law over our marriage rights to preserve privacy and respectful boundaries.

After many years of avoiding discussing this problem, I decided to finally assert my concerns politely by explaining to your mother in passing, "I understand how close you are with your mother. However, we need to define our boundaries. Do you agree that she neglects our privilege to enjoy personal space too often? I don't want to shut your mother out. However, I am your partner and need your loving support too."

Your mother listened and acknowledged my concerns, but I have no idea if she ever delivered my message to your grandmother as nothing seemed to change. As both of you were preparing to enter high school, this remained a nagging undercurrent of resentment. Particularly during the later years of our marriage. My displeasure held an aura of reality that this issue of discontent would never be resolved. Looking back, I should have recognized that my plea was not taken seriously as your mother had no desire to communicate my exasperation. My effort to express my heightened discontent had fallen on deaf ears. It crossed my mind that your mother might be losing interest in me.

In such circumstances, considering that we had lived through marriage counseling and family therapy, I was somewhat lost regarding chasing after the perfect solution to the matter in question. It placed me in the position of being subjected to making a choice. I did not want to make any hasty decisions based on preconceived notions or limited knowledge. Therefore, I decided to judge any future intrusive occurrences on their merits.

Consequently, going with my gut, I took the path of least resistance, thinking that taking a conciliatory course of action would be best.

As you, Johnny, were going to enter your first year at College Park High School, your mother was registering for Cal State University Continuing Education Program, eager to complete her four-year bachelor's degree in mechanical engineering.

Your mother wanted to wait to enter this program until she felt comfortable that you were old enough and could be safely left at home unsupervised. Even though your mother had confidence in your physical and emotional maturity level to be left to your own devices, she would have Mama June stop by to check in periodically when both of us were gone for long periods.

Regarding your mother pursuing and finishing her college education, I fully supported her personal and professional growth. Before we married, we both embraced shared values around the importance of education. I never felt ambivalent or apprehensive about your mother continuing her education. We worked together with stated goals and strategies to meet the objectives of her aspirations. Your mother supported me through school and reminded me it was her turn. It was a burden I was happy to share. Several times, I provided writing help for your mother, completing her college essay paper assignments. My intentions to show my wholehearted support were virtuous and faithful. My thoughts were high-spirited, thinking that providing encouragement and supportive action to help Robbin realize her dream would pay dividends toward a better relationship and future for our family.

In the ensuing days, we got the news that our revered church friends, Rob and Christie, were moving out of state. Rob got a job promotion offer from his company requiring a move to Washington State. Learning that our good friends were moving was unsettling. Besides our friendship, we had a deep spiritual connection and enjoyed getting together and sharing life's experiences. I remember your mother customarily declaring during an invite to our home, "We need our Rob and Christie fix." As you might expect, your mother's reaction was profound sadness and emotional withdrawal.

WHAT A TALE MY THOUGHTS WILL TELL: WORDS NOT TO BE FORGOTTEN

Having no control over the circumstances, your mother was coping with how to view and feel about the situation. I recall overhearing Robbin desperately asking Rob and Christie over the phone, "Is this final? Do you have time to reconsider or decline the offer?" The tone of your mother's question conveyed a deep-rooted love for our friends and her sorrowful perception of abandonment and loss.

At that moment, I couldn't help but read between the lines. My humanistic and rudimentary psychological analysis instincts took over as I thought about Robbin's sad emotions and how they might have a concealed meaning that was intended but not directly said. I remember fearing, could the loss of this friendship affect our marriage?

The proverb "Hindsight is 20/20," meaning it is easier to understand the implication of something after it has already happened, is powerfully relevant. Looking back, this was the start of many subtle but disconcerting incidents that indicated that your mother's love for me was receding and becoming inaccessible. Borrowing a lyrical phrase from Gordon Lightfoot's captivating song, "If I Could Read Your Mind," I was becoming a ghost she could no longer see. Unfortunately, I did not recognize this degradation soon enough. Instead, it happened slowly but steadily over time. As a result, the sweetness we used to share was becoming nothing but heartache.

Afraid to confront my negative intuitions, I would retreat or withdraw to a safer place. My subconscious would protect me by justifying explanations, telling me, *Don't face up to this possible reality. This feeling of emotional abandonment and uncaring will pass. My attachment to and love for my wife is significant. The thought of losing her love again would be unbearable.* Good or bad, it was my way of safeguarding my relationship with your mother. I knew if I were to lose your mother's love again, it would be a love that would never return. Any connection is better than no connection at all was my mindset. This pattern of waiting for the storm to blow over without any communicative intervention would repeat itself again and again.

Meanwhile, my career climbing the corporate ladder, with its prolonged absences, would become even more prevalent. Stimulating new advancements, corporate assignments, and international travel destinations became commonplace during your high school years. I am sure you both remember UPS paying for family travel, hotel, and food expenses so that you and your mother could visit me during weekend idle time, whether it was my nine-month assignment in Atlanta at UPS's Corporate Headquarters or my extended stay in Vancouver, British Columbia, while aiding lawyers during an international business expansion mission or my off-and-on two-year stint in San Luis Obispo helping coordinate and manage the start-up of a new phone center. These new opportunities and exciting destinations allowed my family to enjoy and take on new experiences. I appreciated UPS's efforts to maintain a sustainable work-life balance for my family. We certainly enjoyed the brunches at the Cliffs Hotel in Shell Beach or our delicious steak dinners together at the famous F. McLintock's Saloon and Dining House in Pismo Beach at their expense.

Being away from home so often, I tried to make your visits memorable and unique. Regarding your mother, I knew that my travels made it even more challenging as she was entering the final stages of completing her college degree work. As a result, I would often surprise her by setting up a private female masseuse at the Cliffs Hotel for a nurturing deep, touch massage.

Interviewing the massage therapist in advance, I wanted to ensure that the room space's physical environment had the type of decor that would put my wife at ease, making her feel comfortable and relaxed. I wanted everything to be perfect. The room's natural dim lighting and the incorporation of soothing elements of decorative plants, rocks, candle scents, decorative pillows, and a tinkling water fountain met my expectations of a free-flowing calm setting. As a romantic gesture, I prearranged for a warmhearted greeting card to be left near the massage table with a fresh bouquet and an assortment of chocolate truffles with a bottle of Moet & Chandon Brut champagne on ice. Above all, I wanted my love note to express the tenderness and emotional yearning pulling at my heartstrings during this moment.

The day before your arrival, staying up late into the night while the rest of the world was sleeping, I was in deep thought, striving to come up with the right words to evoke a loving reaction from your mother. I considered how much we had to overcome to mend our marriage and how I continued to have an unabated feeling that there was a gaping hole in our relationship. That something was missing. Abruptly, I thought back to the purity and uncomplicated innocence of my companionship with my childhood sweetheart, Nancy.

I remember when she gently opened the palm of my left hand to secure her final affectionate message before moving away. And how her words, "You are here," handwritten inside the drawing of a heart had stirred my deepest emotions—hoping that my sentimental pondering and the thoughtfully written phrase would have some impact on Robbin. My childhood memory inspired the words written within my crayon-sketched heart. "There's nowhere in the world I would rather be than here in your heart."

I can't say that my words had much impact other than strengthening my negative subconscious hunches as Robbin never mentioned my written message. She thanked me and acknowledged how much she enjoyed the massage's relaxing nature and tension release. However, I wasn't looking for gratitude or an explanation of the calming and satisfying results that the rubdown delivered. Be that as it may, I wanted my written words to give rise to a deeper connection with my wife. I wanted mutual endearment. My wife failed or didn't care to fulfill my basic need to feel loved, to be cared about, or to be valued as a life partner by completely ignoring my message. It was painful and undermined my sense of confidence about our future happiness.

Are you aware of the famous phrase "What's good for the goose is good for the gander"? It means what is good for a man is equally suitable for a woman or what a man can have or do, so can a woman have or do. After graduating from college, your mother's quest for independence and self-determination quickly resulted in her acquiring a job with H.D. Rueb, a structural engineering firm based in Pleasant Hill. With constraints now being lifted, life became much more liberating, and she had the promise of something else. The things she had missed and sacrificed during motherhood—a rewarding career, travel, and contributing to society—were now available.

No matter the dynamics of our relationship, we never had a block in communication regarding her desire to complete a four-year college degree or reenter the workforce. I was always encouraging and had her back, supporting every aspect that involved her career fulfillment. My actions were speaking loud and clear that I appreciated her motherhood contributions and was committed to her happiness. The rhythmic flow of the hypothesis "Happy wife, happy life" echoed in my mind.

As I gave our future together more thought, one thing that became clear was that a bridge-building compromise would have to be forthcoming to maintain our compatibility. Or, at the very least, keep us from growing apart. After nearly fifteen years of marriage, it was evident that Robbin and I started recognizing that no two people are the same. As a result, I consistently bent and twisted myself into uncomfortable thoughts, rationalizing, suppressing, and ignoring the painful reality that my wife might fall out of love with me.

I thought, *Could our differences eventually lead to dissolution?* I mulled over the question, *Did we get married too young?*

We found everything about each other alluring, stimulating, and charming when we fell in love. We were so attracted to one another that we discounted and repressed any thought that a particular fault or incompatibility could raise the alarm. At the beginning of our relationship, I remember how we couldn't bear to go anywhere without each other. However, as time passed, shortly after marriage and children came into our lives, something changed. Our fundamental identities took on new responsibilities and priorities, which led to a lack of connection within our relationship over several years. I can't help but think or speculate that whatever shortcomings I possessed in your mother's mind, she found it increasingly difficult to tolerate my unsuited limitations. She wanted something different which could explain her justification or need to have an extramarital affair. However, love was not blind in my case. I loved your mother unconditionally. As I have said previously, she was the love of my life. Accordingly, I did not want to lose her and wanted to hold onto the hope of love.

WHAT A TALE MY THOUGHTS WILL TELL: WORDS NOT TO BE FORGOTTEN

There is nothing worse than unreciprocated love. When you give your heart and soul to someone and they don't seem to care or when friends become a priority or when your spouse ignores any willingness to spend time alone with you, it is painfully tormenting. Now, with much more wisdom and reflective reasoning, I can't help but believe the betrayal of infidelity abruptly tossed me into the psychological bias of giving more credence to what was giving me pain in our relationship instead of happiness.

Robbin became unwilling to share herself with me, leaving me feeling that she might intentionally attempt to drive us apart. She became emotionally unavailable, thus, stealing the joy out of my life. It was a subtle but penetrating emotional starvation. My initial instincts perceived the signs as I endured a restrained but constant heartache.

During the last three years of our marriage, your mother sought a significant portion of her emotional needs outside of our relationship. Whether it was time spent with her mother, four-day getaway trips to be with her best friends, Kim and JB, in San Diego, or enjoying quality time with friends instead of me during our family vacation excursions. Your mother seemed to be happiest when hanging out with them. Unfortunately, your mother did not miss my presence in her life. As a result, I was consistently being pulled into the anxiety of disappointment, disillusionment, and neglect. The glimpse of the world I thought I would be living in, with someone I desired to grow old with, was fading.

While we were on a family vacation at Salt Springs Reservoir, did you ever find yourself asking "Why is Mom going fishing with Bob McArthur instead of Dad?" or "Why can't we go together as a family to visit Kim and JB in San Diego? Why is Mom going alone?" I surmise that you observed your mother's interactions with me at various times and found them utterly different than the idealized version you would expect from a loving married couple. How often did you notice your father sitting alone, casting a shadow from the glowing and crackling flames of the campfire while at our traditional Trinity Lake campsite? I recall waiting hours for your mother to return from gallivanting with her friends. I would wait, feeling anxious about wanting to make love with my wife until finally falling asleep in our tent—alone.

Emotional detachment and neglect are painful. I felt useless and unwanted by my spouse. The absence of consideration and awareness to fulfill my needs for emotional attachment left me feeling abandoned and unloved. I considered if my wife's lack of connection with me was a result of her attachment wounds stemming from her incestuous relationship with her father. I rationalized that your mother, in all likelihood, never learned how to have a healthy attachment relationship in childhood, influencing her adulthood behavior. Because of the sensitivity of her childhood trauma, communicating my theory to your mother was unfeasible in my mind. A vague rationale for her conduct would be challenging to express and could make matters worse. Therefore, I decided to stay unhappily married. Always wanting to believe that things will get better, your security or the threat of harm by depriving you both of a secure, nuclear family influenced my decision to hang on.

Hoping that a good day would come along to remind us why we fell in love, our fifteenth wedding anniversary was upcoming. Wanting to make Robbin feel special and that she was a priority, I pursued plans to spend a romantic weekend getaway at the Alila Ventana Big Sur Luxury Hotel. The hotel was nested between Carmel and San Simeon, with unmatched dramatic views of the Santa Lucia mountains, redwood forest, and Pacific Ocean coastline. Unbeknownst to me at the time, Robbin was making plans for us to join Kim and JB on a Royal Caribbean Cruise to Baja, Mexico. The fact that Robbin wanted to spend our wedding anniversary with friends was a clear indication and red flag that your mother was losing interest in me and our marriage. Spending quality time alone with your spouse is a hallmark of a flourishing, loving relationship. It is the building block to maintain romance, intimacy, and a meaningful emotional connection that most married couples enjoy on such a special day. When my wife suggested that we spend this special day with friends, it was a sobering slap that made me recognize that something was seriously amiss.

WHAT A TALE MY THOUGHTS WILL TELL: WORDS NOT TO BE FORGOTTEN

Robbin emphatically said, "We have never been on an ocean liner. I have always wanted to go on a cruise. Let's go to the Alila Ventana on another occasion."

Communicating your feelings is fundamental to a relationship. However, the foundation of trust being shattered through adultery is difficult to overcome. You build protective emotional walls that don't allow you to divulge the deepest parts of your heart and mind. As a result, I felt marginalized as if I no longer had any influence on my wife's decision-making. Communicating my wants and needs became a back-burner issue.

Any negative or argumentative response to Robbin's request could cause a problem. Therefore, it was safer to disengage from expressing my utter disappointment. Unfortunately, I fell into the bad habit of internalizing my feelings and holding back from communicating my anxieties. Conforming to the status quo was safer than facing the fear of rejection or a failed marriage.

When choosing a life partner, I was looking for someone who would offer the emotional connection and security that humans seek and need—empathy, friendship, solidarity, passion, and purpose. In its purest significance, marriage allows the union of two people to thrive and provide a greater sense of meaning and purpose to life.

I have always believed that marriage is a transformative act that transcends day-to-day emotions. Marriage is the beginning of a family and a lifelong commitment. Furthermore, the sacrament of marriage is a covenant that mirrors the union between God and his church. In other words, even a toxic marriage is worth fighting for and saving if both spouses make that commitment.

At the same time, when marriage is not done well, when your bond and feelings have gone through long periods of apathy and indifference, you experience the pain of emotional detachment and a profound sense of apprehension. My gut was telling me that my marriage was at risk. Unfortunately, our getaway four-day Mexico cruise did nothing to ease this fear.

Robbin spent most of her time with Kim and JB. Even the most basic attachment a husband would expect from his wife was nonexistent. The lack of emotion and concern for my need to receive shared love and acceptance was palpable. Her need to spend time with others was a lurking problem. My feeling of profound rejection was distressing and painful. I had an aching hole developing in my heart.

In truth, even though I thought I had resolved some of these issues through our joint therapeutic sessions and finding financial security (after just nine years of being promoted into a UPS management career, we saved well over a quarter million dollars in UPS stock and 401K funds), I wondered how I could repair or survive a complex and entangling malfunctioning marriage.

The presence of conflict between your mother and I was never an issue. We rarely disagreed or argued. Do you ever remember an outburst or fight between your mother and I regarding our unfulfilling relationship? The obvious response would be no. Most couples, I would assume that value their marriage, would fight or disagree from time to time because they view their relationship as valuable. You fight for your sense of being loved and respected. In contrast, your mother never fought for our marriage while I was hanging on to the status quo, not wanting to cause a disturbance.

An example of your mother not fighting for our relationship has been forever chiseled into my memory bank.

During a gathering of friends at a Walnut Creek discotheque, an attractive woman approached our table while Robbin was in the ladies' restroom. She sat in Robbin's seat next to me and said in a playful flirting manner, "There must be something wrong with my eyes. I can't take them off you."

I laughed and took her lead on as harmless and amusing. Consequently, this accompanied some casual banter initially but led to some personal questions being asked that left me feeling uncomfortable. I pointed to my left-hand ring finger, indicating that I was married. Suddenly, Robbin returned to our table without even batting an eye that another woman was flirting with me as she took a vacant chair. Jealousy is never healthy in a relationship. However, it always bothered me whenever Robbin gravitated her attention toward other men or vice versa.

Being jealous meant that I cared and that I loved my wife. Yet in this situation, your mother didn't even give a second thought that a beautiful woman was having a flirty conversation with me. Instead, she incredulously said something along these lines to the woman, "Go for it, have a good time." The emotionally detached reply from my wife was excruciatingly painful. It ripped away at my emotional security.

Your mother and I became withdrawers for different reasons. Looking back, I am assuming that your mother withdrew because she felt resigned that our marriage was not worth the effort to salvage, that she had given up hope and no longer loved me. In comparison, I pulled back out of my desire to protect and maintain our relationship. Instead, I would prefer solitude or my career ambitions as a distraction from my worries. In some respects, I felt overwhelmed by feelings that I was not good enough, which exasperated my need to feel safe, thus giving rise to avoidance and seeking seclusion. The emotions of unworthiness and indignity were cruelly heartfelt. I, therefore, became idealistic in my silence and sadness, hoping for the best. I started disconnecting to reduce stress.

A few weeks after our return home from the cruise, we received some dreadful news. Our best friends, Dennis and Marlene Voss, were moving to Kent, Washington. Dennis had accepted a relocation offer from his shipping-container company. I remember feeling deeply sad when Dennis informed me of his new job opportunity over the phone. Dennis was my best friend during this phase of my life. We had so much in common, and he always had a way of making me feel happy. He felt like a brother to me.

As you know, Dennis and I shared our love and joy for baseball as your mother and I played on his coed softball team for several years. We enjoyed family vacations, waterskiing on Trinity Lake, or playing cards at their home. Dennis and Marlene's friendship was a gift as our families participated in many memorable gatherings. I viewed their friendship as being vital to my marriage's well-being. They were our anchors to normalcy. Their move was a devastating, unreplaceable loss that exacerbated an already tenuous relationship between your mother and I.

I started channeling most of my ambition toward my professional commitments as my job gave me a break from the pressures of an uninterested spouse. Work took my mind off the demands of home life and the dispassionate attitude I tolerated from your mother. At work, I was recognized and felt appreciated. I can't remember when my wife thanked me for being hardworking and meticulous about helping with domestic chores, such as laundry, cleaning, washing dishes, or maintaining the front and backyard landscaping. At work, I was acclaimed and rewarded for my efforts through promotions, pay increases, and praise from my boss. My relationships and interactions at work were emotionally stable, positive, and satisfying. For example, it was gratifying when junior associates would seek my advice and counsel. On many occasions, this would lead to close relationships giving rise to socializing during a lunch break or after hours to discuss work-related issues, becoming more enjoyable than returning home. I was no longer rushing home after work as my job reinforced my identity and need to feel valued and respected.

Over the next several months, this negative pattern repeated. Gone were the days when I looked forward to and couldn't wait to get home to be with my beautiful wife. The daily ritual of spending quality time with my wife, discussing our respective jobs, and your high school experiences over a glass of wine vanished. Instead, my home became a space of uncomfortable silence and unshared love. My defense mechanisms intensified as my mother-in-law visited three to four times a week. When I arrived home at a regular hour after work, I often saw her Honda Accord parked in front of our house. My overly involved mother-in-law was crossing boundaries causing a building resentment and bitterness. I would question myself, saying, *Jesus, this is way too much. Why is she coming over so often?* Finally, my growing animosity, frustration, and stress caused me to avoid entering my home after a long day at work after seeing her vehicle parked in our driveway.

Seeking refuge, I would end up at the Arnold Drive McDonald's or Taco Bell parking lot enjoying a Big Mac meal or a Cheesy Gordita Crunch while listening to KNBR Sports radio, staying put until I knew she would be gone. Coming home late was my way of avoiding confrontation.

WHAT A TALE MY THOUGHTS WILL TELL: WORDS NOT TO BE FORGOTTEN

I found myself in this withdrawal state not because of diminished love for my wife or the thought that my Robbin wasn't worth the effort. Instead, my internal reaction to not being emotionally bonded or loved by your mother raised my psychological defenses. I had always wanted to be Robbin's hero. The shame and fear that I was not worthy of her love were heartbreaking, triggering me to pull away and protect myself against intense feelings of rejection. I was afraid that voicing my feelings or thoughts would be dismissed or allow her to say "I want a divorce." We were deadlocked. I was regulated into a state of hopelessness as your mother showed no interest in our marriage.

Looking for relationship help or advice, I started spending time on a social media chat room that offered support 24-7 to discuss relationship issues within a community of impartial participants. Right or wrong, I thought this would be a safe place to anonymously speak your heart without the intimidation of someone judging you. It was an alternative to seek advice from other people experiencing similar difficulties without disclosing my identity. I started exploring an online site called "Anonymous Relationship Help Online Chat." I found that most of the people that joined were very comfortable sharing their relationship difficulties and being receptive to receiving some practical guidance. I never agreed or felt ill at ease that online chatting was "cheating on my wife" while keeping it a secret. Only when a particular woman started showing interest and asking personal questions, such as "What do you look like? Are you married? What is your occupation?" led to sexy innuendoes. I immediately decided to stop participating.

I only mention my decision to use a chat room during this phase of our marriage to reveal how desperate I was to gain opinions and insights from others facing similar obstacles in their relationships. I needed human connection and interaction. There's a point in our lives when our values and belief systems are strongly challenged. You feel lost, shaken, and out of control. I struggled with how to cope with the fear, misery, insecurity, and sadness of potentially losing the love of my life and our family bond.

As we were nearing the end of the Christmas holiday season of 1994, I thought about how the holidays are all about celebrating the values that bring us together in life. I hoped that Christmas's happiness and unity would help revitalize our appreciation for one another's presence in life. To inspire and stir an atmosphere of love and kindness, I pondered how to recreate this sentiment within Robbin's heart. My contemplation prompted my memory of a heavenly scene your mother and I experienced at the Christiana Inn Restaurant during our honeymoon. As we looked out our wood-framed table window, waiting for our dinner order to arrive, we noticed a white blanket of snow starting to accumulate on the ground and surrounding pine trees. We were in transfixed wonderment as we watched how beautiful the snow was, fluttering down with such elegance and grace. The beauty of that moment took our breath away as the spellbinding vision of nature portrayed the desire for our shared human love that night.

My inspiration to reawaken our bond of love came to me instantly.

Music! The universal language.

My imagination was to use music as a window into the deepest region of my heart and as an expression for the atonement of my despair. I was hopeful that the sequence of appealing sounds and words from the melody would influence Robbin's emotions, creating an illusionary perception of the importance of the love we once possessed. You will undoubtedly remember me repeatedly playing the following song late into the night before Christmas Day. You will now understand why as you read the following lyrics:

Winter World of Love
Engelbert Humperdinck

My love, the days are colder
So, let me take your hand
And lead you through a snow-white land
My love, the year is older
So, let me hold you tight
While away this winter night

WHAT A TALE MY THOUGHTS WILL TELL: WORDS NOT TO BE FORGOTTEN

I see the firelight in your eyes
Come kiss me now before it dies
We'll find a winter world of love
For love is warmer in December
My darlin', stay here in my arms
Till summer comes along
And in our winter world of love
You'll see, we always will remember
That as the snow lay on the ground
We found our winter world of love

Because the nights are longer
We'll have the time to say such tender things
Before each day unfolds

And then when love is stronger
Perhaps, you'll give your heart
And promise me we'll never part, oh, no
And at the end of every year, I'll be so glad to have
  you near

As time went on, nothing changed. Accordingly, it became hard to ignore some of the more troubling indicators that something was awry as mother-in-law visits became even more frequent. I couldn't help but think Robbin was discussing our marital unhappiness or planning to end our marriage with her mother. More than once, I felt awkward as if I had walked into a private conversation as your mother or grandmother would abruptly stop talking or lower their voices, not wanting to be overheard. Robbin's reliance on her mother's advice for decision-making or emotional support made me feel insignificant and ignored. I thought, *Why can't we have the freedom and autonomy to make our own decisions? Why is Robbin asking her mother for direction instead of me?* I am sure that Mama June had no problem offering her solicited wisdom. Not knowing what they were talking about, I couldn't help but feel threatened by my spouse's behavior. In reality, Robbin's actions communicated a lack of respect for my judgment and for being a part of her life.

Outside of our onerous marriage circumstances, my work at UPS was stimulating. Having completed special assignments in Canada and Mexico, I was given a new position working with senior leaders at UPS's Regional Office in Pleasanton as the East Bay district congressional awareness coordinator. My responsibilities included a broad range of administrative and advocacy duties supporting government relations and fast-paced legislation that could potentially affect our industry.

The position required various aspects of tracking transportation industry legislation, attending congressional town-hall meetings, local lobbying, articulating a defenders' position on complex federal transportation policy issues, and providing fact sheets/briefing memos. In addition, I got to work with US House of Representatives members, Congressmen George Miller, Pete Stark, and Victor Fazio.

It was invigorating as I learned more about our political and legislative processes. Congressman Miller, in particular, educated me on how congressional action is typically planned and coordinated by party leaders in each chamber. Moreover, once a law is enacted, Congress has the prerogative and responsibility to provide oversight of policy implementation.

My foundation of personal persistence and relationship building led to many sustained face-to-face meetings with Congressman Miller and his staff at his local district office in Martinez. Maintaining and establishing consistent contacts, I arranged for Congressman Miller to visit our Concord UPS Package Delivery Center. Returning the favor, Congressman Miller's staff invited me to his annual birthday bash at the Concord Sheraton Hotel, which allowed me to meet other notable democratic political luminaries, such as Diane Feinstein, Barbra Boxer, and Nancy Pelosi.

In many ways, my fulfilling job provided the only supportive environment where I could feel secure and appreciated. Exciting assignments, respectful coworkers, and colleagues working together to reach goals helped renew my self-esteem and a sense of purpose. My work experience was satisfying compared to my stressful and troublesome marriage life. Such thoughts stayed with me as I devoted more time to pursuing my professional success.

It was right around this time that I received an unexpected but thought-provoking workplace phone call from Daneen, my friend and UPS associate from Cleveland, Ohio. I hadn't heard from her since we said goodbye to one another at the Kansas City International Airport. Her voice was soft, alluring, and suggestively flirtatious. After updating each other on our UPS career paths and personal lives, she inquisitively asked, "So, are you still happily married?"

After a short pause, feeling awkward and not wanting to answer that question honestly, thinking fast, I thought that humor might give me a reprieve. I responded with a Henny Youngman one-liner, "You know what I did before I got married? Anything I wanted to." It worked.

Daneen laughed and changed the subject. She said, "I will be flying out to the Bay Area in a couple of weeks to visit with relatives. Can you arrange some time to hang out or go to dinner?"

I smiled and responded, "Absolutely, it's a date!"

After we hung up, I sat in my office, trying to make sense of my ignited emotions. I felt electrified in anticipation. I couldn't wait to spend some time with Daneen. Looking back, I presume that the jolt of positive energy and proposition of connection coming from a woman other than my wife was captivating and, in some respects, seductive. After enduring years of unmet needs, rejection, and being disregarded by my wife, I must admit that my desire to feel loved and experience a woman's affectionate charms excitedly effectuated my choice to consider committing infidelity for the first time. Then I started planning to make it happen.

I began justifying the reasons for wanting to commit a mortal sin and breaking the covenant of my marriage vows. My thoughts were never about retaliation or tit-for-tat. It was all about my needs not being met in marriage. I figured, *Robbin probably wouldn't care if I strayed anyway.* That kind of thinking or reasoning is a potent motivator. How could my heart not be stirred? I prayed to God about my ambition. The Bible teaches, "The blood Jesus shed on the cross covers all sin." Rationalizing that "all sin" must mean that even infidelity is forgivable, I asked God for absolution beforehand with a repentant heart.

As planned, this kicked off several sustained, intimate phone conversations with Daneen. I was getting my romantic needs met, getting aroused from our lustful exchanges.

"Trust me. I love that you are married. I am attracted to the thought of being your mistress," Daneen said.

"You're good. No, you're bad," I said.

"Resistance is futile. I will cherish the memory of you with your clothes off forever," Daneen responded.

"Until we meet again," I said.

Quietly, as you, Jessica, were preparing to enter your first year of high school and Johnny, his junior year, I planned to take Daneen boating on a Saturday afternoon with my brother, Frank. Later, for our evening entertainment/one-night stand, I obtained dinner and an executive-suite reservation at the Lafayette Park Hotel.

As fate and luck would have it, the planning worked perfectly as your mother was enjoying a weekend away with Kim and JB in San Diego. I felt comfortable and confident revealing the extent of my intentions with Frank as he became my only trusted confidant, keeping him up-to-date with all my marriage dilemmas. Frank always had my back whenever I placed myself in a precarious position. Moreover, including Frank in my plan would provide a "cover" and an excuse to eliminate suspicions.

On a beautiful and warm early September Saturday afternoon, Daneen and Frank met me at the Hogback Island Boat launching ramp, providing access to the Sacramento River Delta. The same water recreation area that we as a family enjoyed over and over again. With its grassy picnic areas that sloped down toward the delta waterway, Hogback was always a place of peace for me. Being surrounded by water and listening to the boat ripples splashing the shoreline or the sound of ski boats whizzing by, it was a relaxing sanctuary.

Daneen looked alluring as she arrived in her black bikini with a long, sheer, white-laced beach kimono swimsuit cover-up with a drawstring. Fashioning a wide-brimmed floppy straw sun hat and Ray-Ban designer sunglasses, she was a sensual vision of glamour and beauty. I was held captive in her warm embrace as we greeted each other. Then I noticed Frank in his usual modus operandi eyeballing with a half-opened mouth.

We enjoyed the uninterrupted time, the warm sun with no one around, just us and the calm water. After taking turns waterskiing, we savored the homemade sandwiches, club crackers, asiago cheese, and merlot wine Daneen furnished while floating down the river.

Being kissed by the sun, Daneen's skin absorbed a gorgeous radiant glow. As Daneen and I locked deeply into each other's eyes, everything around us faded. I noticed her suggestively biting her bottom lip as her pensive look melted into a soft smile. Our gaze lasted several seconds without saying a word, connecting our humanity. The promise of love was written on her face. Accordingly, my breathing became more rapid as the sexual tension swelled. Finally, with a sense of longing, it was time to leave and get ready for our dinner date.

I chose the Lafayette Park Hotel because of its warm and welcoming ambiance. The decor was eclectic and cozy with a romantic European flair. The private dining room embraced sophisticated wood tones and shapes accented by a nearby stone fireplace, bar, and cottage-style wall sconces, which made for a relaxing and picturesque environment. Our small round intimate table for two was covered with luxurious white linen and centered with a gold-dipped glass candle vase that added decadence and a gorgeous dimension to the table. As I pulled out her chair, Daneen commented and approved of the timeless elegance of the restaurant's atmosphere and the luxury of her plush, deep, dining chair. As our waiter approached, he poured the champagne I had ordered in advance without saying a word.

Daneen looked both sexy and classy in her open-back ruffle dress. The sheer material and asymmetrical design with a slight V-neck exposing a bit of cleavage were stunning.

First, I complimented her by saying, "Your beauty cannot be ignored." Then I made a toast, "Champagne is known for having positive effects on women."

Daneen responded, "I only drink champagne when I am in love."

Daneen's words, "When I am in love," found me suddenly lost in thought as we rattled our fluted glasses together and took a sip of the bubbly. Suddenly, my original thoughts of having a sensual encounter were interrupted by feelings of extreme guilt. Daneen's toast tapped into the most profound undercurrents of my psyche. For a moment, time stood still. Then my introspection caused me to ask myself, *What the hell are you doing?*

My poor judgment, opportunity, and lack of self-control led me here, I said to myself. At that moment, no matter how troubled my marriage relationship might be, I realized that my actions would be hurtful, inappropriate, and wrong. Coming to my senses, I comprehended that I could never emotionally remove myself from the thought of breaking my vows. I did not want to cause Robbin any pain. The action of cheating is not a valid response to the unmet emotional connection with my wife. I determined there is no justification for infidelity. I love my wife.

After dinner, as we entered the lavishly appointed executive suite, I held up the room key and said to Daneen, "Enjoy your stay, my compliments."

With a soured look of disillusionment, she asked, "You're going to join me, aren't you?"

"No, I don't want to do this. I am so sorry if I lead you on," I responded.

Daneen stood motionless for several seconds. Then, with "puppy dog" eyes, she tilted her head slightly with a pleasing but sad expression that evoked pity and said "Please stay," reaching out with her hand.

I took her hand, held it tightly, and responded, "Let's leave this as an emotional amour remembrance."

As Daneen let go of my hand and slowly closed the door, she said, "If we ever meet again." She kissed her palm and blew it my way before closing the door.

During the drive home, I could not stop thinking about how my conflicted emotion, desire, and expectation for sharing some heart-rendering intimacy with someone other than my wife could have potentially threatened my marriage. Even though I decided not to have sexual contact with Daneen, I still violated the monogamous companionship principle I valued so highly. It was the only point in my life when my values and belief system were challenged. I was emotionally unfaithful to Robbin by pursuing affectionate fulfillment elsewhere. I crossed the line and felt remorseful about my lack of conviction. I never disclosed my moment of weakness to your mother.

A few more months passed as our negative cycle of disconnection from one another remained unexamined and unchanged, impacting our happiness. Neither of us attempted to validate our feelings. Your mother never became blaming, critical, making threats, or telling me how to improve or change. Instead, she was unresponsive and seemed unwilling to open up and share her feelings. Yet bleak as things looked, I still hoped we had a chance to sway things toward a more secure connection.

One thing felt certain, week by week, I felt the air going out of the balloon of our relationship. But then, when word got to us that our close friends, Bob and Patty, were filing for divorce, it felt as if our relationship balloon had deflated entirely. I remember your mother having long discussions with Patty, sharing ideas about their feelings and attitudes concerning divorce. I feared their conversations would lead Robbin to believe in separation's benefits, which could eventually influence and compel her to become more receptive to divorce. My only reassuring thought was that our children and keeping our family together were more important and would counter the perilous viability of our marriage.

By the beginning of March 1996, I had an overwhelming feeling or sixth sense of intimate peril that the end of my marriage was inescapable. My clairvoyance and precognition were confirmed. The slightest glimmer of light at the end of the tunnel turned into total darkness as your mother asked for a divorce.

The chambers of my heart had never felt such sorrow. As I mentioned in my introduction, I was emotionally and physically staggered. My painful emotions catapulted me into a stage of denial. I did not want to come to terms with the fact that my marriage was ending. I tried negotiating with your mother to save our lifelong commitment to one another. Devastated and feeling beaten and battered mentally, a sense of grief and loss accompanied my thoughts as I considered what life would be like without the love of my life. I did not want to say goodbye. Separating from your mother would compromise a significant part of my emotional identity.

Robbin did not indicate hope for reconciliation. The pain I felt accurately measured how much I loved your mother. After a week of pleading and stubborn persistence being opposed to divorce, my request finally broke through as Robbin arranged a meeting with Father Tom at St. Michaels and All Angels Church. Your mother insisted that we drive different vehicles to the prearranged consultation. I was hopeful that Father Tom would impart some spiritual counseling advice about the sanctity of marriage that would reverse and heal your mother's mindset. The health of my family was of utmost importance. I was optimistic that Father Tom would find a common direction and solution for us to work toward a settlement of our differences by explaining what the church teaches about the sacrament of marriage.

Because of the seriousness of your mother's request to meet with Father Tom, I assumed we would be holding our meeting in a formal setting, such as his rectory or church office. But instead, the doors opened to the colloquial church meeting hall. The surge of an unclean and smoldering odor of old flowers and tile polish mingled with the depressingly cold and damp surroundings. The starkly unoccupied room caused my optimistic anticipation to turn into forlorn self-doubt as Father Tom pulled up a couple of metal stacking chairs.

As I took a seat, Robbin decided to stand next to Father Tom. After an informal greeting, Father Tom started our meeting with a prayer. I will never forget the opening words of his prayer,

> *God of infinite love and understanding, pour out your healing Spirit upon John, as he reflects upon the failure of his marriage and makes a new beginning.*

WHAT A TALE MY THOUGHTS WILL TELL: WORDS NOT TO BE FORGOTTEN

Predictably, those words were stunning as my anger started to simmer. I guessed that Robbin and Father Tom had met beforehand and decided how to orchestrate the narrative of the meeting. A part of me wanted to get up, grab Father Tom, and implore, "What are you talking about? A failed marriage? A new beginning?" Nonetheless, having respect for the clergy, my better angels decided that grabbing a man of the cloth would be unbecoming and inappropriate. However, his words forced me to stand up abruptly out of my chair as he noticed my frowning expression of resentment.

After he finished, it was my turn to speak. I started from the beginning and told the story of what brought us together and what first attracted us to one another. I remained optimistic, explaining the heartening aspects and qualities I admired about Robbin and how we fell in love and gave birth to our family heritage. I urged reconsideration and reconciliation, advising that the scars and consequences of divorce will disrupt our lives and our children's lives forever. I pleaded that divorce would weaken the bonds between our children and us. Finally, I asserted that our marriage issues were not points of no return.

I said, "I love my wife and want to make our marriage work."

Father Tom asked your mother, "Robbin, would you like to respond?"

Instead of talking to me directly, Robbin leaned closer to Father Tom, raising her hand near her mouth as she whispered something into his ear. I remember Robbin's body language and demeanor displayed resistance as Father Tom unbelievably said, "John, Robbin does not love you anymore."

That was it. With my anger now boiling over, the wounds inflicted upon my heart were bleeding out. I walked out silently. It is hard to overstate how disrespectful and devastating those words were from a man who must act as a mediator and representative of the divine being. Rather than being a bridge-builder between God and my humanity, he decided to speak on Robbin's behalf with an insulting tone. Why didn't your mother have the courage to say those words to me? I can only imagine that your mother told Father Tom while whispering in his ear, "I don't love him anymore."

Have you ever heard the phrase "The last straw that broke the camel's back," meaning that a series of unpleasant events makes you feel that you cannot tolerate hurtful situations any longer? In other words, your mother's choice of action, indifference, and complete disregard regarding my love for her broke my heart, spirit, and will to fight for my marriage any longer. I finally realized that mending our marriage was hopeless and that many questions would remain unanswered.

I was optimistic that your mother and I could work together to minimize the emotional pain and financial toll that divorce can cause. Looking back, I remember our first meeting to discuss splitting personal property, retirement accounts, possessions, UPS stock/401(k) holdings, and child custody.

Sitting at the bar counter at TR's in downtown Concord, I requested fifty-fifty child custody. In addition, I asked your mother not to attach my UPS retirement income through a Qualified Domestic Relation Order (QDRO). I agreed to all her other demands.

My reasoning was justified. Your mother did not have to work for most of our marriage, I paid for her continuing education degree, and she was an only-born child who would receive a lucrative inheritance from her mother. In contrast, I came from a large family with four other siblings, and my parents' estate would be meager since they could never invest money toward financial planning. Nevertheless, my hopes were shattered as I received divorce papers (petition and summons) from Robbin's lawyer citing irreconcilable differences and her unreasonable appeals.

Unfortunately, this led to a contentious and contested divorce as I had to seek and hire legal counsel. Even though your mother filed a "no-fault" irreconcilable differences submission for divorce, she also demanded excessive spousal support and child custody percentage and would not relinquish her QDRO rights. Disagreeing with Robbin's requests, I tried to reason and make peace with her to avoid expensive lawyer fees and court litigation. She refused. Even mediation failed. To this day, I will never understand what caused your mother's aggressiveness and unwillingness to compromise. It was as if she was trying to punish me intentionally. Why? I agreed to

WHAT A TALE MY THOUGHTS WILL TELL: WORDS NOT TO BE FORGOTTEN

get a divorce. Throughout our marriage, even during noncommunication, I always treated her with the utmost respect and consideration. In my heart, I believe her litigation-happy lawyer deliberately escalated her emotional conflicts, controlling Robbin's attitude and influencing her desire to fight, with disputable motives to increase the value of the case to pad his wallet.

After spending over ten thousand unnecessary dollars on legal fees to protect me from an uncompromising soon-to-be ex-spouse, our divorce court proceeding commenced. Subsequently, following some inadmissible and ridiculously presented personal hearsay statements by Robbin's lawyer, the judge's final judgment ruled in favor of my lawyer's oral arguments that a lower spousal support amount was justified and decreed me a fifty-fifty child-custody percentage.

Divorce is a brutally painful and life-changing transition. I placed all my trust in Robbin. Everything felt overwhelming as I tried to cope with severe emotional swings. The next few months, I spent grieving the loss of the woman I treasured and adored.

She left me. The promise and pledge we shared through the years were severed. I knew I would never be the same. The keynote themes of heartbreak, sorrow, pain, and regret repeatedly played within my heart. I now stood alone. My self-esteem and identity were linked to my love for your mother. Yet when I looked into your eyes, I could see the concern and sadness hidden within your souls. I had no choice but to begin moving on from a failed marriage.

Over the years since my divorce, you both have witnessed or heard of my struggles with human frailty—two more marriages, two more divorces spanning fifteen years of predestined failure.

Fighting to find some connection and dreaming that I could start a new beginning of loving tenderness, I became the great emancipator, a rescuer of burdens. Searching to revitalize my self-esteem and self-worth, I began to take on the woes of two divorced mothers who did not have my best interests in mind. I fell into a pattern of having a lot of empathy for others who were suffering. I wanted them to need me. I was intuitively aware of their vulnerabilities, so I swooped in to be their knight in shining armor, thinking that by saving others, I could save myself from the emotional pain of my past.

I did not listen to your warnings. Jessica said, "Dad, Donna does not have your best interests at heart. She is a sugar baby." Or when Johnny questioned my common sense after I asked Dora to marry me, "Dad, what the hell are you doing? I don't know you anymore."

Having tied up my life trying to save others, I rebelled against your appeals. Your words hurt me deeply and caused a chain reaction toward alienation. With a sense of dread surmising that I was losing my son, I asked if you would be my man of honor at my wedding. I remember your initial hesitation and awkward reluctance but gradual acceptance. Consequently, our estrangement became more pronounced as I honored Dora's request to move closer to her family in Texas.

While writing my life story and sharing my journey through the multitude of disordering life transitions, I can't stop thinking about a quote I recently read, by Tupac Shakur, that captures my feelings at the ripe old age of seventy years old.

Death is not the greatest loss in life. The greatest loss is what dies inside while still alive.

My dreams and hopeful expectations died inside me when your mother asked for a divorce. Something broke inside when my son said "I don't know you anymore." Divorce ends dreams and expectations and fractures family bonds. Estrangement, in many ways, is a slow death that breaks you down. Special memories that would seem to last forever become inundated with confusion and self-assessment. With so many unanswered questions, I wondered if your mother ever saw me for the man I was. When Robbin looked into my eyes, could she know what was inside? Did she ever care? It is hard to put the depth of my feelings of dysfunction, sorrow, and pain into words. Losing your mother's love is an anguish that lingers.

Why did she fall out of love with me? Was I an embarrassment to my son and daughter? Why do my kids resist spending time with me? Tupac was right. The most significant loss is what dies inside. Having to deal with multiple divorces and child alienation will shorten my life span. Several times over the years, I have thought, *Why or how could this happen to me? I love my ex-wife and children.* You discover that nothing is more painful or draws your life more clearly into a retrospective point of view than the loss of a wife's and child's love. My abandonment from you is a direct result and consequence of the pain of losing the love of my life.

Not unlike your mother, you never communicated to me that I ever let you down. You never told me that I wasn't there for you. You never said "Dad, I need you." You neglected to express your feelings. During the early years of my marriage with Donna, I did everything in my power to include both of you in our lives. However, you both resisted most of the time. As soon as child support had expired, you both decided to move back in with your mother, who chose to purchase a home with her new husband, Tom, inside the dead-end cul-de-sac, less than five hundred feet from our corner house. During my eight years of marriage to Donna, we considered ourselves lucky if we got to enjoy your presence ten times a year. Donna and I were often left to wave hello while maintaining our front-yard landscape as you passed by quickly in your vehicles. Or me having to deal with the gut-wrenching sadness whenever seeing your mother and Tom together as they drove by.

Accordingly, even during the holidays, we were granted about an hour of your precious time. Thus, your long absences and lapses in communication made us feel isolated, irrelevant, and unessential. I never received a phone call from either of you asking, "Hey, Dad, what are you doing today? Would you like to go for breakfast together or maybe to the movies?"

During my English literature days in college, the iconic German novelist, Thomas Mann, was required reading. A famous quote of his seems fitting, "Speech is civilization itself. The word, even the most contradictory word, preserves contact—it is silence which isolates."

It was hard for me not to think that your mother might have undermined my relationship with you, causing the long periods of silence. Did she upgrade her new spouse into being more of a parent to you by focusing on the bad days she shared with me while ignoring the good? Although I never wanted to believe this, my mind visualized her downgrading me as an aloof and uncaring father. When you begin questioning your doubts and your thoughts wander to the more distrusting elements of human nature, it highlights the internal struggle you live through while dealing with the noncommunication, isolation, emotions, and pain that divorce and parental alienation spawn.

Once you both decided to move away to attend college, I knew our time together would be even more scarce. I did my best to stay in touch by phone or help write some essay papers for you. During school breaks, I noticed a slightly improved relationship as Johnny would invite my brother, Frank, and I to join him and some of his friends at the local billiard pub. Or Johnny would accompany me to watch the 49ers game at Uncle Frank's house. As Donna's daughters entered elementary school, Jessica developed a close relationship with Lauren and Chelsea. However, I always sensed a fog of skepticism regarding Donna. Your level of trust and acceptance concerning her never materialized.

I did not discount what feelings you might have dealt with while attempting to adjust to your mother and father deciding to remarry. I felt Johnny's emotions the day I married Donna. It was a rare occasion as my son broke down crying as he hugged me, saying, "I love you, Dad." My instincts told me that my son's sadness came from the understanding that he would never have his original nuclear family back together again. Jessica, on the other hand, had built such a close relationship with her mother that I believe Donna would always be viewed or considered an outsider in her mind. Unfortunately, I can only speculate as we neglected to reach out to each other and communicate these inherent feelings.

As three more years passed, we stayed in the same cycle of infrequent visits, phone calls, and human connection. Your unavailability was highly problematic and hurt me deeply. I viewed this as another betrayal. Regrettably, during this time, I could not attend my son's graduation commencement ceremony from San Diego State University as I was out of town on a work assignment for UPS. Even though I let Johnny know in advance that I could not make flight arrangements in time to attend, I am sure that my son's disappointment was unutterable with agitation. It did not help that Johnny gave me a late notice of the graduation date, just one week in advance. Nonetheless, this exacerbated an already tenuous relationship with my son and daughter.

After asking Donna for a divorce—I should have listened to your earlier warnings—I evolved into blaming others, rationalizing excuses, and justifying my actions. I was out of typical character as I attempted to cope with two life-changing transitions again. I was confused, hurt, invalidated, and felt misunderstood. Indeed, this eventually led to almost no contact with my children. No returned phone calls or visits for an extended period. I started asking myself, *Why have my children turned against me? Where did I go wrong? Was Robbin using coercion tactics to convince them that I was not a good parent? How did I contribute to my child's need for distance?"*

Without much lag time, I met my third wife, Dora, working as a nurse at Mt. Diablo Hospital in Walnut Creek one year later. Shortly after I retired from UPS in 2008, after thirty-four years of service, we were living together within six months and planning our wedding and eventual move to San Antonio, Texas. Regardless of the reasons, voluntary or involuntary, I knew my decision would have profound implications that could potentially disrupt our connection to one another more seriously. When I informed my son that I was getting married again and had plans to move away, this was when he alarmingly asked, "Dad, what the hell are you doing? I don't know you anymore."

Those words cut into my soul like a serrated knife; my son, whom I love, nullified my existence. I was not only hurt but felt resentment and anger. His words indicated that I had failed and wasn't there for him. Cats in the cradle?

My son's words undoubtedly shaped my thinking about moving away from my family. Being reserved and reflective, sensitive to criticism or rejection, my move to San Antonio could provide an outlet and escape from my emotional turmoil. Suddenly, my focus turned to a new life. I looked forward to moving into my new 4,800-square-foot minimansion and starting a stimulating management career with Enterprise Holdings Inc. Our estrangement was kicked into high gear as my emotional reaction would amplify the worst instincts of subjective decision-making.

A perfect example of my misjudgment and imprudence was when Dora and I attended your wedding. I remember having conflicting emotions about handling being in the presence of your mother, her husband's family, and your grandmother. During the ceremony, I did not feel like I was present.

I can't remember if I talked to you or your bride, Jamie. I never spoke to your mother and reluctantly acknowledged your grandmother with a half-hearted wave of my hand from a distance. My depersonalization was wrapped around my feelings of realizing that I was no longer an essential part of your life. Observing your loving interactions as you embraced and kissed your mother before the formal mother/son dance or watching your happiness while interacting with new family members, I felt out of place and awkwardly ill at ease. The ceremonial roles a groom's father typically upholds, making a short speech and being asked to make a toast to the happily married couple, were intentionally avoided. I told Dora "Let's go" as we left the celebration early.

My center of attention was now wholly rejuvenated to start my new life with Dora.

I was instantly lovestruck by Dora's Brazilian heritage, innocent and gentle heart, and large extended Christian family. Additionally, Dora's nuclear family included three sons. Hence, I fell into the same trap of wanting to provide a better life for a family where I could play the superhero role. As you know, my need to be needed did not go well. Dora and I divorced after only three short years of marriage. Reflecting, I genuinely believe that the agony, heartbreak, and torment of losing Robbin's love caused me to lose my self-identity. I was so gosh-darn lost; not even God could find me. Attempting to save others bridged a gap to seek a sentimental connection and regain a sense of self. Turning around my role as an enabler and human-mistake machine into a personal self-development lesson was still years away. Over those fifteen ill-fated years with Donna and Dora, my love for your mother never left my heart. I needed her love beside me.

WHAT A TALE MY THOUGHTS WILL TELL: WORDS NOT TO BE FORGOTTEN

Our emotions and feelings are often used interchangeably, and words cannot thoroughly convey the weighty emotions and feelings I experienced and want to express. That is why I use music as a form of expression. Music binds us in a way that language rarely does. Music is the window to the soul. Another quote comes to mind.

> *Without music, life would be a mistake.*
> —Friedrich Nietzsche, *Twilight of the Idols*

Harve Presnell performs a beautiful ballad on youtube.com called "They Call the Wind Maria." It is a song about a lost and lonely man asking the wind to blow his lost love back to him. The lyrics and alluring melody evoke the true sense of emotion and restlessness I felt during those fifteen years. I hope you seek out the song to watch and listen (Harve Presnell—"They Call the Wind Maria," remastered) as I have always longed for Maria to blow the love of my life back to me.

Once Dora moved out, living alone in a minimansion seemed redundant. Wanting to downsize and save some money, I sold the house within six months and moved into a luxury apartment as I continued my rise among the ranks at Enterprise.

Enterprise, the largest rent-a-car company in the world, was a stimulating and fast-paced environment. It was a pleasant change of pace, and the work was fun. Quickly, I found myself being a mentor to young inexperienced college students looking to gain management experience. After my long and diverse management career with the largest parcel delivery company in the world, Enterprise was a perfect fit. The work fulfilled me at a higher level. I identified and became enmeshed with the company's core values of integrity, honesty, fairness, accountability, customer service, and teamwork.

These values were in sync with my values and significantly shaped how my career with Enterprise would become my identity and inspiration through its foundation and culture of providing highly influential recognition for employee success, thus, rebuilding my self-esteem, self-worth, and prestige. I fell in love working for this organization. In some ways, my passion for my work encouraged distraction and compensated as a buffer/distraction from my still-grieving heart compounded by child-alienation issues.

Then I got an unexpected phone call from my daughter. In a rare and genuine expression of emotion and human connection, you say, "Dad, I miss you. I want to come and spend some time with you." Your heartfelt words reminded me of your love even though we were apart. So wanting to make the most of our time together and share my tender love for you, I planned an extravaganza of events to pamper you. I tried to prop you up and place you on a pedestal to remind you how special and critical you are to my existence. The pure joy and fulfillment of sharing that experience with you will remain in my heart forever. I have never felt closer to you before or since.

For months to come, we would share more frequent phone conversations and plans for another visit. Maintaining a consistent connection with my daughter would require nurturing and attention. I never forgot to inquire about how Johnny was adjusting to married life, hoping he would also reach out to me.

My career growth with Enterprise would sustain my perception of normalcy for the better part of the following two years. But then another reversal of fortune happens, another shift. I received a phone call from my brother that our mother's health was seriously declining. She was diagnosed with congestive heart disease. Her heart was enlarged, and her lungs were starting to retain fluid, causing her shortness of breath. With or without treatment, Frank told me that our mom's condition would progressively get worse. So I thought to myself, *How many disruptions in life does one person have to face?*

Devastated by the news, I promptly asked my boss for a relocation back to California. Enterprise happily granted my request and found me a business management position within Group 30 in Sacramento, about an hour and a half drive from your homes in Martinez and Concord. I started making plans for my move. I reached out by phone informing you of my mother's condition and asking my son to help move my belongings into my new luxury apartment in Rancho Cordova. I noticed some hesitancy and annoyance in your tone as you asked several questions before finally agreeing to help me. Recognizing that it was our first contact since I moved to

WHAT A TALE MY THOUGHTS WILL TELL: WORDS NOT TO BE FORGOTTEN

San Antonio, I understood how our infrequent communication most likely contributed to your reluctance.

Moving back to California did not improve our relationship. Over the next eight years, we continued our staunch adherence—sticking to the blueprint of scarce phone contacts and minimal visits.

Particularly, after I met Gina and decided to move into her home in El Dorado Hills in 2013, eventful life-changing circumstances were the only happenstances that brought us physically together. I can count our get-togethers on one hand: the day I went to the hospital for my first grandson's birth; when I visited Johnny's home for my grandson's first birthday, presenting him his first San Francisco Giants baseball hat; Jessica visiting El Dorado Hills to introduce her new boyfriend; and my mother's passing in 2015. I remember reaching out to you, Johnny, asking, "I would like to see you, Jamie, and my grandson. Would you like to join us for my roomate's fiftieth birthday celebration?" Your response sounded like you were making excuses to find a way to say no politely.

Not surprisingly, that was our last communication. Even my father's death in 2018 failed to bring us together, paving one of the many pathways to our estrangement.

As I hung up the phone that day, it occurred to me that Robbin's warnings had come true. As the lyrics from the song, "Cat's in the Cradle," reminded me,

> *I've long since retired, my son's moved away*
> *I called him up just the other day*
> *I said, I'd like to see you if you don't mind*
> *He said, I'd love to, dad, if I can find the time*
> *You see, my new job's a hassle, and the kids have the flu*
> *But it's sure nice talking to you, dad*
> *It's been sure nice talking to you*
> *And as I hung up the phone, it occurred to me*
> *He'd grown up just like me*
> *My boy was just like me*

Once the COVID-19 pandemic spread in 2020, after twelve wonderful years with Enterprise, I decided to choose early retirement at the age of sixty-eight rather than facing the risk of infection or getting seriously ill as people over sixty-five represented over 85 percent of all deaths. Having so much time on my hands motivated me to reflect on my past. I pondered my accomplishments, reminiscence on memories of loved ones, and looked back to find the purpose and meaning in life. Spontaneously, I started writing.

While looking back, I was most troubled and realized how my inhibitions, anxieties, tireless work ethic, and propensity to seek seclusion during the emotional turmoil of the past and present had contributed to our estrangement. I found myself reviewing every parental mistake. It has taken over two years to compose my story to unblock and overcome my inner obstacles while explaining how life's transitions steer our paths. Knowing that time is short and the door is slowly closing on my life, I wanted to tell my story by avoiding blaming, criticizing, or defending anyone. Additionally, openly discussing my human vulnerabilities through telling the truth with humility and self-reflection hopefully demonstrates my willingness to make amends. Finally, writing from a personal storytelling point of view rather than an idealized self-centered version was crucial to my integrity.

Although I realize that most parental skills are passed down from generation to generation, those skills are constantly shaped by social and cultural forces. As a result, parenting is a tinderbox of eventual and unavoidable mistakes. Therefore, I want you to know that I genuinely did my best. I have always desired the best for you. If I could go back in time and start from what I know now, I would have done it differently.

Consequently, I lay in bed at night, knowing I had made many unfortunate decisions and carelessly misplaced priorities. I am sorry for the ways I let you down as a father. Thank God you have had the great fortune of a mother who has given lifelong love, devotion, and selfless dedication.

Some final thoughts.

WHAT A TALE MY THOUGHTS WILL TELL: WORDS NOT TO BE FORGOTTEN

Regarding your mother, I wanted to be her beloved partner for life. My love for her will forever remain within the deepest regions of my heart. Our ending was more complex and confusing because I never reached closure. I often found myself ruminating and obsessing over Robbin while being married to others. There were too many unanswered questions. Unable to completely understand why our relationship ended the way it did has caused an internal struggle. My only safe place was to retreat to isolation or seek avoidance. I am not making excuses, but the pain of being near your mother in any situation was unbearable and is positively connected to my poor judgments and choices. I mentioned earlier how I avoided talking to your mother during Johnny's wedding. Jessica, do you remember the great lengths I employed to avoid being seen by Robbin while attending your college graduation ceremony? Or the time I twisted myself into a pretzel to steer clear of your mother's presence at the hospital during the birth of my grandson? These are just a few examples of me turning away from opportunities to spend more quality time with you. My dysfunctional behavior interfered with the amount of face-to-face time we spent together because of my broken-heart syndrome. I will always love your mother. It was too difficult to face and overcome the torment of my feelings. I am sorry for this weakness of character. Physical pain always diminishes. The loss of hopes and dreams are true setbacks, and the pain from a lost love never dies.

As I have said many times, she was the love of my life. Some people ask, "What is the true meaning of life?" For some, it is derived from a philosophical or religious point of view. For others, it may be about happiness. But for me, the meaning of life is all about love. To live is to love. Even though your mother fell out of love with me, my love for her will always be unconditional and unending. The love we did share will always endure and sustain meaning in my life until the day I die. The loss of your mother's love changed my life forever.

As Carl Jung said in his last days, "The sole purpose of life human existence is to kindle a light in the darkness of mere being." He continued, "The least of things with a meaning is worth more in life than the greatest of things without it."

Over most of my life, I have always found peace of mind through music. Music has always provided me with a safe space to feel the emotions of happiness and heartache and give a timeline for recollecting memories. Music has helped define my life. Even today, there are two songs that I listen to daily that provide me a sense of contentment and peace of mind from my problematic past and present. So if you could indulge me, I would like to revise the lyrics to the following two songs that are dear to my heart to help expand your understanding of my love for you all.

Gordon Lightfoot wrote the first song in 1969. It is a personal song about the breakup of his first marriage. He beautifully weaves several themes about a love gone wrong.

If You Could Read My Mind
Gordon Lightfoot

With my minor revision of the lyrics, this version for my ex-wife, Robbin

If you could read my mind, love
What a tale my thoughts will tell
Just like an old-time movie
About a ghost from a wishing well
In a castle dark or a fortress strong
With chains upon my feet
You know that ghost was me
And I will never be set free
As long as I remain a ghost, that you can never see
If I could read your mind, love
What tale would your thoughts tell
Just like a paperback memoir
The kind the publishers sell
When you reach the part where the heartaches come
The hero would be me
But heroes often fail

WHAT A TALE MY THOUGHTS WILL TELL: WORDS NOT TO BE FORGOTTEN

And you won't read my book again
Because our ending is just too hard to take

I never wanted to walk away like a movie star
Who gets burned in a three-way script
Enter number two, the intruder, to play the scene
Of bringing all the bad things out in me
But for now, love, let's be real

I never thought I could act this way
And I've got to say that I just don't get it
I don't know where we went wrong
But your feeling's gone, and I just can't get it back

If you could read my mind, love
What a tale my thoughts will tell
Just like an old-time movie
About a ghost from a wishing well
In a dark castle or a fortress, strong
With chains upon my feet
But stories always end

And if you read between the lines
You'll know that I'm just trying to understand
The feelings that you had back then

I never thought I could feel this way
And I've got to say that I just don't get it
I don't know where we went wrong
But the feeling's gone
And I wish we could have gotten it back

The second song was originally written by Barry Mann and released in 1980. The song portrays a family or couple that remembers their past and the difficulties they faced together. It is a beautiful song that reminds us that the true meaning of life is love. I love the remake version performed by Aaron Neville and Linda Ronstadt.

Don't Know Much
Aaron Neville and Linda Ronstadt

With my minor revisions of the lyrics, this version is for Robbin, the only true love of my life, and my children, Johnny and Jessica

Look at my face
I know the years are showing
Looking over my life
I still don't know where it's going

I don't know much
But I know I love you
And that may be
All I need to know

Look into my eyes
They've never seen what mattered
All of my hopes and dreams have been
So beaten and so battered

I don't know much
But I know I love you
And that may be
All I need to know

So many questions
Still left unanswered
So much
I've never broken through

WHAT A TALE MY THOUGHTS WILL TELL: WORDS NOT TO BE FORGOTTEN

And when I feel you within my heart
Sometimes I see so clearly
The only truth I've ever known
Is my love for all of you

Look at this man
So blessed with a family of inspiration
Look at my soul
Still searching for salvation

I don't know much
But I know I love you
And that may be
All I need to know

I don't know much
But I know I love you
That may be
All there is to know

As I have gone through life, I have noticed that choices and decisions grow more complex and life-changing during the later stages of existence. I suspect that God's plan, whatever it is for me, works on a much larger scale than my mere mortal understanding. Therefore, I will rely on scripture. From Matthew 7:7, "Ask, and it will be given to you. Seek, and you will find. Knock, and it will be opened to you."

Not knowing if we will ever see each other again, I hope my words resonate and reside in your hearts. The unavoidable consequences of life's transitions, choices, and decisions determine our paths in life. When you reach my age, you realize how quickly life moves on. In an instant, years of happiness and sorrows have already become memories. Maybe it's time to forgive our past and move on to a love we have only dreamed of.

JOHN EDWARDS

    This is the story of who I am. It is the story of my life. I have described my high and low points, and now we have reached a turning point in our separate lives. If we never connect again, know this,

> *I don't know much*
> *But I know that I love you*
> *That may be*
> *All there is to know.*

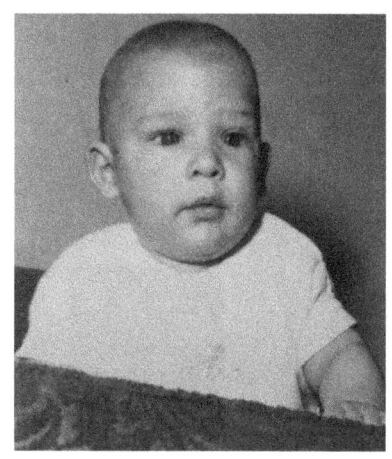

WHAT A TALE MY THOUGHTS WILL TELL: WORDS NOT TO BE FORGOTTEN

My Telly Savalas Baby Picture—1953

The Twins—Frankie and Johnny—2 years old, 1955

The Brylcreem—Clark Gable Hair-Do—I was five years old entering Bay School Kindergarten. Year 1958.

St. Joachim's Catholic uniform sibling photo. From left to right: Judy, John, Frank, Mary, and Susan in the blue dress. Photo taken in 1962.

John Edwards—Major League Baseball All-Star Picture—12 years old. Year, 1965.

Mom and Dad Photo. Dad's pet name for Mom was, "Dee Dee Baby Boo Boos"

WHAT A TALE MY THOUGHTS WILL TELL: WORDS NOT TO BE FORGOTTEN

High School Varsity Baseball Coach Verl Thornock—My mentor and Arroyo High School legendary coach.

John Edwards—Arroyo High School Senior Class Graduation Photo. Year, 1971.

Varsity Baseball Team Picture. I am in the back row #42. 1971. We had the most talented team in the HAAL that year, but did not meet expectations.

Edwards Family Photo taken in 1977. Back row left to right: Judy, Susan, Frank, John. Front Row left to right: Dad, Mary, Mom.

Modeling Photo—I was 25 years old, just before meeting the love of my life, Robbin. Year, 1978.

Groomsmen Wedding Photo—Left to right: Mike Grover, Rob Caisse, John Edwards, Brother Frank, and Bob Grover. The happiest day of my life. That day, I was the luckiest man in the world. Year, 1979.

WHAT A TALE MY THOUGHTS WILL TELL: WORDS NOT TO BE FORGOTTEN

Generational Family Photo (Great Grandparents, Aunts, Uncles, etc.) Back Row right-hand corner of the photo, is my gorgeous wife Robbin holding recently born daughter Jessica and Myself holding my son, Johnny. Photo was taken in 1982.

John Edwards with his amazing daughter Jessica. John was living in San Antonio, Texas at the time working for Enterprise Holdings, Inc.—2010.

My wonderful children—Jessica and Johnny. Photo taken in 2007.

Handsome son Johnny and his beautiful wife Jamie
at Trinity Lake, Northern California.

WHAT A TALE MY THOUGHTS WILL TELL: WORDS NOT TO BE FORGOTTEN

Time passes back quickly. John Edwards with his best friend, Mike Grover. I have known Mike since I was five years old. The picture was taken recently at our 50-year Arroyo High School Class Reunion (2022). We had to delay our senior class reunion one year because of the COVID 19 pandemic.

My high school sweetheart and girlfriend, Debbie Blanchard. Our shared moments and loving memories will always remain in my heart.

There is a short passage in my book about my best friend, Mike Grover, and his girlfriend, Andrea Fike. A touching and charming picture of them during their high school dating days.

There is a passage in my book describing when my father and I go to a Buick dealership in San Leandro, California to purchase my first vehicle, a 1973 Opal GT.

WHAT A TALE MY THOUGHTS WILL TELL:
WORDS NOT TO BE FORGOTTEN

Corporation Book Illustration

JOHN EDWARDS

I am a longtime San Francisco Giants fan. Growing up, my baseball idol was Willie Mays.

When I am not writing, I find time to play golf. I am passionate about improving my game.

WHAT A TALE MY THOUGHTS WILL TELL: WORDS NOT TO BE FORGOTTEN

We meet so many people in life, but we connect to the heart of very few. Ronnie Lott, my favorite 49er player, is an inspiration, and you cannot help but feel connected to his passionate nature. Mr. Lott exemplified the heart and courage of a champion. He often says about a winner's heart, "If my heart can inspire my will, then I can achieve anything."

About the Author

John Edwards grew up in the small Bay Area bedroom community of San Lorenzo, California, a twin son of a Korean War veteran turned patternmaker for the Alameda Naval Air Station. After a school career that included St. Joachim's Catholic, Arroyo High School, Chabot College, and the prestigious St. Mary's College of California. He married young, at twenty-six, and settled in Martinez, California. Growing up, he was fascinated with Professional Sports and American History, which led to meeting such notables as Willie Mays, Reggie Jackson, John Brodie, Kenny Stabler, John Madden, Lon Simmons, Bill King, and former Congressional Representatives George Miller, Pete Stark, and Vic Fazio.

Before becoming a full-time writer, John had a long and distinguished Business Management career for two of the most preeminent organizations in their industry, United Parcel Service and Enterprise Holdings, Inc. In *What a Tale My Thoughts Will Tell, Words Not to Be Forgotten,* John explores and chronicles how joyous and traumatic life transitions shape our choices and decisions, ultimately leading us on a path of understanding. A California Bay Area native, John Edwards lives in El Dorado Hills and works for another world-class organization, Safeway.

Printed in the USA
CPSIA information can be obtained
at www.ICGtesting.com
LVHW050011110424
776970LV00018B/317